WHEEL FEVER

WHEEL FEVER

How Wisconsin Became a Great Bicycling State

Jesse J. Gant & Nicholas J. Hoffman

Wisconsin Historical Society Press

Published by the Wisconsin Historical Society Press
Publishers since 1855

© 2013 by the State Historical Society of Wisconsin

For permission to reuse material from *Wheel Fever*, 978-087020-613-9, please access www.copyright.com or contact the Copyright Clearance Center, Inc. (CCC), 222 Rosewood Drive, Danvers, MA 01923, 978-750-8400. CCC is a not-for-profit organization that provides licenses and registration for a variety of users.

wisconsinhistory.org

Photographs identified with WHi or WHS are from the Society's collections; address requests to reproduce these photos to the Visual Materials Archivist at the Wisconsin Historical Society, 816 State Street, Madison, WI 53706.

Cover: Detroit Lithograph Company, 1895. Library of Congress Prints & Photographs Division, LC-DIG-ppmsa-08935
Back cover: Milwaukee County Historical Society

Printed in the United States of America

Designed by Authorsupport.com

17 16 15 14 13   1 2 3 4 5

Library of Congress Cataloging-in-Publication Data

Gant, Jesse J.
  Wheel fever : how Wisconsin became a great bicycling state / Jesse J. Gant and Nicholas J. Hoffman.
    pages cm
  Includes bibliographical references and index.
  ISBN 978-0-87020-613-9 (pbk. : alk. paper) 1. Cycling–Wisconsin–History. 2. Wisconsin–History. 3. Wisconsin–Social life and customs. I. Title.
  GV1045.5.W62G36 2013
  796.6'409775–dc23

                    2013007080

∞ The paper used in this publication meets the minimum requirements of the American National Standard for Information Sciences—Permanence of Paper for Printed Library Materials, ANSI Z39.48-1992.

Contents

To Randy and Marcy Gant
and Kristi Helmkamp

FOREWORD

Why a book about cycling in late nineteenth-century Wisconsin? Granted, the bicycle is widely considered one of the greatest inventions of all time, cleverly exploiting the clean and abundant supply of willpower to provide cheap and efficient transportation, not to mention healthful and enjoyable recreation. And those were the crucial years that witnessed the transformation of the first crude miniature carriages into something very much resembling contemporary bicycles. But, still, why focus on Wisconsin?

The authors of *Wheel Fever*, Jesse Gant and Nicholas Hoffman, explain that Wisconsin has become a leading cycling destination for outdoor enthusiasts, offering beautiful scenery, an inviting rolling terrain, and a vast network of cycling paths reclaimed from abandoned railroads. They further assert that the current popularity of cycling has something to do with the state's long infatuation with the sport, dating back to the original boneshakers of 1869.

As a bicycle historian who learned how to bicycle in the capital city of Madison less than a century after Joshua G. Towne introduced the sport to the state, I am, of course, partial to the book's premise. But some might question whether the book's geographical scope is sufficiently broad to tell the story of cycling's rise.

The authors, both passionate riders and loyal native sons, readily concede that the state's historical ties to the "mechanical horse" are not particularly striking. After all, the first waves of "velocipede mania," emanating from France, struck the eastern seacoast before making their way west in the late 1860s. And the bicycle revival a decade later, triggered by the introduction of the British "high wheeler," likewise started in the East, with Boston serving as its hub. To be sure, Wisconsin did keenly experience the great bicycle boom of the 1890s, but so did every other state, notably neighboring Illinois, home to the manufacturing center of Chicago.

Still, there is a Wisconsin-based story to trace and tell, and the authors have done so with admirable skill and devotion. It would be a great mistake to infer that this book is narrowly focused or strictly of regional interest. On the contrary, it gives an excellent overview of bicycle development during a crucial period when the curious two-wheeler was still vying to prove its lasting value.

The narrative also explores broad themes that would greatly influence the development of the nation as a whole, such as the birth, growth, and operation of an important industry, the rise of—and resistance to—women and black cyclists, the campaign for better roads, and the establishment of a popular spectator sport.

Moreover, as it turns out, the Wisconsin-rooted characters presented here were highly representative of their peers elsewhere. Joshua Towne may have been a clerk at the Milwaukee office of the American Express Company, but he was also the spiritual brother of hundreds of young office employees the world over, for whom the velocipede represented an exciting and alluring new way to exercise, travel, and socialize. Only a year before Towne's exhibition, E. Vallot of Paris wrote Pierre Michaux, the pioneer bicycle manufacturer of the same city, asking for a payment plan. "I have about 85 colleagues," he pleaded. "Most are young people, and the majority of those would certainly become buyers if offered such terms."

Similarly, Terry Andrae, a.k.a. "The Flying Badger," was in many ways a typical wheelman of the 1880s. Young, athletic, and privileged (his father's factory in Milwaukee produced bicycles and tricycles), he was an ardent proponent of the new-style bicycle with its towering and daunting profile. Unlike the discredited boneshaker, it truly was a roadworthy, if accident-prone, vehicle, though it renounced any aspiration to serve as the "people's nag." On the contrary, it was unabashedly recreational in nature, deliberately imposing and exclusive. For Andrae and similar devotees on both sides of the Atlantic cycling offered speed, adventure, and glory.

Despite its elitist nature, the high wheeler laid the technical and social foundation for the great bicycle boom of the 1890s, a phenomenon that would touch nearly every segment of American society and shape the nation's course for decades to come. And as the title *Wheel Fever* suggests, the boom era is in fact the heart of this book. Many of the Wisconsinites we meet here were not only representative of their generation but were also genuine players on the national scene. The Janesville-raised temperance leader Frances Willard, for example, wrote a popular book encouraging women to take to the wheel. And Milwaukee-born racer Walter Sanger dominated the competitive sport at its peak.

This is also the part of the narrative where the authors present their most compelling research and analysis. They show how the cycling movement, even as it grew to include ever-larger cross sections of the American population, was still very much a product of its times, subject to powerful reactionary forces bent on suppressing its liberating and democratic tendencies.

I thank and congratulate Jesse Gant, Nicholas Hoffman, and the Wisconsin Historical Society Press for producing this valuable and welcome addition to cycling literature.

David V. Herlihy
Boston, Massachusetts

The publication of *Wheel Fever: How Wisconsin Became a Great Bicycling State* was made possible, in part, by a generous grant from the **Sally Mead Hands Foundation**

Acknowledgments

It is a tremendous pleasure to thank the people who helped bring *Wheel Fever* into existence. We first started thinking about this book during the summer of 2009, and—as is often the case with this kind of work—we have incurred many debts. We would like to take this opportunity to acknowledge those who helped us, directly and sometimes indirectly, along the way.

We start with the number of excellent mentors and teachers we have worked with these past few years. Scholars and writers who taught us to become better historians include: Jasmine Alinder, Bill Cronon, Jack Dukes, Kristen Foster, Michael Gordon, Susan Johnson, Will Jones, Steve Kantrowitz, David McDaniel, Aims McGuinness, Steve Meyer, Jennifer Morgan, Monica Rico, Amanda Seligman, and Daniel Sherman. Michael Gordon, in particular, deserves our special thanks. He made this a better book not only by laboring through a number of early drafts but also by challenging us to expand our thinking whenever and wherever it was possible. We also want to offer a special thanks to David Herlihy, our foreword writer, who read an early version of the book, travelled to visit us in the middle of Hurricane Sandy, and has proven himself to be a wonderful friend and supporter. Finally, Greg Bond wrote a PhD dissertation examining race and sports in the late nineteenth century that we found helpful for our analysis. All have inspired us to become better thinkers and writers, and we are grateful that they have invested so much time and energy in us.

University archival staff has also been crucial to making this book possible. We would like to thank Fred Burwell and Josh Hickman at the Beloit College Archives; Erin Dix at Lawrence University; Andrew Prellwitz at the Ripon College Archives; Matthew Appleby at the Mills Music Library, University of Wisconsin–Madison; Michael Doylen, Christel Maass, and Ellen Engseth at the University of Wisconsin–Milwaukee; and last but certainly not least, Jennifer Bumann and Joshua Ranger at the Forrest Polk Library, University of Wisconsin–Oshkosh. The staff at the Firestone Library, Princeton University, kept a steady flow of interlibrary loan materials moving in 2011.

The Wisconsin Historical Society (WHS), the Wisconsin Historical Society

Archives staff, and especially the Wisconsin Historical Society Press all deserve sincere thanks for believing in this project and supporting it from day one. Kathy Borkowski, Elizabeth Boone, Jane De Broux, Laura Kearney, Kate Thompson, Barb Walsh, and John Zimm of WHS Press all put energy into helping make this book happen in some way, and we know that it would not have been possible without them. Jesse has worked as an editorial assistant with WHS Press since his first semester at UW–Madison, and is grateful for the support its staff has offered over the years as this book developed. Nobody could ask for better colleagues. Our editor, Sara Phillips, guided the book through the development process and consistently pushed us to hone our arguments, streamline our points, and express our thoughts in the clearest language possible. Managing editor Diane Drexler and production editors Mike Nemer and Jere Foley helped with the text design and made sure the book made its many production deadlines along the way. Kristin Gilpatrick and Anna Wehrwein helped with the book's marketing and were always receptive to the ideas we had for thinking about what it meant to "do" public history. We would also like to thank Andrew White for organizing the art program and Joel Heiman and John Nondorf for their help on the book's images. A number of the WHS Press staff involved with this book in the earliest stages have since moved on, but we remember the help they gave us: Caroline Bohler, Mallory Kirby, Shannon Sampson, and Susan Tierney deserve our thanks for being enthusiastic supporters of this book. Our copy editor, Melissa York, also a former staff member, helped get the final drafts of our chapters into shape. Last but not least, we would like to thank marketing coordinator Melanie Roth, who was probably the first person to hear about this project, and who never doubted it would one day make a nice addition to the WHS Press catalog. In addition, Michael Edmonds, deputy director of Library-Archives at WHS, helped digitize the *Pneumatic* at a crucial part of the writing stage, and for his hard work to help us meet deadlines, we are extremely grateful.

A number of staff members at smaller local institutions, public libraries, and museums also offered assistance. We would like to thank Terry Bergen, Matthew Carpenter, Emily Rock, and Patty Wagner at the History Museum at the Castle in Appleton. Matt Carpenter read a number of early drafts of the book and continually challenged us to dig deeper. We would also like to acknowledge Kurt Sampson, Dodge County Historical Society; the staff at the Rock County Historical Society in Janesville, especially Laurel Fant and Michael Reuter; Cynthia Nelson and Tom Schleif at the Kenosha County Historical Society; Jane Lang of the Neenah Historical Society; Sharon Clothier, Scott Cross, Deb Daubert, and Brad Larson of the Oshkosh Public Museum; Karen Braun at the Racine Heritage Museum; and Alli Karrels of the Deke Slayton Memorial Space and Bicycle Museum. The front desk at the Oshkosh Public Library was always helpful with our various requests, and the staff at the Janesville Hedberg Library helped make it a worthy research destination.

Given the importance of Milwaukee to our story, it makes sense that we found some of our most important help there. Sarah Hopley, Amanda Koehler, and Jeff Kollath played vital roles in connecting us with a number of crucial Milwaukee County Historical Society photographs, objects, and research leads, while the staff at the Frank P. Zeidler Humanities Room at the Milwaukee Public Library patiently accommodated our research in photographs, city directories, and manuscript collections. Claudia Jacobson, Al Muchka, and Dawn Scher Thomae of the Milwaukee Public Museum helped put us in touch with a number of rare photographs and Milwaukee-based cycling publications and clippings.

Local parks staff, historical organizations, and online history projects also helped bring *Wheel Fever* to life. We would also like to mention Kenneth Germanson of the Wisconsin Labor Historical Society, who reviewed our section on labor and industry, and Emily Pfotenhauer of Wisconsin Heritage Online, who invited us to submit early portions of our research for an online audience, giving us a valuable opportunity to publicize our work at an early stage.

For all the Wisconsin connections we've made, we cannot claim that this is an entirely homegrown project. Rich Malley of the Connecticut Historical Society helped us find an important image of Colonel Albert Pope, while Kara S. Vetter of the Indiana State Museum helped us locate several images of Major Taylor. Pryor Dodge shared pieces of his wonderful bicycle collection. Staff, students, and librarians at New York University have also helped us become better researchers and thinkers.

A number of area cycling businesses and cycling organizations also helped with this book in ways large and small: Gwen Sargeant at the Appleton Bike Shop; Rob Gusky of the Fox Cities Cycling Association; the South Shore Cyclery in Cudahy; Michael's Cycles in Janesville; Susan Hostetler of the Budget Bicycle Center in Madison; Scott Reilly of the Bicycle Federation of Wisconsin; and Ben's Cycle/Milwaukee Bicycle Company. A good portion of the book was written at the Black Water Coffee Company in Beaver Dam, following quick brainstorming breakfasts at nearby Walker's Restaurant and Bakery. We would like to thank the hardworking waitstaff and baristas at each for putting up with us as we seized their tables, loitered for many hours over photocopies and laptop screens, and muttered to one another about "cranks" and "scorchers."

Without the encouragement and support of our many good friends, we know that this book might never have been possible. Our special thanks go out to: Bill Albertini, Simon Balto, Matt Barbee, Rob Baumann, Ervin Beck, Matt Christman, Joe Fronczak, Michael Gabrick, Brian Hamilton, Michael Horne, Curt Huibregtse, Amanda Izzo, Rob Jach, Erick Jacobs, Ann Kloehn, Ben Looker, Ann Negri, Kate Negri, Andrew Rakowski, Kate Riordan, Jenna Rolle, Michael Sonn, and Brian Wissbeck. We are especially thankful to our Milwaukee friends for offering places to rest, good company, and many laughs during research visits. The Revolting Masses, Princeton's History Department softball team, took Jesse in as an adopted member during a key part of the writing period in 2011, providing much-needed writing breaks. We would also like to thank the many graduate students in the UW–Madison Department of History who have helped with this project and the many others we are involved with.

A number of fellowships and grants helped this book come into being. From the University of Wisconsin, fellowship support came from the Graduate School, the University Chancellor's Office, and the Department of History. Travel support for research also came from the University of Wisconsin's Nelson Institute, including the Center for Culture, History, and Environment. The Everett Helm Visiting Research Fellowship at the Lilly Library, Indiana University, and the Jacob Price Visiting Fellowship at the William L. Clements Library, University of Michigan, were both helpful in introducing the authors to collections housed outside of the Badger State.

We owe our deepest debts to our families. Marcy Gant, Jamie Gant, and Randy Gant; Rick Lutenski and Pam Lutenski; James Hoffman and Jane Hoffman; Ben Helmkamp, Brenda Helmkamp, and Andrew Helmkamp—all of these and many, many more have provided love and support through the years, and we hope that this book makes them proud. Our partners in crime, Emily Lutenski and Kristi Helmkamp, each know what they have meant to this book and deserve our most heartfelt thanks.

Jesse Gant and Nick Hoffman

INTRODUCTION

How Wisconsin Became a Great Bicycling State

On a recent summer night, an array of battery-powered bike lights pierced the darkness, signaling the arrival of several bicyclists at City Park in Appleton, Wisconsin. Dressed in athletic gear, helmets, reflective vests, and Lycra, some with their bikes decorated by flashing LED lamps and strands of battery powered holiday lights, they gathered for an evening ride. The group—men, women, and children—met to encourage new riders and to gather with neighbors and friends to plan future rides and events. They rode representing groups like Fox Cities Greenways, Fox Cities Cycling Association, and the Bicycle Federation of Wisconsin. Circling the park's Ring Dance fountain, the twenty riders cast off in a long line of lights and ringing bells, slowly cruising through area neighborhoods and parks, alerting all who might see and hear to their presence.[1]

Appleton's moonlight ride in June 2012 brought the city's bicycling community together, but it was hardly a new step for bicycle advocates at work in Wisconsin and throughout the United States. The ride continued work that has been going on in the state for almost 150 years. Swap the modern LED lamps for acetylene-powered brass lanterns, the bikes themselves for some oversize high-wheel "ordinaries," and those magnificent Lycra shorts for some military-style wool uniforms and kepis, and you basically have a historical reenactment of what happened in Appleton and throughout the na-

The Oshkosh Bicycle Club and other state cycling organizations gathered to promote their sport at the Milwaukee Bicycle Meet on July 3–5, 1880. Wisconsin's bicycle advocacy began organizing formally during the high-wheel era.

Courtesy of Oshkosh Public Museum

tion during the last three decades of the nineteenth century. As Wisconsin residents continue to push bicycling in new directions, it seems important to reflect on what historians have called the "first bicycle boom," which grew from humble origins in the 1870s and 1880s before exploding as a national phenomenon in the 1890s.[2] What lessons can be learned from the successes and mistakes of the state's pedaling pioneers? Early racers like Terry Andrae, Marshall "Major" Taylor, and Walter Sanger are all but lost to modern memory. Imagine their marvel had they been able to experience today's bike paths and technologies. What might they have said about Wisconsin's ongoing love for all things bicycle?

That Wisconsin has made a significant contribution to bicycling culture is hard to deny. Recent data suggests that an estimated forty-nine percent of Badger State residents bike for recreation and other purposes, making cycling one of our most popular outdoor activities. Several leading bicycle manufacturers are located in Wisconsin, and the state is a national leader in total bike-path mileage. Wisconsin is also home to a historically powerful bicycle lobby. This advocacy helps the state host hundreds of bicycling events each year, drawing visitors from all over the world. The health, environmental, and economic benefits of biking are by now well known, and its popularity continues to soar. In 2010, a study by UW–Madison's Nelson Institute for Environmental Studies showed that bicycling has even become more popular than deer hunting, the most iconic of all Wisconsin's great outdoor traditions. In fact, bicycling has become so popular among Badger State residents that it generates an estimated $1.5 billion dollars annually for the state's economy. As we began the research for this book, these insights helped suggest that this was a story worth investigating further. We wanted to know more about how it all came to be.[3]

Numbers, of course, only tell part of the story. They do not explain how bicycles got to Wisconsin in the first place. Nor do they explain how they were popularized or how cyclists created such a tangible culture around the sport. Indeed, the numbers only hint at the ways Wisconsin cycling rose to prominence. *Wheel Fever: How Wisconsin Became a Great Bicycling State* looks beyond the numbers and takes a broad historical view of how Wisconsin became a top national cycling destination. It examines the early history of cycling politics and culture in the Badger State to explain why bicycling has become so important to Wisconsin's identity. As one of the first state studies of its kind, the story told here helps to illuminate how cycling contributed not only to the development of Wisconsin, but also to the making of the modern United States.[4]

Historical discussions of politics and culture matter to this discussion because it was people power, in the end, that made Wisconsin a great place to ride. Cycling advocacy ultimately drove the creation of Wisconsin's historic ties to the sport. In highlighting the importance of advocacy, however, we do not mean to suggest that all who played a role managed to do so equally, nor that it was a solely homegrown phenomenon. While Wisconsinites have made several notable contributions to the sport, a number of the state's early cycling advocates and a good number of its key technologies originated from outside the state, illustrating Wisconsin's many debts to other parts of the country, as well as to immigrant and international developments. We should also stress that Wisconsin is

Lacking a pannier, this man carried goods under his arm as he cruised through Black River Falls, ca. 1897. Early cyclists saw the utilitarian potential bicycles had for daily travel.

WHi Image ID 45631

a great bicycling state, but not *the* great cycling state. Our story is as much about the state's limitations and failures over time as it is about its many triumphs. By no means do we see this as the only state history of cycling that deserves to be written.

Wisconsin's bicycling advocacy, like the nation's, came from many different directions. Two key groups have been most significant. The first is bicycling's more egalitarian tradition, which cheered not only cycling's simple joys, but also its affordability, practicality, and efficiency. Cycling advocates like Frances Willard and Edith Shuler pushed for women's entrance into the sport and served as two of its earliest diplomats.[5]

Though they had great appreciation for what the bicycle does for the individual, their real interest lay in its capacity for spurring democratic change. Susan B. Anthony, in an often-cited line, captured this view well in 1896 when she said, "Let me tell you what I think of bicycling. I think it has done more to emancipate women than anything else in the world."[6] More recently, egalitarians have highlighted bicycling's health and environmental benefits. What unites their vision of the sport through time is their longstanding optimism about bicycling's wide-ranging positive effects for broader society. Although women have often historically constituted the clearest egalitarian demographic in the United States and elsewhere, men throughout cycling's history have, to a far lesser degree, also stressed the utilitarian possibilities of perfecting what was often called the "poor man's horse." Such men and women have worked hard to expand the democratic potential of the sport, ensuring that all people have a chance to ride wherever and whenever they want.[7]

Opposite them stands a group that historically has been less willing to stress bicycling's collective benefits. Bicycling's conservatives, often white men of the middle and upper classes, have worked to restrict or otherwise constrain the spread of bicycling. Their motives vary and often cannot be explained by simple charges of racism, classism, or sexism, even when these factors have clearly played a role. In the world of late nineteenth-century American politics, the reality was that limiting the scope of cycling's access often yielded advantages for the sport's more privileged riders. The League of American Wheelmen (LAW), founded in 1880, often used the "respectable" standing of its elite membership—wealthy white males—to call for narrow and usually self-interested legislative changes. Careful to protect the sport's benefits from those who might expand them in more democratic directions, conservatives have typically favored a vision of the sport that stresses recreation and competition, often at the expense of the sport's broader benefits for society. They have more readily identified with feats of athletic prowess than with stories of freedom and mobility. As such, conservative advocates have helped promote the sport's more professional, competitive, and masculine aspects. Long-distance racing, track racing, and competitive long-distance touring have long been their domain. They have been united by efforts to keep bicycling's historically insular culture a key aspect of the sport's enduring appeal.[8]

Bicycling politics were not "formal" politics when the sport first started in the last years of the 1860s. Instead, bicycling gave rise to a distinct culture that slowly became assimilated into the larger political world of both the state of Wisconsin and the nation. Organizations such as the conservative LAW arose and effectively mobilized bicycling politics, but in doing so they stamped bicycling with a culture of exclusion—and reactionary inclusion—that would continue to be its legacy in years to come. In other words, the cultural tensions that arose within the cycling community had few wide-ranging electoral implications at first, but as the sport's power and numbers grew, it became increasingly entangled with national electoral politics. In a dramatic turnaround from the outsider status most cyclists encountered in the 1870s, presidential campaigns in the 1890s would actively court the LAW vote, turning to bicyclists for help in canvassing neighborhoods. By 1900, both parties, particularly the developing "progressive" wing of the Republican Party, were using bicycles in their campaign speeches, buttons, and ribbons to signal their friendliness to the new cycling community. Although the conservative lobby had greater political power throughout the period, the egalitarian vision remained powerful as it continually exposed the limits and constraints of the sport, demonstrating democratic possibilities in a deeply unequal society.

Between 1870 and 1900, then, egalitarian and conservative cycling interests vied for supremacy in Wisconsin and nationwide, but neither gained a true upper hand. Instead, they together forged the basic contours of what might be called today's recreational cycling mainstream. Between 1870 and 1900, egalitarians managed to open up the sport to unprecedented numbers of working-class women and men. This effectively upended the manly, refined, and aristocratic culture that had dominated cycling since the early 1870s. Conservatives, meanwhile, managed to hold onto their control of the bicycling industry and professional venues like racing despite ongoing challenges from women, people of color, and members of the working class, who challenged their outsider status. Yet by 1900, egalitarians had failed to secure the ideal of providing everyday people with a cheap, practical, and reliable form of everyday transportation. Conservatives, too, had failed to bolster their sport against the challenges that arose from below, ultimately ceding their aristocratic perch at the top of the nation's cycling hierarchy to growing numbers of working- and middle-class men, and, especially by the middle 1890s, throngs of middle- and upper-class white women.

Some early riders envisioned the bicycle as a "poor man's horse." Augusta Wilhelmy symbolized this transition as she sped past her sister Elizabeth on their family farm south of Manitowoc, ca. 1895.

Courtesy of Manitowoc Public Library

Though the sport radically expanded by 1900, it ultimately fell short of becoming truly accessible to Wisconsin's masses, even as such a change seemed within reach. As a result, bicycles largely became a mode of leisure and recreation for the white middle class, and there they remain to this day—utilitarian only in the sense that they are useful for this privileged demographic. When "cyclist" comes to mind, Americans today imagine someone who does it by choice, often in his or her spare time or for competitive reasons. Yet in 1880s and 1890s Wisconsin, many believed cycling would soon become a normal way of getting around—much like how we assume the car is a perfectly natural form of transportation today. It may be hard to imagine from today's perspective, but despite the "manly" stereotype early conservatives worked so hard to promote, the sheer number of women and working-class bike riders in this early period made it difficult to think of the sport as purely recreational.

For these reasons, while the bicycle has been celebrated for its role in breaking down gender and class barriers, early cycling typically reinforced dominant power structures. In this way, it eased the adoption of a far more hierarchical "civilized" technology, the automobile. By the middle of the twentieth century, the white middle class had forgotten the early challenges leveled by egalitarians in the 1890s, and cycling was cemented in the American psyche as a leisure activity. Examining the 1890s cycling boom reminds us that alternatives to today's car-dominant society have existed in the past and that bicycling has not always been imagined as simply a leisure option for the middle class in America. The story of the twentieth century might be thought of, to some degree, as the story of how Americans came to see the automobile, not the bicycle, as their most viable private transportation option.[9]

After a hard rain, roadways could become impassable, like this street in downtown Wausau, ca. 1900. The LAW advocated for improved roadways for commerce, travel, and smoother cycling.

WHi Image ID 35988

Bicycling advocates pushed their love affair with cycling a long way in the last part of the nineteenth century. Egalitarians extended bicycling access to women, children, and people of color. But they also helped speed a growing transition away from more public forms of transportation like railroads and steamboats to more privatized forms of individual transport.[10] Bicycling, in the end, effectively showed the white middle class that it could call upon government to secure a range of infrastructure benefits, but that these benefits did not have to extend beyond the color line or the picket line. That so many continue to push for the further incorporation of cycling into our daily lives is not only a testament to the lingering challenge and promise of the egalitarian ideal, but a testament to how pervasive private transportation options have become in the United States. As both attitudes continue to compete for attention within the world they helped create, they remain relevant to our most pressing policy discussions, particularly in regard to transportation and energy.

Struggles between Wisconsin's cycling advocates crystallized in the "good roads movement" of the late nineteenth century. Organized in 1895 through the Wisconsin League for Good Roads, the movement called upon a range of institutions and organizations, most importantly government, to improve both Wisconsin's and the nation's

THE VELOCIPEDE BELLE.

Women were among the first cyclists in Wisconsin in 1869. Men first saw women cyclists as novelties in velocipede acts and later challenged their access to the sport.

University of Minnesota Library, Hess Collection, Illuminated Western World, March 13, 1869

roads, from small county and city streets to the most heavily traveled national roads and highways. The movement made appeals to both parties in an intensely partisan climate, and managed to build a complex coalition of supporters. Egalitarians, of course, saw good public roads as something all people could use; good roads vastly expanded the mobility enjoyed by women and working riders. As historian Michael Taylor has shown, they also expanded the potentials for democratic expansion through canvassing, door-to-door petitioning, and pamphleteering. Conservatives also found elements of the good roads movement appealing. Good roads provided a way for manufacturing and leading industry men to improve their infrastructure, lending a tremendous boon to area businesses through improved shipping and transit. Improved roads also deepened individuals' enjoyment of the sport, offering opportunities for racing and touring as tracks increasingly converted to concrete and roads to macadam (crushed and broken rock) in the late 1890s and early 1900s.[11]

What did these struggles actually look like on the ground? And what shape have they taken throughout Wisconsin's history? As we explore in chapter 1, bicycles first became popular in Wisconsin in the first years after the Civil War in the form of the "velocipede," a human-powered vehicle with two or more wheels.[12] Opinions as to what the new technology meant diverged greatly. Some residents, evidencing an emerging egalitarian view of the sport, celebrated it as a practical, fun, and efficient transportation solution for the common man. Others, reflecting what would become a more conservative argument, blasted it for being unwieldy and potentially dangerous, quickly relegating it to recreational or pure entertainment status. At their most extreme, naysayers worried the new machines would corrode the American family. These first debates over cycling, often expressed in ordinances against the use of the newfangled machines on city sidewalks, would come to shape the future of the bicycle in Wisconsin. Out of these overcharged conversations the early dynamics of Wisconsin's bicycling politics slowly came into view between 1869 and 1879, and with them the early struggles over bicycling advocacy began to take a coherent shape.

Wisconsin's early bicycle advocates fought their first meaningful battles during the "velocipede mania" of the late 1860s, when French blacksmiths and engineers introduced pedals to two-wheeled contraptions called "hobbyhorses," developed by a German engineer working in the early part of the nineteenth century. The addition of pedals to these simple designs created a wave of international interest, and soon "velocipedes" were seen from Paris to San Francisco. Egalitarians had the early edge. They celebrated the creation of a poor man's horse that adherents said would liberate mankind from the tyranny of transportation dependence, and they peddled around Paris streets together, male and female alike, scandalizing the French public in the process. Young women would also play a key role in popularizing the velocipede in Milwaukee, Wisconsin.[13]

It was there that the first recorded bicycle ride in Wisconsin's history took place when a young man named Joshua Towne rode one of the new French designs through Milwaukee's streets in February 1869. Advocates like Towne soon realized, however, that the poor condition of the state's roads made velocipede riding a viable option only in indoor rinks. Early velocipede riders, perhaps no more than a few dozen in those early months of 1869, were further encouraged to take their riding indoors by the passage of several local ordinances that often explicitly banned "velocipedestrians," as these early riders were often called, from the sidewalks and streets. This inauspicious beginning put the fledgling bicycling community on the defensive, and for a while it appeared the velocipede mania would be just another fad to come and go.[14]

Banished from the streets, early cycling advocates in Wisconsin turned their attention to Europe in the early 1870s as a series of innovations helped spur the development of a faster, more reliable, and certainly more comfortable bicycle. Aided by the development of rubber tires, wheels with metal spokes, and improvements in handlebar and saddle technology, bicycles underwent a dramatic change during the 1870s and 1880s, as we detail in chapter 2. Commonly called "ordinary" bicycles or simply highwheels, these machines were characterized by their massive front wheel, which required riders to literally run and jump aboard them because of their extreme height. While tremendously dangerous, the new machines were also extremely fast and exceptionally comfortable when measured against the velocipedes, the infamous "boneshakers" of the earlier era. Bicycles moved back into the streets with the help of a new and enthusiastic fan base—a transition that would have a dramatic effect on the shape of the sport in the coming years. In Wisconsin, the key development on this front occurred on July 2, 1879, in Racine when two men from the East, described as "young men who came from Boston" in local papers, rode through the city's downtown near Racine's present-day Monument Square.[15]

This description of the sport's eastern ambassadors is significant because it highlights how quickly the nation's white men seized on the sport, forming a bloc that would become vital to cycling's longstanding conservative advocacy. As we discuss in chapter 3, it was this group that ultimately started the work of cordoning off cycling's benefits

from others, allowing early white male riders to begin molding bicycling's benefits for riders like themselves. In fact, the amateur cycling clubs that became popular in Wisconsin borrowed directly from all-male clubs already common in Europe and throughout the American East Coast. In 1880, men in Rhode Island formed what would become the era's leading advocacy organization, the League of American Wheelmen (LAW). Wisconsin's men were slower to organize, but they shared the belief that cycling was a white man's sport, and they protected access to it in a variety of ways. By 1882, a group known as the Milwaukee Cycling Club appeared in Milwaukee's streets, donning militaristic uniforms and riding with drill-like precision. Others followed. Clubs such as these wore badges, sang club songs, and decorated elaborate clubhouses where the men gathered before and after rides. In this way, Americans increasingly saw bicycling as a white and "respectable" male pursuit.[16]

Privileges such as these also ensured that when conservative advocates called for more bikes and better roads, bicycle manufacturing would reflect the tremendous opportunities afforded to white men of the era and not women or people of color, who were often banned from business ownership and access to equal facilities. Wisconsin thus became home to a burgeoning bicycle industry in the 1880s, an industry that often profited from the labor of children and other groups while advancing the profits of a few captains of industry. White men benefited from the business connections they had with industry leaders in the East and overseas, connections that were often fostered

Bicycling's growing popularity fostered an expanding market for shops and factories. In Sheboygan, ca. 1900, this bicycle shop even included an area where riders could safely park their machines while running errands.

WHi Image ID 2002

through cycling organizations like the League of American Wheelmen. Oshkosh's Jay Hinman Bicycle Agency and Appleton's William Groth Bicycle Agency and Repair Shop all became vendors for East Coast manufacturers like the Pope Manufacturing Company of Hartford, Connecticut. Not until the last half of the 1880s did a true Wisconsin-based bicycle industry develop when Julius Andrae and Sons began producing bikes for Wisconsin's residents. In part, the Andrae men helped build their local dominance through the formal endorsement of Milwaukee's all-male amateur cycling clubs.[17]

White men's control of the sport and its industry was persistently challenged from a variety of directions from the beginning, however. In the last part of the 1880s, as detailed in chapter 4, the dominance of the daredevil and yet gentlemanly culture that surrounded the high-wheel was forced to accommodate thousands of new riders as a new, safer frame—called, simply, the "safety"—entered the market. The introduction of the safety meant that, after the initial high prices dropped, scores of working-class consumers could not only afford bicycles but also enjoy cycling without fear of crashing. By 1889, descriptions of "ladies' bicycle parties" appeared in Milwaukee newspapers. Women worked to secure many of the same cycling benefits that men had secured for themselves. They published books and manuals describing how to fix and maintain their machines, such as Maria E. Ward's *Bicycling for Ladies* (1896). They studied maps in order to navigate cities and towns on their own and organized riding clubs when

Loaded with camera bags and picnic baskets, this group of cyclists is prepared for a day of riding, ca.1895. Conservative Americans feared the bicycle would corrupt young men and women, leading to immoral activities.

WHi Image ID 98626

men ostracized them from area wheelmen clubs. Some, such as Kate Parke of nearby Chicago, even submitted patents to the US government offering new bicycle designs.[18]

Nonwhites, workers, and women continued to challenge white men's control of the sport in the late 1880s and early 1890s, a key theme of chapter 5. This advocacy from below led to many gains for the sport's egalitarians at first, but ultimately fueled a backlash of conservative advocacy that put an end to bicycling's democratic high tide by 1900. The backlash began in earnest when the LAW forbade black membership in

Ho-Chunk tribal member Jim Carriman posed for Charles Van Schaick at his Black River Falls photography studio in 1905.

WHi Image ID 60614

1894.[19] Wisconsin's black and Native communities were decidedly small compared to the demographic power of the state's white and European immigrant populations, but blacks and other nonwhites enjoyed cycling even if they were not formally allowed to participate in its mainstream culture. Unfortunately, few Wisconsin-based records survive to tell us much about black or Native cycling communities in the state or how they might have fought for access to the sport, although our research did turn up a few notable photographs that indicate such communities existed. Further than this, black newspapers such as La Crosse's *Wisconsin Labor Advocate* and Milwaukee's *Weekly Wisconsin Advocate* and

Wisconsin Afro-American provided coverage of bicycling's growing popularity among nonwhites during this period.[20]

As we discuss in chapters 6 and 7, early advocates also drove demand for new bicycles in Wisconsin and elsewhere. Wisconsin's bicycle manufacturing boom helped democratize the sport by providing affordable machines to the working class, but it also exploited the state's workforce with poor working conditions, low pay, and long hours. Companies like A. D. Meiselbach, Beebee, and Sercombe-Bolte employed a workforce comprised of hundreds of men, women, and children. Factory operations built and customized bicycles, constructed frames, wove handgrips, and fabricated brass lanterns. Recognizing that conditions were unfair, employees organized in the Bicycle Workers and Allied Mechanics Union. In some instances, workers went on strike to demand greater working rights and reverse the unfair labor practices common in bike factories during the boom. The boom quickly passed, however, as producers filled an oversaturated market with cheap machines. Lingering effects of the Panic of 1893 and continued poor labor relations sent a good number of local bicycle and component manufacturers into bankruptcy and their workers to the unemployment line by the end of the decade.[21]

The era's tremendous inequality also helped shape the nature of the good roads movement in Wisconsin. The leaders of Wisconsin's bicycling industry recognized by the early 1890s that cycling would have no future in the state if roads were not improved. This led, at least in part, to the formation of the Wisconsin League for Good Roads. Leading the effort were men like Otto Dorner, who became one of the state's most important good roads advocates at the age of twenty-six. This good roads "apostle" would ride his bike to communities outside of Milwaukee to lecture on the significance of road reform. Farmers who had initially opposed good road reform for fear they would bear the tax burden slowly came around, as Wisconsin followed models in other states in which all levels of government shared the cost. Yet it was only with the emergence of the automobile that comprehensive road reform in the state would truly

Women such as Margarite Grimm of Oshkosh, 1899, were expected to wear full-length skirts while cycling. Bicycle manufacturers added a drop frame, chain guards, and rear-wheel netting to protect flowing skirts.

Courtesy of Oshkosh Public Museum

begin. Wisconsin's legislature voted in support of state aid for roads throughout the 1890s, but a constitutional amendment for state highways was not enacted until 1908. Nonetheless, cycling and legislative cooperation helped pave the beginning of that key transition, and wheelmen like Dorner were crucial to making it happen.[22]

Continued calls for expanded access to roads helped lead to new restrictions by the sport's leadership, as we document in chapters 7 and 8. White men tightened their control over the industry and expanded their presence over the sport in a variety of ways as the boom deepened. Many used touring to enhance entrepreneurial opportunities as journalists and travel writers depicting exotic locales, an opportunity that was near to impossible for women and nonwhites. Though some women did embark on epic cross-country and even worldwide tours, for example Annie Londonberry (born Annie Cohen Kopchovsky), who rode around the world between 1894 and 1895, for the most part the long-distance quest was a privilege afforded only to middle- and upper-class white men.[23] Such men also upped their racial and gender antagonisms during this period, as Milwaukee's *Pneumatic*, easily the most popular of Wisconsin's bicycling magazines, details in several racist and sexist examples. The *Pneumatic* frequently published jokes about the state's nonwhite riders, as when it covered a Chinese man nicknamed "Sam Wing" who was seen riding his bike, "Yellow Fever," in Green Bay during the last half of the 1890s. Area wheelmen could turn to the pages of the *Pneumatic* for updates and news concerning local LAW-produced minstrel shows. It also published a series of stories admonishing women to give up riding. Women, many men feared, might use the bicycle to solicit romantic encounters, and the *Pneumatic's* pages make their anxieties

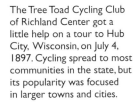

The Tree Toad Cycling Club of Richland Center got a little help on a tour to Hub City, Wisconsin, on July 4, 1897. Cycling spread to most communities in the state, but its popularity was focused in larger towns and cities.

Richland County History Room

clear. One particularly incensed male writer noted in July 1896 that "the bicycle is a menace to marriageable young men." The threat of a mobile, independent young woman on a bicycle caused significant discomfort.[24]

Another way to re-secure white male dominance of the sport was through the professionalization of racing, a key theme of our final chapter. Racing had been a popular part of cycling's identity since the days of velocipede mania, but in the last part of the 1890s, it rose to new heights as a form of white middle-class leisure and entertainment. Wisconsin's connections to racing ran deep during this period. Milwaukee's most famous racer, and quite possibly the most accomplished Wisconsin bike racer in history, was Walter "Wooden Shoes" Sanger. Sanger was very much a child of the first bicycling boom. Born March 13, 1873, in Wisconsin's nineteenth-century cycling epicenter, Sanger rose to fame in Milwaukee's streets by crushing his opponents with his tremendous speed and raw physical power. His bitter defeat at the hands of a black racer from Indiana, Marshall Walter "Major" Taylor, however, helped put his illustrious career into a decline, and by the early 1900s Sanger could no longer claim the celebrity status he once enjoyed. Told together, Taylor's and Sanger's stories illuminate the complicated ways race and professional bicycle racing became entangled in the last part of the 1890s.[25]

As the story told in *Wheel Fever* shows, Wisconsin's early bicycle boom ultimately helped expand the sport's popularity nationwide. The number of cyclists in the United States, with Wisconsin's help, went from a few hundred thousand in the early 1890s to several million by the middle part of the decade. This tremendous growth laid the foundations for the sport into the next century and beyond. No element of modern cycling has gone untouched by the scope of this original boom. The conclusion, finally, brings this history back into the present, and explores the ways Wisconsin's more recent decades have been shaped by the experiences discussed in the book.

ALL writers have to make decisions about what goes into their books and what gets left out. Early on in our research, we realized that the richness of our source material for the first boom, vastly outweighed anything we might put together on Wisconsin's second boom which started in the 1970s and continues today. More importantly, we realized that on almost every point, from the public sector's involvement in supporting cycling to bicycling's longstanding popularity and embrace at the grassroots, particularly among women, it was almost impossible to understand the sport today without first understanding this early history.

This book is very much about the origins of bicycling in Wisconsin, and why those origins still matter. Though historical, it is also a story of deep personal meaning to both of us. We have both benefitted from a number of Wisconsin's modern bicycling advocates. Jesse's father, Randy Gant, was diagnosed with type 2 diabetes back in 2001. His grandfather had lost both of his legs to the disease when Randy was a young man, and Randy resolved to do whatever he could to avoid the same outcome. For several weeks after the diagnosis, he started his long road to wellness by walking from his home in rural Rock Township in southern Wisconsin to the nearby city of Janesville. He walked several miles each day, capping off his journeys with a round of coffee with friends. Feeling stronger, he then dusted off an old bike he had kept hidden away in a shed. He rode a few times each week until he felt confident he could make it to work. By the end of 2002, a year out from his diagnosis, he was able to commute more than twenty miles each day round-trip. In time, his doctors informed him that many of his symptoms had begun to fade. He started riding longer distances, pushing himself until his old bike literally fell apart. He simply bought a new one and continued on.[26]

Nicholas's parents, James and Jane Hoffman, also ride bicycles for health and recreation. They often cruise the streets of Oshkosh aboard their bikes and take advantage of Wisconsin's many trail systems. When Nick was growing up in Hillsboro, his mother and father often enjoyed the benefits of the nearby Elroy-Sparta State Trail, then in its early years, but already an inspiration for riders with its system of tunnels and pastoral vistas in the Driftless region. By the 1990s, James had become an avid road cyclist, circling Lake Winnebago with coworkers from Jacob Shapiro Elementary School and partaking in a regular half-century ride on weekends. Seeing his father's Trek road bicycle from a young age inspired Nick to ride alongside his father on the WIOWASH Trail and complete his first out-of-city ride to Winneconne. James's ease with distance riding remains an inspiration to Nick. Today, his parents continue to ride often during the summer as an easy and effective means of health and relaxation, taking advantage of the growing bicycle lane infrastructure available in Oshkosh.

All of us are indebted to this history in one way or another. Wisconsinites between 1870 and 1900 helped lay the foundations for what would become a great bicycling state. For a little more than thirty years, residents of the Badger State joined increasing numbers of riders throughout the United States to grow bicycling's presence. During this crucial time, Wisconsin went from a place where bikes and bicyclists were literally laughed off the streets to a place where, on any given day, individual riders could join hundreds of their neighbors gathered for bike parades, commemorative rides, and even races down the streets. Cycling had become so popular that by 1895 Wisconsin boasted one of the largest bicycling communities of all the western states. As the *Pneumatic* reported, "Michigan, Ohio, Colorado, Illinois, and other Western Divisions which, in former years, have looked down on this state with contempt, because it was weak in num-

Bicycle mechanics were highly skilled, as demonstrated by this worker fixing a violin inside the Leslie Warner Bicycle Repair Shop in Black River Falls, ca. 1897.

WHi Image ID 28923

bers, now find the tables turned." Wisconsin was nowhere near the nation's leader in terms of its number of riders, but regionally, at least, none could compare. The foundation for a future great bicycling state had been built.[27]

This was a significant triumph for the state's riders. The density of the state's ridership soon translated into a movement, with new calls for reform to the state's roads serving as its rallying cry. The movement, both in Wisconsin and outside the state, ultimately changed America's expectations of its road infrastructure, lending credence to the notion that all public roads should be kept to a certain standard and that government had a central role to play in making sure there was widespread access to them. As one of the rare sports that depends upon the quality and accessibility of public spaces like roadways, parks, and other venues, the study of bicycling can be helpful in understanding the struggles that have occurred over those spaces.

Still, what is made in one generation can be unmade in the next. Wisconsin has actually slipped in the League of American Bicyclist national rankings over the past several years. Wisconsin fell from its highest rank of number two in 2009 to its most recent rank of sixth in 2012.[28] When it issued its most recent report card, the League (formerly the League of American Wheelmen) indicated that Wisconsin had fallen in the rankings for failing to keep up its infrastructure spending. Indeed, Wisconsin has fallen well behind states like Washington and Oregon in the most recent national rankings. This is likely to remain an ongoing concern for a state that has seen drastic cuts to its state budget over the past several years. Ultimately, state residents will have to decide whether the public values they have shared since at least the time of the Civil War are still valuable and worth protecting or whether the demands of fiscal responsibility will ultimately undermine the strength of their public spaces and institutions.

It makes sense, then, that a sport so intimately linked with contests over public space would have its origins in the nation's streets. Wheel fever would soon grow to include the din of thousands of cyclists singing songs while on out on parade, but those days were yet to come. The true story began with the almost imperceptible sound of creaking wood on ice. It was January 1869 and a young man was about to ride a machine people had never seen down a frozen Milwaukee street.

CHAPTER 1

Velocipede Mania

"All hail! then to the velocipede. We welcome the
distinguished stranger to our city."

Milwaukee Daily Sentinel, 1869[1]

The story of how Wisconsin became a great bicycling state began in earnest on January 7, 1869, when Joshua G. Towne peddled his velocipede—the wood and iron forerunner to today's bicycle—in what is believed to be the first ride in state history. It is easy to imagine Towne bouncing clumsily down the frozen midwinter streets of Milwaukee, crashing into icy ruts as his "boneshaker"—a name later used to describe these simple machines—creaked and groaned underneath him. Towne made for such a peculiar sight that local newspaper reporters even turned out to witness his ride, making him something of a local celebrity on the spot. "Were [Towne] not so modest as to induce the belief he would decline the honor," the *Milwaukee Sentinel* noted, "we should expect to see him elected mayor next spring by a unanimous vote." Towne never did manage to ride his velocipede to the mayor's office, but this was an important moment in Wisconsin's history nonetheless. His rickety, squeaking journey helped set into motion changes that would transform life throughout the state of Wisconsin in the coming decades.[2]

By simply going for a ride, Towne demonstrated how enthusiasm alone helped start Wisconsin on the path to becoming one of the world's top cycling destinations.

Towne had rather unwittingly helped start a statewide "velocipede mania," a term Wisconsin residents used to describe the state's early and widespread zeal for the new technology. This enthusiasm was intensely felt, especially as the first machines arrived, but the mania faded almost as quickly as it had bloomed. Between January and May 1869, Milwaukeeans, and then Wisconsinites more broadly, fell under the spell of the velocipede. For these five months, there seemed to be no cure for what it unleashed.

Winslow Homer expressed high hopes for the velocipede in the pages of *Harper's Weekly*, showing baby New Year welcoming 1869 aboard one of the new machines.

Harper's Weekly, January 9, 1869

New private rinks and riding schools grew to accommodate novice riders. Entrepreneurs came forward with innovative designs and patents. Nothing seemed capable of bringing it to an end. When the end did come, velocipede mania crashed in a dramatic fashion. By the summer of 1869, cities and towns could no longer point to a single velocipede making its way down a nearby street. Nor could they find a single indoor rink where they might try their own hand at riding the machines.

What can explain this swift rise and fall? The answers are multiple and complex. In the end, the velocipede's failure foreshadowed what was to come in cycling throughout Wisconsin in the coming decades. While the mania's immediate impact quickly faded and velocipedes and their riders effectively disappeared from Wisconsin's roads and towns by the end of that summer, velocipede mania did provide the foundation upon which Wisconsin's later embrace of cycling would be built. The story of the velocipede's dramatic rise and fall points to important but long-overlooked lessons about Wisconsin's history. It suggests that deep divisions have characterized state politics, and the challenges of bicycle advocacy, from the start. While the mania did not immediately create political debates that then became electoral issues for Wisconsin's citizens, it did force a serious reconsideration of who belonged on the roads and what those roads ought to do for the public. The mania also demonstrates that while Wisconsinites may have embraced the possibilities and opportunities the velocipede symbolized, the state was still a long way from becoming a premier cycling destination. State residents first had to *make* their state into a place where cycling could flourish.

As Wisconsin transitioned to a peacetime economy in the aftermath of the Civil War, there was little to suggest that cycling in any form would ever catch on in the Badger State. The state lagged far behind in many of the industrial developments already seen throughout Europe and other parts of the United States. In manufacturing, in particular, it trailed most of its most neighbors at the regional, national, and international levels. Nonetheless, as bicycling historian David Herlihy has helped illuminate, Wisconsin did share important connections with the industrializing world, particularly France.[3] Those who called Wisconsin home in the late 1860s were entangled in an emerging global marketplace. When new velocipede designs appeared in Paris in 1867, almost two full years before Towne's Milwaukee ride, Wisconsin's connections to this market made the state particularly well situated for the further incorporation of European-made goods.[4]

Wisconsin residents were keenly aware of new European technological innovations, including the velocipede. Many recognized that the new French-designed model marked an important improvement upon an earlier and more primitive machine called the "hobbyhorse." Developed by the German engineer Karl von Drais in 1817, the hobbyhorse resembled a velocipede in that it shared a number of basic components, such

Americans believed the velocipede was a technological marvel and by 1869 saw the hobbyhorse of 1818, illustrated in *Harper's Weekly,* as an old-fashioned curiosity.

Harper's Weekly,
March 6, 1869

as a wooden frame and two wheels. To operate a hobbyhorse, riders essentially walked or ran while seated atop the bar linking the two wheels, using their feet to balance as they bounded along. The application of bacon grease sometimes helped smooth the friction caused by the grinding of the wooden axles. In addition to adding a metal frame, the new French design added pedals to the hub on the front wheel, enabling the velocipede rider to have a much more efficient and comfortable ride. The rider then balanced between two wheels while using his or her feet to propel the velocipede forward. Pedals also enabled the rider to go greater distances without his feet and legs getting as sore or tired. Unlike a modern bicycle, however, the velocipede lacked such basic design elements as pneumatic tires made of rubber and a central chain drive to connect the bike chain to gears on the front and rear wheels. More importantly, velocipedes featured an entirely different kind of frame, one that was ill suited for the pedaled propulsion common in modern bicycles. Velocipedes had eliminated the need for a rider's feet to touch the ground, but they were still a ways off from what we would recognize today as a bicycle. Riding a wooden-wheeled velocipede also proved extremely uncomfortable over long distances, despite its many improvements over the hobbyhorse.[5]

Wisconsinites also demonstrated their early interest in and enthusiasm for the mania by tapping into a growing scientific and technological print culture. Simply by following the latest news and updates in magazines and newspapers and familiarizing themselves with a new print market meant explicitly for outdoor enthusiasts, state residents could track European design developments with ease. One of the first names Wisconsinites learned to associate with the velocipede was Pierre Michaux. Before 1867, Michaux had toiled as an obscure Paris blacksmith making parts for carriages. With the marketing of his new velocipede design, he gained a much wider notoriety. Michaux's expensive and often-unwieldy machine was not without its critics. So many earlier European hobbyhorse designs had failed to deliver on the promise of a cheap and reliable means of individual transport that a healthy dose of skepticism seemed destined to plague Michaux's sales wherever his product appeared, first in Germany, then France, then in England. His addition of pedals inspired at least a few to rethink their skepticism, however. Perceptions in Wisconsin and throughout the United States changed for the better when reports from abroad showed early velocipede riders were able to maintain an eight-mile-per-hour pace using the new Michaux design. Reporting on these developments for American readers and consumers, *Scientific American* noted that pedals "completely change[d] the character of the vehicle. . . . It glides along as though it were alive." Not everyone, however, bought into the trend. "It's just Paris at play again. First balloons, now velocipedes—one more capricious fantasy," the French *Journal Universel* wrote.[6]

A hobbyhorse being propelled by a rider, perhaps at a Milwaukee velocipede rink.

Milwaukee Public Museum Photography Collection

Young urbanites from Milwaukee to Paris expressed such an enthusiasm for the velocipede that it immediately became clear that cycling's future, whatever shape it might take, would be forever linked with this crucial demographic. This was especially true of young urban dwellers who enjoyed both the leisure time and the disposable income to afford the new machines. As had been the case throughout Europe and America's Northeast, the velocipede's most enthusiastic supporters hailed from the young, moneyed, and mobile ranks increasingly found in the industrial cities. Towne was a typical early advocate, given that he was both young and gainfully employed through his work as a clerk for the American Express Company. Young urban women, too, played key roles in popularizing the velocipede. Starting in the summer of 1867, a group of young

Velocipedes were individually made by hand, utilizing the skills of a blacksmith and a wheelwright. The earliest machines were wood with just a few iron parts, but by the spring of 1869 some were made entirely of iron.

Courtesy of Budget Bicycle Center, photo by Joel Heiman

people rode their new machines through the grounds of the Paris Exposition, showcasing the new technology to commentators from all over the world. Herlihy has suggested Michaux's design may have failed to find a market at all were it not for this small group of early boosters who started riding in public by the cascades in the Bois de Boulogne, an expansive park on the city's west side not far from the location of the original Michaux shop, becoming more common throughout Paris in 1868. *Le Sport*, a French sporting magazine, wrote, "On your velocipede! That is the rallying cry loudly repeated of late by a few intrepid Parisians, fanatics of this new means of locomotion."[7] Early advocates, including a small but growing class of young Wisconsin urbanites, embraced the velocipede as a solution to the age-old problem of how to get from here to there in the quickest and easiest way possible.

These demographic patterns eventually helped animate the beginnings of cycling politics in the Badger State—those adamantly for and against the new technology. The French public established an important precedent when it reacted with hostility toward many of its first velocipede riders throughout 1867 and 1868, a hostility that would be echoed in Wisconsin the following year. Many referred to velocipede riders as "fanatics." Others said they suffered from a debilitating "mania." Newspaper reports often ridiculed the machine. Not long after the first "velocipedestrians" stormed Paris, a French correspondent for the *New York Times* spoke about the new technology to

American audiences. The reporter said the machine gave riders "the comical appearance of flying through the air." The *Times* adopted a similarly flippant tone in its coverage of female riders. Reporters worried it would "force adoption of the bloomer." Such a statement suggested how strange the sight of female riders was at the time, particularly when women began touring cities alone on their velocipedes or in packs escorted by large groups of male friends.[8]

By the end of 1867, a handful of new velocipede manufacturers had sprung up across France. In December, just eight months after the new design appeared, nearly a hundred riders rode as a group on an excursion to the palace at Versailles. For all the showy display, however, it still remained unclear whether the velocipede would truly catch on. Many complained of injuries sustained while riding the machines. And because the velocipede was expensive, only the upper and upper-middle classes had the time or money to really perfect the art of riding. This meant that when it finally arrived in Wisconsin, the velocipede was easily dismissed as a whimsical plaything for the rich, not a serious transportation alternative for everyday people.[9]

Women widely embraced velocipede mania, however, and helped demonstrate that the fad could not be so easily dismissed as a rich man's toy. The early and open participation of French women in the velocipede mania in Paris certainly contributed to the enthusiasm American women brought to the velocipede boom. Female participation opened doors, but it also led to complaints from early critics, especially men, who dismissed female riding out of hand. A male-led backlash over female participation stressed the various dangers the velocipede might pose, not only to gender norms but also to women's bodies. The *Appleton Crescent*, for example, admonished women

Unlike in the United States, women velocipedestrians in Europe were more accepted and even participated in races on the streets of Paris in 1869.

Harper's Weekly, December 19, 1868

Velocipedestrians were a common sight on city streets and parks in the Northeast before the sport became popular in Wisconsin.

Harper's Weekly, December 19, 1868

to properly button their dresses and skirts when riding velocipedes, so as not to "detract at all from the appearance of an ordinary walking costume." It added that men ought to "right her" if they witnessed a woman wearing improper clothing in public.[10] As a result, instead of celebrating the machine as a transportation alternative for the masses (a "poor man's horse," regardless of sex), male riders increasingly adopted a more conservative tone. Indeed, the mania slowly lost its subversive edge as advocates fell back into existing notions of manhood and womanhood. Both men and women, critics maintained, had been threatened by the radical potential of cheap and easy-to-use individual transportation.

The divide deepened as racing events, sponsored by manufacturers, began to gain in popularity. Racing showcased the virtues of competition, while velocipede long-distance riding highlighted athletic endurance. Velocipede trick riding, too, provided a venue for demonstrating mastery over the machines. No longer did advocates emphasize the velocipede's broad utility as a practical transportation option for working people. Instead, the velocipede fell into the service of offering competitive opportunities that would later help speed the sport's male-dominated professionalization. Though early pamphlets were published to celebrate the democratic potentials of the velocipede while teaching the layperson how to ride, the early trend pointed away from using the velocipede as a way to change the fundamental nature, place, and meaning of transportation itself.

Wisconsin's business community provided ample support for these more specialized, competitive, and enormously popular venues. Velocipede riders organized races and other demonstrations using local business sponsorships, but these events increasingly occurred away from the city's public streets and parks where no tickets were required for admission. The sport moved to privately owned spaces, including indoor rinks—again following France's lead. In 1868, the French manufacturer Michaux and his associates sponsored the sport's first recorded races. They occurred in the Paris suburbs at Saint Cloud, and featured events pitting between three and seven racers against one another at a time. The winners of the races averaged a speed around fourteen miles per hour. Shorter races, with their explosive speed, were far more popular than longer rides. Even so, in July 1868, a Favre-built velocipede was used in a race against a horse and buggy over the course of forty-five miles to Toulouse on rough, rural roads. The horse won by only twenty-five minutes.[11] And in November 1868, a women's race held at Bordeaux drew thousands of curious spectators to a local park. Onlookers openly fretted that the women were wearing unusually short skirts.[12]

When velocipede mania did reach the United States, Wisconsin was well ahead of the curve in adopting it, particularly for a western state. Back east, the mania had already started in earnest during the summer of 1868, well in advance of Towne's first ride through Milwaukee. Eastern cities including Boston and New York were treated to the velocipede's debut as three of the Hanlon Brothers, part of a famous nineteenth-century acrobatic troupe, raced velocipedes on stages across the country for ticket buyers. The machine proved popular, and soaring demand led to the creation of a small velocipede industry, the first step in what would become a booming domestic bicycle trade in the United States. Several New York manufacturers, many of them (like Michaux) previously employed as carriage makers, started producing velocipedes for American consumers. While demand continued to escalate, costs for American-made velocipedes remained high. In 1868 and 1869, the average price for a velocipede was $75 to $150, while Pierre Lallement's new patent on the machine added an additional hefty surcharge after February 1869. White Union soldiers three or four years before had earned just thirteen dollars a month. There was no guarantee it would ever catch on with the growing middle class in the United States, particularly in emerging consumer markets like Wisconsin. New Yorkers, however, did have the capital on hand to participate. In the fall of 1868, Manhattan became the nation's velocipede epicenter. Velocipede races were held there in November, and Central Park became the nation's most popular early cycling destination. The young artist Winslow Homer got so caught up in the fever that he depicted the year 1869 arriving on the back of a velocipede. It was not long before races were also planned in Cincinnati, Chicago, Detroit, San Francisco, and Milwaukee.[13]

When a few new velocipedes were finally shipped to Wisconsin in 1869, it should come as no surprise that they arrived first in the state's major shipping and industrial center, Milwaukee. When Towne unveiled the state's first velocipede in January, he helped introduce a trend that would soon sweep the smaller towns and cities of the countryside. Most Wisconsinites probably read about the velocipede's appearance in their local newspapers, such as the February 5 clipping in the *Milwaukee Daily Sentinel* that announced a "velocipede exhibition" planned to be held at a nearby gymnasium alongside other gymnastic and acrobatic performances.[14]

Reading the accounts, it becomes clear that many Wisconsinites greeted these early machines with a heavy fog of suspicion and skepticism. As Wisconsin's bicycling culture developed over the course of the ensuing decades, these tensions never fully disap-

In this illustration from *Harper's Weekly* in spring of 1869, the artist imagines potential uses for the velocipede by police, salesmen, soldiers, and regular men and women.

Harper's Weekly, May 1, 1869

peared. Accounts again and again stressed how dangerous velocipedes were. It would be a mistake to read these stories as purely cautionary or reactionary, however. The whimsical tone of many early accounts, combined with the very real injuries riders sometimes sustained, made for compelling local coverage that only helped further the curiosity that became characteristic of the velocipede mania as it reached the far corners of the state. People seemed to have an endless appetite for stories of the odd velocipedestrians and their strange exploits, especially when a little blood, laughter, and tears filled the columns. In February, for example, not long after Towne's informal debut, the *Daily Milwaukee News* ran a story about a Cincinnati "lad" named George Grier who crashed through a hatch in the floor of a fourth-story velocipede school, suffering wounds that observers feared were fatal.[15] The warming spring air, however, finally made velocipede mania more than an abstract in a newspaper. By late March, Wisconsinites fell under the velocipede's spell through direct experiences and encounters with the machines and their riders. They were a common sight at "every hour of the day," the state's newspapers reported. "As soon as warm weather shall give us firm roads, we may expect to see everybody straddling his velocipede," an account from March 5 boldly declared.[16] The increased number of riders on Wisconsin's streets only led to new questions and dilemmas, however. Slowly but surely, velocipede mania gave way to new concerns about regulating exactly where and when these peculiar velocipedestrians should be allowed

How to Mount a Machine

SOON AFTER THE first velocipede appeared in Milwaukee in 1869, local newspapers published these tongue-in-cheek instructions for would-be riders, with the assumption that anyone with enough gall to mount a velocipede would be male. A reporter for the *Milwaukee Sentinel* offered the following:

1. Avoid all liquids which tend to unsteadiness. Divide your pennies so that an equal number shall occupy each pocket. Place your hat squarely upon your head (it might be well to carry a spirit level, the better to accomplish this). Either leave your watch with your uncle or buy another for your other vest-pocket, in order that the weight of one may not throw you out of balance. Also avoid tobacco, unless you place a quid in either cheek, and be sure that your cigar be held in the center of your mouth; also part your hair in the middle.

2. Mount your machine. If you don't succeed at first, try again; it's good exercise for a beginner. In this connection it might be well to suggest that the learner get himself upholstered. The limbs may not work as freely, but it saves the skin.

3. Balance yourself. This may seem a trifle difficult at first, but it becomes quite easy after you learn how. . . . If you are practicing in the presence of ladies, or even a promiscuous company, act as graceful as possible. If you tumble over, repeat it, smilingly. Never get red in the face, it may be taken advantage of by spectators, who often think such things funny.

4. After having acquired the art of balancing yourself, raise your feet to the cranks and push out. The faster you push out the better, provided you'll keep at it. Don't stop, unless you come in contact with something you cannot surmount, in which case, if you still maintain your seat and your [*sic*] upright, back out with all the grace you possess. Never allow your bicycle to get on top of you; it learns its bad tricks, besides being bad for the projecting angles of your anatomy.

5. When you conclude that you have mastered the forward motion in a straight line, try your hand at a curve. These curves should be as long as possible at first, since a new rider is very apt to obey the law of inertia and continue to move in a straight line after the machine is turned into a circular one.

6. [By] having learned all sorts of forward motions, if you are desirous of putting on

How to Mount a Machine

a few more emotional frills, try the backward motion. Don't be too confident of astonishing anybody but yourself by this movement; it requires something more than cheek to make it a success. You will find your bicycle inclined to lay down. This must be guarded against, since it takes the poetry all out of the motion, and is not exactly what might be called a triumph of genius.[1]

to ride. Riders also took a keen interest in these questions, opening what would become a key dynamic within local and statewide cycling politics.

In important ways, the development of early Wisconsin bicycling politics simply echoed patterns already established in France, throughout Europe, and along the eastern part of the United States. Much of early cycling's politics reflected broader social anxieties of the time. Early French criticisms about the unmanly and unwomanly tendencies the velocipede seemed to encourage mirrored some of the same anxieties expressed by people in Wisconsin. Newspaper editors worried about the velocipede's effects on good and upstanding Wisconsin men. As one editorial in the *Daily Milwaukee News* put it, "The velocipede may make a temporary plaything for boys of larger growth, but as to settling down into a sober, steady, everyday practicability, we are quite willing to risk our judgment or reputation for prophecy in the negative." Commentators pointed out that the machine's lack of efficiency would only suit those rare men in superb physical shape. "When we reflect . . . that the whole effort of this utilitarian age is to get away from labor, and not into it, we can guess what the fate of the velocipede will ultimately be," the *Daily Milwaukee News* predicted.[17] By March 1869, Wisconsin's residents could also look to the velocipede's story in Paris and New York and assume that the velocipede was probably more suited for the confines of the city, not well equipped to handle the state's rough rural and country roads.

Those Wisconsinites who were more optimistic about the velocipede's promise found new ways of using it to entertain themselves. Their efforts helped resurrect the velocipede's increasingly troubled image. One of the most common strategies involved establishing an indoor velocipede "rink" or "school." There, local riders and specialists might perform tricks and other feats for a paying audience while also teaching locals the basic skills they would need in order to ride the machines on their own. The first such rinks appeared in Milwaukee but soon spread to other parts of the state. An advertisement in the *Milwaukee Daily Sentinel* for March 26, 1869, announced that the local "skating rink" would soon be converted to accommodate a new velocipede riding school, led by a transplanted New Yorker, very much a velocipede booster, named C. D. Veazie. It is difficult to know whether these schools aimed to spread the velocipede gospel to a wide segment of the population, or whether they were meant from the beginning to serve as a kind of boutique entertainment for the well-off.[18]

Whatever their intended purpose, velocipede rinks nevertheless offered chances to make cycling more respectable in the eyes of a still-skeptical general public. At an indoor Wisconsin rink, it was not uncommon to see amateurs trying their hand at the machines alongside a few local celebrities. Civil War veterans were particularly common as guests of honor. On April 2, riders at Veazie's newly opened Milwaukee

Learning to ride a machine indoors at a rink was a treacherous affair, as demonstrated in this print showing a velocipede riding school in New York City.

Harper's Weekly, February 13, 1869

rink helped raise money for veteran Gilbert H. Bates, who was introduced to the admiring crowd as the "hero of the flag march from Vicksburg to the sea."[19] A former Union soldier, Bates had recently walked through the postwar South carrying a United States flag and no money, betting friends that the goodwill he encountered among defeated southerners would demonstrate the desire for reconciliation between North and South. He appeared at Milwaukee's velocipede rink dressed in the same uniform he had worn during his march and talked throughout the evening to the riders and guests about the highlights of his journey. Patriotic and wholesome appeals such as his helped build Wisconsin's growing enthusiasm for the mania.[20]

To meet the increasing interest in velocipedes, indoor schools also opened throughout Milwaukee, building upon the small cottage industry of ticketed exhibitions and shows that were also held in the rinks. On April 3, an advertisement announced the opening of the first school. Veazie, already the operator of the city's first rink, was named as the school's director. Lessons could be had for fifteen cents.[21] To encourage enrollment, Veazie turned this time not to patriotic pride, but to the charms of a young woman. On April 10, the *Milwaukee Daily Sentinel* reported that the "celebrated female velocipedist" and trick rider Edith Shuler of Chicago would help open Milwaukee's rink.[22] On April 16, only a few weeks after the velocipede riding school was announced in

Professor Veazie advertised his Velocipede Riding School in the Milwaukee newspapers in 1869 to attract potential riders and curious spectators.

Daily Milwaukee News,
April 3, 1869

VELOCIPEDE
RIDING SCHOOL.

On and after Saturday evening, April 3, 1869, the undersigned will open a school in the

SKATING RINK,

Where instructions in Velocipede Riding will be given.
THIS SATURDAY evening the first public EXHIBITION will be presented, and classes formed for future instruction. Admission 15 cents.

apr3dtf   C. D. VEAZIE, Director,

The earliest image of a man or woman bicyclist known to have ridden in Wisconsin is of Edith Shuler of Chicago. She appeared in advertisements for the Milwaukee Skating Rink in the *Daily Milwaukee News.*

Daily Milwaukee News,
April 16, 1869

MISS EDITH SHULER, of Chicago, assisted by Prof. GEO. D. MILES, of New York, will appear at the Skating Rink,

Tuesday Even'g, April 20, 1869.

Admission, - - 50 Cents.

local papers, the *Daily Milwaukee News* announced that Shuler would begin her shows on the night of April 20. The newspaper ran a striking image of Shuler atop her velocipede. It circulated widely, adorning virtually all advertisements for her shows scheduled in the days and weeks ahead.[23]

The increased privatization and commercialization of velocipede riding opened doors for Wisconsin women in sometimes surprising and conflicting ways. Shuler's presence as a performer, for example, carved out a space for her to operate as a kind of entrepreneur at a time when women were discouraged from doing so. The *Daily Milwaukee News* said of the performance of April 20 that Shuler was the "embodiment of grace." It went on, "She is one of the most skillful performers in the country."[24] More than this, the private venue of the rink helped legitimate velocipede riding in ways that were often not extended to those who used the velocipede out of doors, including men. Newspapers told of savvy entrepreneurs putting the machines to use around town in various ways, but revealed that these efforts usually met with failure. When a man selling oranges used a new "tricycle" to peddle his produce about on the city's west side in the midst of the mania, officials debated whether he needed a "one-horse or foot peddler's license," the *Milwaukee Daily Sentinel* reported.[25] Inside the rink, Shuler's shows fell beyond the control of specialized licensing and ordinances.

THE CELEBRATED
AMERICAN IMPROVED VELOCIPEDE.
Patented January 26, 1869.

Mechanics tried to perfect the velocipede with iron frames and wheels that afforded more stability and a gentler ride. The improvements remained unpopular and too costly for most Americans.

Harper's Weekly, March 13, 1869

The velocipede also helped give rise to changes in ideas about manliness, as the velocipede encouraged the development of a new and potent strand of daredevil bravado. In late April, Milwaukee papers carried a story from the *Jacksonville Journal* (Illinois), which detailed the account of a Professor Grove, who, like Milwaukee's Veazie, ran a local velocipede hall on the third floor of a Jacksonville building. When Grove's students started experimenting with a ramp, a man named Dunlap nearly died when he flew out of the building's window. "As soon as he got the velocipede up to full speed," the *Journal* reported, "up he went like a bird [and] away he went, through the window, like a flash, and disappeared." Spectators rushed to the edge, expecting to see a mangled body lying broken on the street below. Instead, he had actually flown across the alley and landed on the roof of a neighboring drug store, and then onto the roof of a bank where he managed to slide off his broken machine before it tumbled to the ground. According to the report, the man jumped to his feet, swung his hat, and gave a cheer. "Mr. Dunlap thinks he is entitled to the champion medal as the most daring velocipede rider in the country," the *Journal* writer laughed. In stark contrast with Shuler's elegant performances, the velocipede gave clear incentive to those men who wanted to claim the machine for a new rough-and-tumble kind of competitive manhood. As desire for competition heated up, the possibility of the velocipede becoming the "poor man's horse" was slowly eclipsed.[26]

In what would also become a key element of Wisconsin's cycling future, the state's natural environment also shaped the course of velocipede mania. Pleasant weather in the spring of 1869 encouraged large numbers of Milwaukeeans to make the trek to nearby velocipede rinks, which remained cool and dry in the absence of intense winter cold or summer heat and humidity. Pleasant temperatures also ensured that the performers themselves would not be plagued by excessive sweat during their performances, something that would have undermined the womanly grace Shuler cultivated during her shows. As April progressed, large crowds turned out in Milwaukee to see indoor trick riding by Miss Shuler and Professor George D. Miles, along with Veazie and Master Lennie Davis. The weather was an apparent non-factor as Shuler and Miles won admiration for their "double riding," which commentators said "showed great nerve and excellent balancing on the part of both."[27] Shuler seemed to draw the most attention of all. "Many of our citizens have doubtless seen in the hotels or show-windows, photographs of a beautiful young lady riding a velocipede," a writer at the *Milwaukee Daily Sentinel* observed on April 20. "All such persons will be pleased to learn that she appears at the Rink this evening, when they will have an opportunity to witness her wonderful performances on the velocipede."[28] As the performances continued, Shuler's celebrity seemed only to grow.

She was back in the papers a few days later after appearing again with Miles, to the delight of the "fashionable audience." The events seemed to combine trick rides with demonstrations meant to showcase the velocipede's utility. The *Milwaukee Daily Sentinel* reported:

> Their feats are truly wonderful, and give the beholder new ideas of the capabilities of the velocipede. An interesting feature of the entertainment were the performances of a quartette [*sic*] consisting of Miss Shuler, Prof. Miles, Mr. Veazie, the genial manager, and Master Lennie Davis, who went through all manner of graceful curves in concert. They will appear again this evening. The price of admission is reduced to twenty cents, reserved seats fifty cents.[29]

The *Daily Milwaukee News*, meanwhile, reported on April 23 that the "audience at the rink last night was large and respectable." Shuler and Professor Miles "seem to perform with greater perfection, if such a thing were possible, each evening." Shuler also rode the velocipede by standing straight on top of its saddle, a feat that editors said was "as difficult . . . [as] riding a horse erect in the ring."[30] On April 24, another strong crowd turned out to see the performers, no doubt lured by continued pleasant weather. "This will be the last opportunity our citizens will have of seeing these artists and they should have a crowded house. The performance is well worth seeing," papers read.[31] Hailed as the "farewell benefit" by the *Daily Milwaukee News*, the rink was supposed to hold its final velocipede show on April 25. As the *Milwaukee Daily Sentinel* reported on April 26, however, the performers were encouraged to do one more performance in the city. "Both of the artists received the heartiest applause," the *Daily Milwaukee News* reported, adding, "We trust they will visit our city again at no distant day."[32] As the crowds for Shuler's shows expanded, the velocipede's popularity reached new heights throughout the state of Wisconsin. Relegated to the indoor rink, however, debates over where velocipedes should be ridden on city streets fell increasingly by the wayside.

Hoping to capitalize on velocipede mania, inventors in Wisconsin also turned their efforts to perfecting new velocipede designs. These efforts helped establish what would become Wisconsin's strong manufacturing ties to racing, a key part of Wisconsin's status as an emerging cycling state. In December 1868, Sylvester A. Wood of Manitowoc applied for a US patent for his version of the velocipede. Wood's patent presented a machine that the *Janesville Gazette* reported might reach twelve to fifteen miles per hour.[33] An inventor and town booster, Wood was involved in several local businesses and worked as a lawyer.[34] His outlandish design was actually a three-wheeled velocipede with a special Wisconsin twist, in that it came complete with skis or "sleigh attachments" for

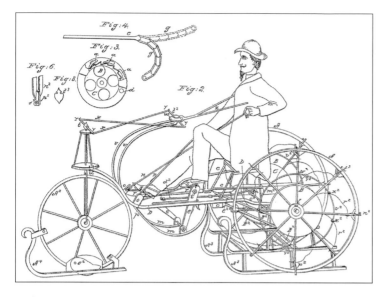

Sylvester Wood's "Improved Velocipede" proposed adding skis—a special design for riders in Wisconsin.

US Patent 85,501, December 29, 1868, courtesy of Google Patents

help with winter riding.[35] In Ripon, a man identified only as "Dr. Hubbard" also designed and constructed a version of the velocipede in January 1869, around the same time Towne debuted the machine in Milwaukee.[36] Hubbard learned about the velocipede while watching celebrity velocipedestrian Charles A. Dana during travels through Boston and New York during the early part of the mania. According to accounts, Hubbard eventually built two velocipedes and taught local young men how to ride.[37]

The success of the New York scene fresh in his mind, Dr. Hubbard also turned his attention to creating a velocipede rink for Ripon's citizens, perhaps hoping to create a permanent venue for his inventions. He located his rink on the second floor of Greenway Hall in downtown Ripon. When they came out to view the place, Ripon's newspapers described the velocipede in characteristic terms as "a vicious looking beast." Lacking a beautiful young woman like Shuler to help sell the machines, Hubbard fared poorly in the local paper. "There was Dr. Hubbard," a reporter wrote, "charging around the hall like an escaped lunatic, straddled of a thing that looked like a cross between a Rock Mountain go-it and a hand-cart. His hair streaming in the wind and his coat tails straight out so you could play marbles on them."[38] The reaction to the velocipede in Ripon mirrored trends common in rural sections of the state. A simultaneous sense of attraction and revulsion seemed to color all accounts of the velocipede between January and June 1869. The only place where velocipede mania seemed to really catch on was in Milwaukee, where women like Shuler helped make the machines respectable in ways that failed to translate beyond the city.

Still, even the hint of commercial success lured many Wisconsinites to form businesses to help sustain the new market. In Oshkosh, William Crawford, a junior member of Crawford Brothers Carriage Company, rode a velocipede manufactured by his business down Main Street as a way to both advertise for his company and test some of the design innovations he hoped to bring to his new product line. As the member of an Oshkosh family with deep ties to the carriage-making business, Crawford was well positioned to become a potential leading manufacturer of velocipedes in the state, as many early velocipede makers, like Michaux, borrowed skills gleaned from carriage production to make the new machines. Though the state's natural environment would later prove a boon to cycling, in the early years poor outdoor conditions often hindered cycling advocacy. Simply traveling down a street in 1860s Oshkosh presented several difficulties for velocipede riders. The city's Main Street had dirt roads, and although occasionally smoothed, it was often filled with furrows in the ground cut from wagon wheels crisscrossing the mud. Crawford tried to select good ground to display his machines, but the poor roads undermined his pitch. Crawford ended his street performance by riding his velocipede down a ramp and up through a building window.[39]

Forced by poor weather and road conditions to take their riding indoors, more of Oshkosh's early velocipedestrians moved their practices to a rink on Main Street. The *Northwestern* announced, "Two of these new fangled go-carts were in training at McCourt's Hall last evening belonging to Frank Waldo, the other to Crawford Brothers."[40] Waldo had moved from Colorado to Racine by 1863, and soon relocated to Oshkosh, where he worked for Rudd and Holden Carriage Company, as well as taking odd jobs as a sign painter.[41] His experience certainly helped his ability to construct a velocipede, although his machine was still described by the *Northwestern* as "imperfect" and "difficult to manage."[42] After two or three days of practice, however, Crawford managed to present an excellent display of riding during an exhibition at McCourt's Hall. He impressed the crowd with his velocipede skills.[43] Slowly but surely, the face of the velocipede mania started to shift as more and more rural men perfected their riding. In small towns and throughout rural parts of the state, the face of the velocipede was becoming increasingly male.

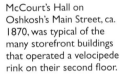

McCourt's Hall on Oshkosh's Main Street, ca. 1870, was typical of the many storefront buildings that operated a velocipede rink on their second floor.

Courtesy of Oshkosh Public Museum

Fancy Riding

SPECTATORS AT THE Milwaukee velocipede rink were astonished by the "fancy riding" tricks performed by the city's first expert
bicyclists. At a performance on April 22, 1869,
Professor C. D. Veazie maneuvered his machine

Spectators were amazed by fancy riding
stunts at velocipede rinks.

Penny Illustrated Paper, September 18, 1869

through the rink, picked up three or four chairs,
and carried them while continuing to pedal.
Master Lennie Davis rode and directed his bicycle with his arms folded so he could not use them
for balance, and Edith Shuler rode her velocipede
standing on the saddle.[1] Fancy riding's popularity continued during the high-wheel craze, and it

later became professionalized as celebrity riders
profited from performances at national meets.

Milwaukee's most celebrated fancy rider was
Lee Richardson, who rose to international
renown for his daring stunts and unrivaled
manipulation of his machine. As the son of L.
M. Richardson, owner of Monarch Bicycle
Company, Lee often traveled with his father to
meets and exhibitions.[2] By 1896, Richardson
began performing fifteen-minute acts at meets
held in Appleton, Sheboygan, New London,
and Chippewa Falls. Among his top early stunts
was the ability to ride backward for an extended
period, a feat he claimed to do longer than anyone in the world. According to the *Pneumatic*,
Richardson had indeed become the "champion
trick rider of the world," as well as a major draw
to races.[3] In Windsor, Ontario, the *Evening
Record* described his stunts between each race
among the highlights of a local LAW National
Circuit meet. "It would be hard to tell all this
clever little kid did with that machine of his,"
the newspaper explained.[4]

Part of Richardson's success was due to his
specially constructed bicycle. His machine had
a sturdier body, wider and stronger tires, and
a fork that could make a complete revolution
without hitting the frame. Additionally, he had
a uniquely designed wheel that was fitted with a

Fancy Riding

A spectator captured this rare snapshot of Lee Richardson performing at the Appleton meet in 1896.

WHi Image ID 98617

changeable gear, which permitted him to leave the saddle, slide his body through the frame, and remount, all while still in motion.[5] During the height of his career in 1897, Richardson traveled to Europe under the direction of "Teddy" Marks, the agent for cabaret singer Yvette Guilbert. Unfortunately his European tour was cut short when he caught pneumonia.[6] After recovering, Richardson continued his fancy riding shows, visiting Europe again in 1899 and finishing many more tours throughout the United States.

Stunt performers also exhibited and competed with modified bicycles in short races between the main racing events. In 1896, Chicago's A. J. Nicollet rode a "giraffe" bicycle in a half-mile exhibition in the time of 1:11 at the Neenah State Circuit Meet. Giraffes (commonly called "tall bikes" today) were unusually tall and incorporated two bicycle frames welded one atop the other. Earlier that year, Julius Andrae and Sons unveiled a four-seated bicycle for similar exhibition races against their personal records.[7] Often these bicycles were made with spare parts

Fancy Riding

Lee Richardson's specially designed bicycle allowed greater manipulation of his machine to perform daring stunts.

Scientific American, May 13, 1899

or recycled older models. By hiring fancy riders like Richardson or Nicollet, early race promoters expected to draw record-breaking audiences to Wisconsin's meets. More importantly, by their ability to control their machines and break the bicycle's known limitations, these fancy riders helped add to the spectacle and wonder of modern bicycling.

As the popularity of the velocipede grew in Oshkosh, rival rinks began opening throughout the city. Abel Neff converted the second story of his hall on Kansas Street into an indoor rink. Benton Brothers Hardware Store sponsored the rink and offered spectators three velocipedes of their manufacture, including a three-wheeled design. Their wooden velocipedes had wider tires than normal designs, but they were infamous for being stiff, unstable, and very uncomfortable. Beginners found the three-wheeled versions easier to ride and therefore safer. A reporter from the *Northwestern* who tested the velocipedes thought the two-wheeled design was easier to mount. Although two wheels required a good amount of practice, the three-wheeled design was "liable to bolt and unhorse you at every turn, unless the greatest precaution [was] taken." Benton Brothers sold their machines for twenty to thirty dollars, or the equivalent of several weeks' pay for a typical state resident at the time.[44]

Velocipede mania generated further enthusiasm throughout the state. On April 1, the *Eau Claire Free Press* said, "Eau Claire is no longer without her velocipedes."[45] Quarter-mile races between two Eau Claire men were held at the city's newly opened rink around April 15.[46] Because they already associated it with Milwaukee and the big-city life, some rural people resented the velocipede's appearance. One report captured this sentiment well when it said, "Already the horses about town, whose services now are dispensable, are beginning to drop their tails and lament over the probability of being supplanted by a new wooden creation of man's device that don't 'eat hay.'" It went on to mention that a local

named Howell Drake, Eau Claire's "hay man," was already threatening "utter extinction to the wooden horse" and "instant death to its propagators." "The storm cloud deepens," editors snickered, "look out for the shower."[47] Drake may have been having a bit of fun with the reporters, or perhaps the reporters were having fun with Drake, but his words nonetheless hinted at a growing chasm between segments of the Wisconsin population.

Part of the growing rift seemed generational. Young people were crucial in spreading the velocipede's appeal throughout the state that spring. The first velocipede ride in Appleton happened on the campus of Lawrence University. The *Appleton Crescent* noted, "A velocipede can be seen almost any day going to or coming from the University." With the campus under the mania's grip, it was not long before new velocipede rinks opened in the city. A new "velocipede school" soon opened in Metropolitan Hall, where lessons could be had "every afternoon and evening, Sundays excepted." An effective ban on Sunday riding would soon become a key part of early cycling culture. Sunday riding remained controversial throughout the first three decades of cycling's rise in Wisconsin. Beaver Dam newspapers also noted that they had seen their first "velocipedists" with the coming of the New Year.[48]

Though the velocipede clearly gave pause to some of Wisconsin's residents when it first arrived, evidence suggests that most of the city's residents welcomed it with open arms. Similar to Milwaukee and Oshkosh, local rinks and schools opened across the state to pave the way for velocipede mania. Outside the city, velocipede mania took on different dimensions. On April 8, the *Eau Claire Free Press* reported more quarter-mile races at the velocipede rink owned by C. E. Johnson.[49] Where notions of womanly grace filled the descriptions of Shuler's performance in Milwaukee papers, the folksy description of the *Eau Claire Free Press* cast the mania in a different light: "The science of riding a velocipede is expressed in a very few words. You 'straddle, paddle, and then skedaddle."[50] Just how long Wisconsinites would straddle and paddle their way on a velocipede remained anyone's guess.

An unknown man poses on an early tricycle, April 23, 1869.

Milwaukee Public Museum Photography Collection

By the end of spring, the velocipede boom had turned into a bust, even as new cities and towns, such as Elkhorn, got their first view of the machine.[51] There were multiple reasons for the velocipede's decline. Perhaps most important, natural conditions throughout the state simply did not favor the widespread adoption of the machines. Out of doors, poor town roads remained muddy and difficult to navigate. Velocipedestrians did what they could to find clean and dry wooden sidewalks, but riding on sidewalks tended only to stir up animosity from pedestrians. In Appleton, a ride on the sidewalks of College Avenue became a daily routine for Mr. Kirkwood. Despite the occasional surprise by neighborhood dogs (quite possibly the first recorded dog chase of a cyclist in state history), Kirkwood's rides through town were uneventful so long as he remained on the sidewalk. When on the sidewalk, however, he risked the ire of men and women walking along the paths.[52] As the summer progressed, it became clear that the velocipede simply was not going to work in most out-of-doors spaces in Wisconsin. Relegated to a few moneymaking shows in indoor rinks whose novelty quickly passed, the heyday of the velocipede came to a rapid close.

Bicyclists imagined creative ways to deal with the treacherous riding conditions in the winter of 1869.

Harper's Weekly, February 20, 1869

Culturally, too, many Wisconsinites expressed resentment toward the machines. If the state was to become a known cycling destination, the public would need to be won over. "The velocipede mania seems to be dying out as rapidly as it sprung up," the *Oshkosh Northwestern* reported as early as February 1869. "The velocipede exhibition at the Rink last week failed to create an excitement." Held at Neff's hall, the exhibition drew only twenty-five people, although one of the lucky guests was given a free velocipede.[53] Late in March, explicitly antivelocipede poems and snippets started appearing in rural and small-town papers across the state. One example, published as "The Velocipedestrian," issued a warning against young men who spent too much time riding their machines. In telling the fictional story of a young rider named "Augustus L.," it created a melodrama in which young Augustus died from over-riding, leaving his bereaved wife behind:

> *Remember the fate our A.L. has just met;*
> *Let this be your warning creed:*
> *Stay at home with your wife, the rest of your life,*
> *And avoid the velocipede!*[54]

The irony, of course, is that the velocipede mania's key diplomat in Wisconsin was female, meaning women certainly did not stay at home waiting for their husbands to abandon velocipede riding. As Shuler and others had already demonstrated, women were just as eager to embrace the velocipede as men.[55] Yet, even as velocipede riders constituted only the smallest minority in the state, they managed to generate a widespread cultural backlash. In Appleton, for example, where only three or four velocipedes were known to exist, and where riders could not have formed a meaningful community, locals insisted on ordinances to ban them entirely from the city's streets. By March, the situation became nonnegotiable, as the *Appleton Crescent* reminded readers of an ordinance that prohibited velocipedes on sidewalks subject to fines. A classic example of overreach, the ordinance suggests just how rabid antivelocipede culture was at the height of the mania.[56]

Increasingly, the battle for velocipede legitimacy was also lost in bigger cities like Appleton and Milwaukee. "Persons may not know it, but they are liable to a fine for riding velocipedes on the side-walks of this city," an Appleton announcement read.[57] On May 12, reports surfaced in Milwaukee that City Councilor Prentiss had submitted an ordinance banning the "running or propelling" of velocipedes on any sidewalk in the city.[58] At about the same time, Commissioner Delano of Milwaukee decreed that the velocipede rinks in the city would be subject to a new tax, comparable to the sales tax paid by city theaters or concerts.[59] Janesville, too, passed an ordinance to ban the "riding upon or using velocipedes on the sidewalks" on June 19, and issued fines of one to ten dollars for those who continued the practice.[60]

In these early stages of bicycle activism, those optimistic about the velocipede's future often wrote impassioned editorials to their local papers to celebrate their potential. Advocates, though few, routinely fought back in the editorial pages of their local papers. One article, signed "A Friend to Progress (On Velocipedes)," rather arrogantly blamed "a few selfish old men" and "another few nervous old females," along with a cadre of "innately ill-natured snub-nosed young snobs" for opposing any new thing, regardless of its merit. These statements captured an important insight into the early politics of cycling in the state. "It is a kindred feeling to that which would control other people," the editorial observed. "Let those who wish, ride; and those who do not, let others alone." The "Friend" of the velocipede yearned for compromise even as he adopted what rural and conservative readers would have felt was an elitist tone. As the "friend" proposed banning velocipede riding from the busiest sections of downtown, and admonished city leaders to give the velocipede a try themselves before they rushed to judgment, he dismissed many of the legitimate concerns state residents had.[61] In the end, however, many people seemed intent on disliking the velocipede no matter what. As 1869 wore on, the velocipede became an increasingly rare sight around the state. Then, it effectively disappeared. Only a few can be found in the state to this day.

Already by the summer of 1869, inventors and designers were busy at work de-signing new improvements for the velocipede. Ultimately, these design improvements would radically transform both the velocipede's design and the early cycling culture of the state. By the early 1870s, a new machine could be seen travelling the streets in Wisconsin. Once again, state residents would be asked to grapple with new changes to transportation.

CHAPTER 2

The Dawn of Wisconsin's High-Wheel Era

"Few people had ever seen a bicycle constructed in the manner of these. . . . Crowds of people satisfied their curiosity by examining them."

Oshkosh Daily Northwestern, 1879[1]

The dramatic end of velocipede mania in 1869 demonstrated that Wisconsin was a long way from becoming an important part of the world bicycling scene. From Paris to San Francisco and many places in between, the downfall of the velocipede reverberated. The market for new machines crashed, leaving storefronts filled with inventories that never moved. By 1872, the *New York Times* reported that unsold machines still cluttered storefronts across Manhattan, noting the "seductively low prices affixed to them." Everyone seemed to have an explanation for the velocipede's defeat. As the *New York Times* claimed in its particularly colorful report,

The real cause of the failure of the velocipede was the tyranny of the small boy. These shameless and exasperating mouthpieces of crude and unreasoning public opinion crushed out the velocipede, and drove its patrons into the obscurity of back yards and private piazzas. . . . Whenever a man presented himself on the street, mounted upon his bicycle, the small boy . . . surrounded him like a poisonous cloud.[2]

Whether it was "small boys," terrible roads, or poorly designed machines that ultimately brought the velocipede down, the mania nevertheless built a small but committed cycling following throughout the United States. It was this core group that lent renewed enthusiasm to the effort to develop a new and improved machine, one that would eventually push the sport in new directions. As new innovations such as rubber tires and wire spokes appeared, a new era in the history of bicycling began: the era of the high-wheel.[3]

Canadian Thomas Dale poses on top of his large fifty-two-inch high-wheel, which he purchased for $150 in 1886. Dale later relocated to Kenosha.

Kenosha History Center

The velocipede's collapse put a halt to the state's cycling culture in the early 1870s, and outside of the handful of state residents who rode the old velocipedes for fun, the future of the sport appeared quite bleak. Newspapers stressed the growing speed of daily life, noting that the velocipede may have been slightly ahead of its time. "That this is getting to be a fast age nobody can doubt," the *Milwaukee Sentinel* reported in 1876. "Legs don't count now-a-days. They're too slow." Reports indicated that velocipede nostalgia was seen, on occasion, in places like Sheboygan. Those with "gray hair" in the community often had to "step aside for safety . . . to let young America and its train pass by." In Waupun, similar reports indicated that velocipede riding was still "all the go," and that "at almost any hour of the day some one [*sic*] is seen mounted on the vehicle."[4] From Watertown also came news of marginal but renewed interest. "We thought velocipedes, or at least hoped so, had had their day and generation," the *Milwaukee Sentinel* joked, "but occasionally may be seen a young shaver mounted on one of them traveling down the sidewalk to the great comfort and convenience of pedestrians."[5] It's clear from these reports that velocipede mania had faded, leaving the future of cycling undecided.

New design innovations helped re-spark this dormant enthusiasm and ultimately led to cycling's rejuvenation. Named for their massive front wheels, "high-wheel" velocipedes (increasingly, these were also called high-wheel "bicycles") helped reposition Wisconsin on the path of becoming a great bicycling state. The transition to the high-wheel started almost immediately after the velocipede's collapse. Because the velocipede simply failed to catch on as a mode of everyday transport for regular people, it was competitive racers often from outside the state who drove the sport in new directions. Armed with improvements to velocipede design that included new and dramatically improved rubber tires (an upgrade to the velocipede's wooden wheels), improved frames, and other enhancements, such men trimmed the times of existing velocipede world records for mile-long races, moving the record from around five minutes almost down to four and a half minutes. Riding what by the mid-1870s were commonly called "bicycles" for the first time, these early racing men likely saved the sport from oblivion. Their success, however, set into motion forces that would eventually open new debates and tensions in bicycling culture, in particular the marginalized role of women against the masculine culture of bicycle racing and clubs.[6]

Wisconsin would again lag behind its eastern neighbors in adopting and accommodating the high-wheel era, however. The velocipede crash effectively slowed cycling's popularity in Wisconsin for almost the entire decade between 1869 and 1879, leaving the key transitions to take place elsewhere. The racing resurgence of the early 1870s took hold not in Wisconsin, but in such places as France, England, and the eastern United States. As public pressure grew for competitors to shave off even more time from existing world records, bicycle manufacturers, many of them former velocipede makers, stepped up to provide the riders with newer and bigger front wheels. The reasoning was simple: riders on a large front wheel gained the advantage of higher speeds, since it took less pedaling to propel a bike with a massive front tire forward. In fact, as wheels grew bigger and bigger, high speeds actually drove a small spike in European bicycle sales toward the end of 1870, stabilizing the end of the velocipede crash.[7]

Wisconsin demonstrated an interest in these developments, but the state fell short in terms of actually participating in them. Reports on advancements outside of the state often carried a characteristic dose of skepticism. When the English Middlesex Bicycle Club, an all-male cycling fraternity, raced 106 miles from Bath to London in August 1874, editors at the *Milwaukee Daily Sentinel* offered Wisconsin readers a full account. Their matter-of-fact report of the race signaled an enduring but cautious interest in the great distance the bikers managed to cover. The reports also hinted that this kind of competition might one day find a market in Wisconsin. Milwaukee editors marveled that the riders made a time "one hour less than the fastest stage coach," and that they averaged a speed of "ten and a half miles per hour." Such achievements might radically transform life and transportation in Wisconsin if they became commonplace, and *Sentinel* editors warmed to the possibilities.[8]

Europeans took a different tack and openly embraced the rejuvenated market, building up a base of bicycling fans who would help revitalize cycling. English and European racing men used special gimmicks, many borrowed from the days of velocipede mania, to lure hesitant audiences to biking events. Many were held outdoors. A favorite kind of early race involved pitting a bicyclist against a horse to see who was fastest. Milwaukee newspaper editors reprinted a story about English bicyclist David Stanton, who bet he could defeat a horse in a five-mile race. Stanton was easily defeated and lost by over a mile.[9] European cyclists had won an important triumph a few months before when it was reported that a rider had in fact beaten a horse in a race from Paris to Vienna in December 1875. The cyclist arrived in Vienna ahead of the horse by almost three days. "The astonishment of the natives, especially when he [the cyclist] lit his lantern . . . is said to be excessive," *Harper's Bazaar* noted.[10] Wisconsin readers likely found these stories fascinating.

European design improvements, faster race times, and a stabilizing cycle market helped rebuild enthusiasm for cycling throughout Europe and the United States. Racing played a key role in shaping this turn because during the early 1870s racers had constantly asked manufacturers for lighter bikes. European manufacturers answered the call in a variety of ways, such as introducing steel in place of iron in bicycle frame tubing. Steel tubing made the new machines significantly lighter and more durable. A good bike usually weighed around forty pounds in 1873, a significant improvement over the hulking iron velocipedes of the late 1860s. This number would dramatically decrease over the course of the 1870s. New bearings in the steering column and axles, too, ensured a smoother ride that required only minimal maintenance. As mile times fell to just over three minutes, the public's interest surged. At the same time, many recognized that American manufacturing was falling behind. The journal *Scientific American*, a reliable source for news in technology and sports, ran what was a common story in 1875 detailing the difference between the bicycling scene in the United States and England. "This is a sport resigned to a select few in this country," it said, "but in England it is extensively practiced." The report went on to offer testimonials from British riders celebrating the innovations that made their bikes easier and more enjoyable to ride.[11]

American manufacturing and labor did undergo profound changes during the 1870s. Many of these changes were driven by a growing sense of inferiority to Brit-

Designers improved the velocipede's stability and speed by enlarging the front wheel while shrinking the rear. These transition models first appeared in eastern cities, but slowly moved west by decade's end.

Harper's Weekly, December 18, 1875

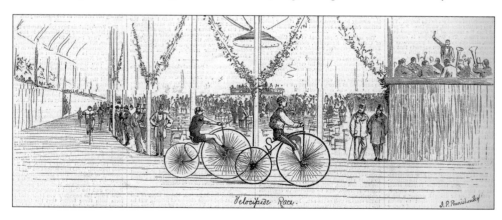

Velocipede Race.

ish and French manufacturers, a sense that often transcended the comparatively small bicycle manufacturing trade. In 1876, US manufacturing received a boost during the massive Philadelphia Centennial Exhibition, where many new American-made innovations were put on public display for the first time. Beginning on May 10, the celebration marked the one hundredth anniversary of the nation's founding, and the technologies on display suggested high hopes for America's growing industrial and urban identity. President Ulysses S. Grant helped perform the exhibition's opening ceremonies. Notable entries included Alexander Graham Bell's newly patented telephone, Thomas Edison's phonograph and megaphone, the top portion of the still-unfinished Statue of Liberty, and the Corliss steam engine, a machine so powerful that it helped power many of the exhibits. Janesville residents Edgar Dexter Tallman, father to one of Janesville's budding cyclists, and Bob Bostwick made their way to Philadelphia to see the exhibits. Tallman and Bostwick likely saw several bicycle displays as they were prominently featured as an example of America's promising industrial future.[12]

Early high-wheel models had straight handlebars, but later models had "mustache" handlebars that better accommodated leg movement.

WHS Museum 1968.642, photo by Joel Heiman

Albert Pope cultivated the bicycle craze by starting Columbia Bicycles, the nation's leading bicycle brand.

Connecticut Historical Society

Pope's new operation in Hartford, Connecticut, shown here, was one of the fastest growing manufacturers on the East Coast.

Scientific American, March 20, 1880

Bicycle manufacturing in the United States had not yet taken hold by the end of the 1870s, but its industrial and manufacturing future could be seen taking shape at the exhibition. One figure at the exhibition who would play a key role in shaping that future was Albert Augustus Pope, a Massachusetts entrepreneur and Civil War veteran. Pope, like many Americans, also had an interest in the cycling news emanating from Europe, and he took in the English exhibitions on bicycle design hoping to study the products to see whether they might be marketed on this side of the pond. Initially unimpressed with the new bicycle designs, he returned home to Massachusetts. Legend has it that when he went for a horse ride in the countryside upon his return, he saw a cyclist pass him on the road. This inspired him to at last see the bicycle's full potential, and he apparently decided to enter the bicycle manufacturing business on the spot. He learned how to ride a high-wheel that summer and opened a riding school at his company, Pope Manufacturing, which had previously made shoemaking supplies. By 1878, just two years after his trip to Philadelphia, Pope was poised to become one of the largest bicycling manufacturers in the country. As a Civil War hero and successful entrepreneur, he also started underwriting publications for bicycling enthusiasts, including *The Wheelman* (later called *Outing*), and awarding prizes to doctors and others who might spell out the health benefits of cycling in books, newspaper articles, or magazines.[13]

If bicycling did become a major domestic industry through the efforts of Pope and others, Wisconsin, whose ties to manufacturing grew exponentially in the 1870s and 1880s, was poised to join in the effort. Yet although it stirred hopes for a cycling renais-

THE BICYCLE FIEND IN THE PARK

sance in the United States, the high-wheel industry was not without its problems. Critics recognized that huge front wheels only partially answered the many design problems plaguing the machines. Massive wheels made the bikes prone to tip over in severe crosswinds, for example, and their height made them very easy to crash. Early cyclists called this "taking a header"—even the smallest bump in the road could force the wheel off course. Still, the big wheel did improve rough rides by smoothing the journey over bumpy surfaces, and the bike's massive height ensured that riders would be safe from the dust clouds that were often kicked up when riding along dirt roads.[14]

In the years and months before Pope entered the industry, reviews of the new European bikes remained mixed in the United States. "Great improvements have lately been made in [bike] form and materials," the *Milwaukee Daily Sentinel* acknowledged. "When bicycles were first introduced there was a disposition to treat them with ridicule. . . . The machines were, of course, rather rough and clumsy." Now, as the paper noted in November 1874, "The weight has been considerably reduced."[15] Still, it seemed unlikely for much of the 1870s that a new bicycle craze would sweep the United States. As *Forest and Stream* proclaimed in 1874,

> The enthusiasm with which this species of exercise [bicycling] has been adopted in England recently seems somewhat surprising to us on this side of the Atlantic, who have been rather apt to classify any person on a bicycle . . . as one devoid of much sense, not to use a coarser term. It [the bicycle] has met its fate in this country. . . . It does not promise to be revived."

The editors could not have been more wrong.[16]

Wisconsin's streets were soon filled with cyclists, and by 1880 they had become a ubiquitous feature of the state's landscape. The story of how this happened begins, once again, in England and France. There, slow improvements were made to bicycle designs throughout the 1870s. To mount the tall machines with greater ease, riders added a small step to the left side of the frame that helped propel them onto the saddle. This

Early cyclists were expected to dress like gentlemen, including this unidentified man, who looks more like he's going to a society dinner than an athletic event.

Courtesy of Oshkosh Public Museum

enabled them to easily mount and dismount, a task that often terrified novice cyclists. The step also enabled riders to develop a method of mounting the bikes by running alongside their machines, placing their foot on the left step, and then pulling themselves up onto the saddle while quickly catching the spinning pedals before the whole thing, rider and machine, toppled over. Riders also mastered an alternative method, which required the bicyclist to put his or her left foot on the step, push hard, and then jump onto the saddle. Needless to say, the dangers these bicycles posed never truly allowed the public to abandon their skepticism.[17]

The smoother and more solid feel that came to characterize the new models during the last part of the 1870s resulted from innovations generated across the manufacturing spectrum. This was particularly true of ball-bearing technology, which developed in part when English inventors inserted a ring of loose, solid spheres within fitted cups that could grip around the ends of each side of the axle. With bacon grease no longer necessary for lubing the wooden axles, ball bearings substantially improved the quality of the ride. Old racing records fell as a result. A rider named F. Cooper established a new world record for one mile in 1879. Another rider, John Keen, earned notoriety for riding eighteen miles in a single hour, and the amateur F. T. East set a new fifty-mile record, finishing in two hours and forty-seven minutes.[18] New records encouraged larger numbers of the public to come to races as riders sometimes logged over a thousand miles over the course of several days.[19]

As improvements to the high-wheel appeared, a small recreational market developed in the eastern part of the United States. For the most part, these new riders were men, both because of the daredevil and competitive culture that clearly surrounded the new bikes, but also because of the social customs that governed the behavior of women in public. The bikes were also very expensive, meaning only the wealthiest residents could hope to afford them. The increasing alliance of bicycling with elite men transitioned the culture of bicycling further away from more practical, everyday considerations toward more specialized uses. Less and less a utilitarian option, early riders engaged in an ongoing process that made the bicycle a leisurely expression of male refinement. With the advent of the high-wheel era, bikes became as much an accoutrement to gentlemanly style and recreation as they were a tool for everyday transportation.[20]

The expansion of the urban middle class in Wisconsin and elsewhere eventually put these machines into thousands of new hands in the United States. Long-distance races and tours also led to a profusion of fraternal bicycling clubs, a step that had tremendous impact on the future of the sport. Again, Europe led the way. In England, huge meets throughout the 1870s drew thousands of cyclists from across the English countryside, and processions stretched for miles when riders rode in formal and compact parade formations. However, the clubs tended to position their riding and participation against the culture that had already taken shape around racing, leading to a new sense of exclusivity. English club members cultivated a kind of bike riding that suggested an air of civilized refinement and gentlemanly self-control. For example, an organization in England named the Pickwick Club only allowed writers in its ranks, and each had to identify himself with a character from *The Pickwick Papers* by Charles Dickens. Other clubs included the Wanderers, who only allowed men with an expressed interest in leisurely touring and who vowed never to race on competitive terms. Thus, while racing saved the sport from oblivion in the wake of velocipede mania, and while racing drove the technological innovations that made the sport more appealing to wider numbers of riders, racing would slowly lose out to gentlemanly refinement. By the late 1870s, the most common bicycle rider witnessed in public was the "man on the bike" who chose to ride his bike at leisure for only moderate distances. This would play a crucial role in shaping the development of bicycling culture in places like Wisconsin later on.[21]

Wisconsin's increasingly working-class and immigrant populations of the late 1870s seemed slow to adopt the machine and the refined culture that came along with it. It is entirely possible that Wisconsin's workingmen were turned off by the elitism of the English clubs. Yet it was a bicycling club that ironically made the sport more accessible and visible. Regarded as the most inclusive of England's riding groups, the Bicycle Touring Club encouraged its members to plan trips, secure cheap hotel rates, and do their own bicycle maintenance in case of crashes or breakdowns. In a tradition common to a variety of nineteenth-century fraternal organizations, the English Bicycle Touring Club also asked its members to don a club uniform, and with the uniform the club issued badges, handbooks, guides, and newsletters. The Bicycle Touring Club also placed signs near especially treacherous points in the road and requested local officials to cover or change the position of sewer grates so as to make bicycle riding safer and easier. Riders in the United States, including those in Wisconsin, adopted many of these initiatives and put them to good use in their own communities. In this way, the elite sport unleashed changes that helped broaden its appeal in the public sphere.[22]

Changes such as these helped generate a growing movement that aimed to extend the enjoyment of cycling to greater numbers of people, including those in places like Wisconsin. As in the example above, elitism often worked in favor of the common rider. England's Bicycle Touring Club wanted, above all, to make bicycling a gentleman's sport, but because being "gentlemanly" often involved showy public presentations, roads everywhere had to be improved. The most popular of the club's events was the weekend "club run," when English riders, cycling en masse, would set out on a Saturday or Sunday (usually a Saturday since public riding on the Sabbath was highly discouraged) and ride at a leisurely pace for an extended period of the day, sometimes covering a hundred miles or more. The main point was to enjoy cycling, of course, but also to demonstrate the respectability of the club through martial display. Riding in unison, the men consciously evoked the strength and precision of soldiers marching in formation, much like a militia parade or grand review. The riders would also ride side by side in a meticulous display of bicycling skill and dexterity, but whenever the roads became too busy or too cluttered with other modes of traffic, they would narrow down to a single-file line as a show of courtesy. Respect for the public was key to early cycling culture. English Bicycle Touring Club members would break their rides up with occasional stops for tea and friendly conversation before heading out again for the afternoon and evening. By nightfall, since their bikes were equipped with oil lamps, they could navigate back to the clubhouse where conversation and other "good times" awaited. Clubs also wrote and performed songs unique to bicycling, and by all accounts these efforts created a tight sense of community cohesion.[23]

Presaging patterns that were soon to take hold in Wisconsin, American men adopted many of the methods used by the British bicycling clubs. Organized loosely and only sometimes as formal clubs at first, they took early velocipede rink tactics to the streets, where performances including parades opened new dimensions within local cycling culture. Yet Americans seemed most enamored when the new high-wheel bicycles demonstrated more practical, everyday uses out of doors—a hope that was idealized in racing venues. Ohioan James M. Mason eclipsed all standing records in the United States by riding well over a hundred miles outdoors in a single stretch. In New York, boosters hosted a new set of indoor high-wheel races at the American Institute Building. The following spring, the first ever outdoor high-wheel competition was held in the United States in New York. Not long after, bikes were on display at the 1876 Centennial Exhibition in Philadelphia.[24]

Spurred on by riding clubs and a growing legion of amateur riders, the bicycling industry began to boom in Europe. By 1880, England had more than one hundred bicycle manufacturers developing products, including more than a dozen in Coventry alone. French bicycle manufacturing also exploded, aided in part by the exploits of Albert Laumaillé of Château-Gontier in central France, who made a celebrated twelve-day ride from Paris to Vienna in 1875. American capitalists, like Pope, were also moved by these developments, and they soon formulated their own plans for bringing the new industry to its shores. A new bicycling era in the United States dawned.[25]

WISCONSIN was slow to capitalize on these innovations and experiences. As new bicycles from Europe slowly entered the American marketplace between 1873 and 1876, New York and Boston were the more reliable fountains of early cycling culture. Entrepreneurs in Boston, particularly, helped spread Europe's bicycling resurgence. Frank Weston, a native of England, and Massachusetts's Albert Pope were busy vying for control of the emerging bicycle trade. Weston launched the *American Bicycling Journal* to help celebrate bicycling and advertise his new wares, while Pope, who had only recently learned to ride, arranged for eight bicycles to be sent to his store from England. Soon he was manufacturing his own line. Pope and Weston faced another challenge: local carriage makers had actually purchased the rights to a number of existing velocipede patents, making it difficult for bikes to be produced. After some complicated and possibly dubious dealings, Pope emerged in 1879 with his enemies subdued and sole control over existing bicycle patents secured. Following the tactics of his competitors, he worked to secure patents related to domestic bicycle production and soon dominated large segments of the US bicycling industry.[26] Soon his ambitions extended well beyond the Northeast.

Bicycling's spread changed the nature of the sport in complicated ways. As the bikes became more and more accessible to growing ranks of American men through revitalized domestic production, the sport changed to reflect its expanding appeal. By 1879, it was clear that a growing bicycle scene was again winning converts in the United States, even though it did not, at least at first, generate the kind of public interest that the velocipede had at the height of the mania. Instead, it became a particularly fashionable accessory among the young and moneyed. Ivy League colleges became important early purveyors and advocates of bicycling culture. At Harvard, as the *Boston Globe* reported, "The 'steeds of steel' may be found reposing in the entries of all the principal dormitories."[27] Pushed along by the appeal these young riders helped generate, sales continued to rise toward the end of the decade.

Posters advertising the latest models appeared on city streets and bicycle shop walls. Wisconsinites preferred the inexpensive and mass-produced Columbia brand shown on this poster, ca. 1879.

Pryor Dodge Collection

David Herlihy estimates that roughly twenty-five hundred Americans acquired bicycles in 1879 alone, and the young men of Boston helped lead the way.[28] In February 1878, influential men in Boston formed the Boston Bicycle Club, the first formal bicycling organization in American history. The Boston Bicycle Club became notable for taking its bikes out into Boston's Copley Square for demonstrations, as men on horseback, children, and even a few ladies stood by in admiration. As the year 1878 rolled on, hundreds of new cyclists took to the streets, inspired by the Boston club's style and success. Most riders bought their cycles from Pope, and new organizations patterned their clubs after the Bicycle Touring Club of England. Together, these showy public demonstrations became a launching pad for an American bicycling expansion. That expansion would not reach Wisconsin until 1879.[29]

Wisconsin was slower to adapt the new machines, but never unenthusiastic to see what they offered. In the Badger State, where many bitter memories of the velocipede lingered, and where ordinances meant to ban riders from the street were still in place, changing public perceptions of the machines was a difficult task. Wisconsin newspapers offered little help, in that they filled their columns with stories detailing the bicycle's resurgence out East and overseas but usually fell short of a full embrace. In 1879, for example, the *Milwaukee Daily Sentinel* told the story of William Rolling's ride from New York City to the upstate town of Saratoga, a ride that covered almost two hundred miles. Rolling downplayed the importance of speed in his riding to the reporters. Instead, he wanted to explore the leisurely joys of long-distance riding, particularly as it allowed him to escape the confines of crowded Manhattan. For most Wisconsinites, the bicycle remained an object of curiosity rather than a complementary component of everyday life. They looked to the East with interest, but still wanted proof that the bicycle offered something tangible for improving their everyday lives.[30]

It should come as no surprise, then, that young men from Boston would be the first to introduce the new and improved high-wheel machines to Wisconsin. On July 2, 1879, one of the first high-wheel rides, quite possibly the state's first, occurred in Racine. The *Milwaukee Sentinel* reported that "two bicycles made their appearance on Main Street (Monument Square) yesterday afternoon." It added, "They were propelled by two young men who came from Boston."[31] Unlike what had occurred with the velocipede, the new high-wheels did not immediately create a sensation in Milwaukee papers. The appearance of these Boston boosters did not generate the outrageous coverage that had characterized the appearance of the boneshaker a decade or so earlier. Wisconsinites of course knew that the new bicycles existed, as the racing and touring circuits in England were commonly discussed. Perhaps the tremendous popularity of the machines out east had helped smooth the introduction of the new technology this time, making the spectacle less bracing, less marvelous.

Outside of Milwaukee, however, the appearance of these new machines certainly did attract attention. Late that month, on July 25, two young men identified in area papers as Edwin F. Brown and Harry S. Farwell from Evanston, Illinois, rode their bicycles onto Main Street in downtown Oshkosh where they attracted "considerable attention." As the *Oshkosh Daily Northwestern* reported the scene, "Few people had ever seen a bicycle constructed in the manner of these. . . . Crowds of people satisfied their curiosity by examining them" as the bikes were put on display in a room at the Beckwith House, a popular hotel. Noting that the "young gentleman" sought no greater fame during their

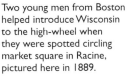

Two young men from Boston helped introduce Wisconsin to the high-wheel when they were spotted circling market square in Racine, pictured here in 1889.

WHi Image ID 40106

leisurely tour, reporters seemed particularly impressed by the presence of odometers on the machines. The young men said they hoped to take in some of the "rural resorts" then popular in that part of the state, and claimed that they were averaging between six and ten miles per hour out on Wisconsin's mostly dirt roads.[32]

State cynics did their fair share to downplay the new machines, however. As they had done during velocipede mania, Wisconsin's newspaper writers cast suspicion on the rising popularity of the bicycle by printing stories of terrible injuries sustained by cyclists. The *Eau Claire Daily Free Press* reported in December 1878 that Reverend Wall, a Wesleyan clergyman, lost control of his bicycle while riding down a hill and "was thrown." He suffered a severe dislocation of his shoulder and "internal injuries" that, as the paper noted, were enough to "keep him out of his pulpit and off his bicycle for some time to come."[33] The *Milwaukee Daily Sentinel* ran a story in 1879 about a young railroad clerk who crashed and died near Philadelphia.[34] When stories of injuries did not stem enthusiasm, editors managed to make their distrust toward bicycles more explicit. A short clipping in the *Milwaukee Sentinel* on July 2, 1880, mentioned that a new steam-powered bicycle had been invented: "This will fill a long felt want. A steam bicycle may explode and kill its rider." As the dark humor suggests, the bicycle had a long way to go in proving its worth to a large number of Wisconsin's residents.[35]

Women had been influential in introducing the velocipede to the state back in 1869, but this time around the high-wheel's propensity for stirring daredevil trickery and tales of heroic rides made the machine a more obvious male consumer choice. The bicycle trip

The high-wheel's popularity spread into smaller Wisconsin communities. Edmund Hanske demonstrates that the town of Kiel had at least one young cyclist, ca. 1880.

Courtesy of Kiel Public Library's "Big Streets in a Little City"

Dressed in athletic clothing, Jim Wilder rode this bicycle in the late 1880s as a member of the Oshkosh Wheelmen.

Courtesy of Oshkosh Public Museum

of H. S. Farwell and E. F. Brown from Chicago to Appleton made front-page news in the *Janesville Gazette* during July 1879, the first summer of the high-wheel's growing boom. "They make about thirty-five miles a day on the journey," the paper noted.[36] In Oshkosh, meanwhile, editors made sure to mention, "It is very interesting . . . to learn that a man using no other motive power than nature has given to him" can cover a great distance, adding that a recent rider in London had covered 1,404 miles in six days. Slowly but surely, Wisconsin's residents warmed to the possibilities bicycles presented.[37]

Almost immediately after the first 1879 rides in Racine by the Boston men, bikes were sent to Wisconsin. An all-male "bycicle" club in Milwaukee was announced in March 1880, echoing developments already well underway in England, France, Massachusetts, New York, and elsewhere. The *Milwaukee Sentinel* noted, "The members of the club have already thirteen bicycles and have ordered ten additional." The club planned to use the machines for exercise, for spending pleasurable evenings outside, for riding on the city's grand avenues, and for racing. These goals provided a telling roadmap for the shape bicycling culture in Wisconsin would take in the decade to follow.[38]

By May, the *Milwaukee Sentinel* was able to report, "Bicycling is becoming very popular in Milwaukee. . . . There are now owned and ridden in this city about twenty of the 'steel steeds,' and this number is being added to constantly." The bicycles were still a peculiar sight for many, however. With reporters noting that they continued to attract "special attention" and "excite a lively curiosity" wherever they went, bicyclists again faced deep suspicions about whether their sport was just a passing fad.[39]

The bicycle's rising popularity in 1880 also helped stabilize the meaning of a new word in Wisconsin's vocabulary. As the new machines became an ever more popular sight, many struggled over what to call them. In the *Milwaukee Daily Sentinel* of August 7, 1880, locals debated the correct pronunciation of "bicycle":

High-wheels would remain popular into the 1880s. Philetus H. Sawyer, ca. 1885, son of Oshkosh lumberman Edgar P. Sawyer, owned a unique lever-driven high-wheel. The machine's name derives from the pedal system that powered the wheels.

Courtesy of Oshkosh Public Museum

Myself and others were, last evening, led to a discussion as to the correct pronunciation of the word 'bicycle,' the name of the new two wheeled machine now so common on our streets. It has up to the present time been commonly pronounced as if spelled 'bi-sickle,' but last evening for the first time I heard it pronounced as if spelled Bi-si-cle (long sound of y in cycle), and on questioning the correctness of the last pronunciation I was informed that it was correct.

The writer wondered, "Will you please decide the question?" *Sentinel* editors dodged an answer. "Custom will decide the pronunciation," was their reply. What they did not seem to fully realize is that the word bicycle was already routinely used outside of Wisconsin.[40]

Perhaps the greatest signal of the bicycle's rising importance in Wisconsin, however, occurred on Election Day during the 1880 presidential contest, which pitted Republican James A. Garfield against Democrat Winfield Scott Hancock. That evening, tens of thousands of Garfield supporters took to the streets in Milwaukee in a showing that reportedly drew thirty thousand people out of their homes. "The Republicans

Jay Hinman, ca. 1885, contributed to Oshkosh's thriving bicycle community. He helped create an LAW club, opened a bicycle agency, and photographed the city's growing cycling scene.

Courtesy of Oshkosh Public Museum

have captured the city to-night [*sic*] with the grandest parade and most inspiring political demonstration ever known in Wisconsin," the *Janesville Gazette* reported. Taken as a sure sign that Garfield would defeat Hancock in a landslide, the paper noted that in addition to covered wagons adorned with decorations, beautiful fireworks displays, marching Civil War veterans, and city streets that were "brilliantly illuminated," bicyclists also appeared. A full "brigade" of almost one hundred bicyclists paraded around the city in a display of Republican support. Only a year or so after they had first appeared in Racine, the new high-wheel machines helped signal cycling's dramatic re-entry into the state's politics and culture.[41]

All evidence seemed to suggest that cycling had found a promising home. Republican Party connections to the emerging bicycle fad, after all, ran deep in Wisconsin. Widely recognized for its role in the Republican Party's creation back in 1854, the small town of Ripon had hosted an important early meeting of disaffected antislavery Whigs, Democrats, and Free Soil Party members in March of that year, just six years before the dramatic election of Abraham Lincoln in 1860 and the fateful outbreak of the Civil War that followed in 1861. Present at that original meeting in Ripon was George F. Lynch, a committed antislavery man who had spent the years since the war working in Milwaukee helping to develop the city's public rail network. In 1867, Lynch secured a patent that helped push ball-bearing technology forward. His innovations were eventually adopted by the bicycle industry, making his inventions part of the story of the bicycle's rise.[42]

As thousands of Milwaukeeans poured out into the streets on Election Night in 1880, the cool autumn air would have been punctuated not only by the burst of fireworks overhead but by the occasional laughs, cheers, and giggles stirred by the remarkable scene of a hundred men gliding by on their massive high-wheel bicycles, quietly

and in graceful unison. As this curious "bicycle brigade" snaked its way downtown, riding in tandem as
lights and flags flashed and flickered over the throngs
of marching Civil War veterans, city residents must
have stood in awe. In that moment, Wisconsin's future
as a great cycling state was slowly coming into view.

Transitional high-wheels from
the early 1870s incorporated
the wood and iron materials
of their velocipede predeces-
sors. The manufacturer and
owner of this highly decorated machine are unknown,
and the bike's handlebars
are a later replacement.

*Milwaukee County Historical
Society, photo by John Urban*

CHAPTER 3

The Rise of Wisconsin's Amateur Cycling Clubs

"Whatever emotion may be surging at his heart, whatever tempestuous yearning at riot in the soul within, the stoic face goes glimmering by us, betraying nothing. . . . He knows his purpose and his destination. That is enough for us."

Milwaukee Daily Sentinel, 1881[1]

The new high-wheel presented exciting possibilities for Wisconsin's budding group of cycling enthusiasts. With a small cycling community taking shape throughout the state, questions centered on how to get the most out of the opportunities the new machines offered. The explosion of amateur bicycling clubs throughout Wisconsin between 1880 and 1885 provided some early answers. These clubs would radically expand bicycling's presence throughout the state and help spread the gospel of its many benefits. By lending the sport a sense of increased legitimacy, they helped establish the grounds upon which bicycling's emerging popularity took hold. In the end, the early cycling clubs of the 1880s, though often exclusive, helped forge the complicated origins of Wisconsin's bicycling politics.

There were many reasons why amateur high-wheel cycling clubs flowered in Wisconsin throughout the early part of the 1880s and why this particular moment became so important to the state's cycling identity. As the decade dawned, a small but growing domestic manufacturing base helped ensure that American consumers had plenty of new wheels to choose from. According to historian Sue Macy, the United States had a handful of bicycle producers in operation by 1885. These manufacturers turned out roughly 11,000 bicycles per year by the middle part of the decade.[2] This was an important development because the slow production of inferior, shop-made designs had helped undermine the velocipede mania of the late 1860s. Public perceptions of cycling had suffered as a result. The new factories turned out cycles of a much higher and standardized quality. The opening of Albert Pope's Massachusetts-based bicycle works in 1878, for example, introduced a new class of machines into the marketplace, effectively lowering the price of new bicycles by expanding their availability to a wider pool of riders. In addition, improvements to high-wheel designs in the late 1870s and early 1880s, including improved steps and mounts, made it easier to ride these sometimes unstable, occasionally dangerous machines. These developments alone were enough to spur the creation of a small but perceptible bicycling community in the United States, including the one that emerged around 1880 in Wisconsin.[3]

While the number of Wisconsin's cyclists increased, there were still lingering questions about the machine itself. One of the early challenges had to do with the design of the high-wheel. While its design did mark an improvement over the velocipede in terms of speed and durability, many critics pointed out that simply adding a larger front

The Racine Bicycle Club, early 1880s, ready for a tour in their riding uniforms.

Racine Heritage Museum Archival Collection

The high-wheel was firmly planted in Wisconsin by 1880, especially in Milwaukee. Groups of cyclists became a common sight on the city's streets.

Milwaukee County Historical Society

wheel did nothing to improve its more fundamental flaws. When a rider hit a bump or encountered a rut in the street, the high-wheel routinely threw its riders violently to the ground. Even a high crosswind, a special plague for riders navigating the Lake Michigan shoreline, could topple the machine. As a result, many who had already been discouraged by the "boneshakers" of the late 1860s and early 1870s had little reason to believe the high-wheel presented anything new. Designers put forward many good ideas for improving, tweaking, and customizing the high-wheel, but few ideas really transformed its essential design. A lack of progress in design exacerbated more common and immediate practical problems. Poor roads continued to limit the likelihood of a widespread bicycling boom. Bad infrastructure (including a lack of repair shops, bike-friendly businesses, and bridges) ensured that the high-wheel bicycle clubs would have limited appeal. Partly for these reasons, bicycling remained most popular in and around Milwaukee and other urban centers, where modern and improved roads made it more enjoyable to ride. As a result, Milwaukee became ground zero for the emerging state cycling scene.

The other dilemma for Wisconsin's cyclists involved winning the public's favor. It proved to be no easy task. After all, by 1880, Wisconsin residents had already initiated a sweeping range of laws aimed to restrict the use of the machine. These measures took a variety of forms. City ordinances regulated questions of access, establishing rules defining *who* cyclists were, *where* cyclists could ride, and *when* they could ride. Indeed, local ordinances mirrored a number of high-stakes tensions in 1880s politics.

Residents made bicycling a political matter from the start precisely because it promised cheap and readily available transportation to anyone who could learn to ride. Cycling also created greater public access to space, opening the door for traditionally marginalized groups, including women, to travel between neighborhoods and even between cities if they so chose, often without men to accompany them. Fears of female riders using bikes to pursue illicit romantic relationships, radical politics, or other acts outside the womanly norm created tremendous anxiety. In a deeply unequal society, cycling opened up the possibility of a new vision of equality that proved frightening to many. Efforts to govern access to cycling's privileges for the benefit of the white middle and upper-middle class would play a tremendous role in how Wisconsin's bicycling culture would develop over the coming years.

IT should come as no surprise that the state's early cycling culture, rooted as it was in Wisconsin's white middle and upper-middle classes, took on many of the beliefs of the culture it became part of. At once progressive and deeply regressive, these ideals took shape during the early 1880s, when cyclists first attempted to challenge legislation aimed at restricting cycling in public spaces. Wisconsin's riders were already far behind the curve, however, in initiating these efforts. The first significant step in this battle occurred many miles from the Badger State. Inspired by the British Bicycle Union and Bicycling Touring Club, amateur high-wheel riders in Newport, Rhode Island, founded the League of American Wheelmen (LAW), commonly called "the League," in the spring of 1880.[4] The development of the LAW forever transformed cycling in the United States. Its influence would soon be felt in Wisconsin.

There were many reasons why the eastern states took the lead in organizing the LAW. First, there were simply more riders in the eastern part of the United States during the early 1880s. Riders filled the streets of places such as Boston, New York, and New Haven in numbers that dwarfed cycling's still-fledgling presence in Milwaukee.[5] Second, eastern riders—partly by virtue of their great numbers—had already taken part in a number of heated political battles with local and state governments throughout the 1870s. They had more experience with political organizing and had lessons they could teach new cycling communities throughout the country. Because riders in cities like New York and Boston had already faced down many of the same restrictions that

Before relocating to Wisconsin from New York, Stephen Babcock was an avid high-wheel rider and LAW member. As a chemist at the University of Wisconsin, Babcock went on to create a test of milk's butterfat content that revolutionized the dairy industry.

WHi Image ID 97378

were common in places like Milwaukee, the League was able to advise new cycling organizations in their fight against antibicycling laws. When it was first organized in Rhode Island, the LAW took on a broad set of goals: promoting equal rights for riders, advocating for better roads, and fostering a sense of community among members.[6] In time, the LAW's struggle for bicycling rights initiated significant changes to the law that ultimately helped pave the way for a national cycling culture. On a more local scale, the formation of the LAW also played a key role in making Wisconsin the premier bicycling destination that it is today. The League's early efforts and successes provided a roadmap for how Wisconsin would transform itself into a place where bicyclists could feel at home.

The story of this transformation started in earnest with the LAW's founding in 1880. Early on, the LAW recognized that the rights associated with bicycling would need the protection of a powerful and vigilant political lobby. Unlike other sports, cycling required widespread access to public space in order to really work. This meant that cycling was especially vulnerable to decisions about public spaces, particularly for roads. Unlike other popular leisure and sport activities of the period such as boxing, horse racing, and baseball, which featured events held indoors or in stadiums, cycling's real potential was out of doors. This was especially true as bicycling became synonymous with touring culture. Yet the political challenges were even greater. With the perceived threat of working-class and women's mobility, early cycling leaders struggled to define basic guidelines regarding when, where, and how one should ride while in public. These were not easy questions to answer, especially as cycling became more and more popular among the general population. The increasing presence of women in the sport, in particular, raised new questions about what was permissible for women to wear and do when out and about town on their bikes.

As Wisconsin's largest and most powerful demographic in the early 1880s, middle-class white men took the early lead in providing answers to these questions. Early Wisconsin riders took an aggressive pro-bicycle stance through their local clubs, often borrowing from practices first established by the LAW and the eastern or English bicycle riding clubs. From the start, Wisconsin cyclists devoured printed materials that broadcasted clear lessons about who belonged in cycling and who did not and who deserved rightful claim over the sport. Biking publications, as a result, eagerly claimed the bicycle as yet another example of the superiority of white "civilization." In 1879, future LAW member Charles E. Pratt published *The American Bicycler*, one of the nation's

Currier and Ives characterized cyclists as pedaling maniacs who gracelessly cruised on city streets, ca. 1880.

Library of Congress, Prints & Photographs Division, LC-USZC2-2477

first serious bicycling manuals.[7] In the book, Pratt celebrated the growth of cycling clubs, manufacturers, and racing events that were in full bloom as the 1870s came to a close. With his regular appeals to the "intelligent public," however, Pratt made it clear he had a particular audience in mind. Bicycling was something the well-to-do might do for leisure and recreation, but it was decidedly not for the rest of the population, particularly women. In this way, Pratt saw bicycling as an emblem of modern America, not because it symbolized a future of transportation equality for all races and creeds, but because it stood for the superior white society America had helped cultivate. Pratt and others like him may have pled for equal access to the cities and roads, but his rhetoric makes it clear that elitist politics underpinned the sport's leadership in these early years. Few early advocates embraced the participation of women, blacks, or other marginalized groups.[8]

Given their many privileges, white middle- and upper-class men were well positioned to lead the development of cycling culture, especially those who hailed from eastern cities with a well-established bicycling community. New York City's wheelmen, in particular, took an important lead in framing the early conversation on bicycle politics. The sheer number of bicyclists in the city made New York, recognized as the epicenter of eastern cycling, a flashpoint for new legislation. New Yorkers had already helped shape Wisconsin's story through nineteenth-century migration and settlement; now their cycling community would further influence the culture of the Badger State. One of the first points of conflict arose when New York City's municipal government passed a number of laws the city's cyclists interpreted as hostile. To offer one example, city leaders made it mandatory for bike riders to dismount every time they approached a team of horses. This was no easy feat in 1880s Manhattan, as horses and carriages clogged the roads at every turn. Incredibly, New York's cyclists were also expected to help carriage drivers lead horses away from oncoming bikes, as carriage drivers often complained, not without justice, that cyclists scared horses. Adding insult to injury, New York's Board of Park Commissioners also briefly considered banning bicycles from Central Park, a move that would have dealt a serious blow to the city's wheeling community. Since the days of velocipede mania in 1869, Central Park had become one of the premier bicycling destinations in the country. Losing park privileges would have cut off one of the wheelmen's greatest resources, both in giving riders a great place to

The Milwaukee Wheelmen pose in their club uniforms outside the Industrial Exposition Building, 1888.

Milwaukee Public Museum Photography Collection

ride and also in promoting the machine to curious onlookers. Hoping to ensure some level of control against these restrictions, New York's wheelmen started interviewing political candidates to make sure pro-bike legislators filled city government positions.[9] These efforts helped establish an important precedent for bike riders throughout the East Coast and eventually Wisconsin.

As in many other places in the United States, Wisconsin's roads were in dismal shape at the outset of the 1880s, plagued by mud, poor signage, and crumbling bridges and sidewalks. Pratt joined a growing chorus of wheelmen when he proclaimed that "every person has an equal right to travel on the highways, either on foot or with his own conveyance, team, or vehicle." His words may have sounded like a call for equality, but it would be a mistake to see the LAW as an advocate for truly equal rights. In fact, he was expressing a common desire that the government could be called upon to improve the lives of everyday people—especially people like himself. An effective way to do so, Pratt and others reasoned, was to use the language of "rights." Whose "rights" they were, and who ought to benefit from improved roads, was in fact very narrowly interpreted by the wheelmen.[10]

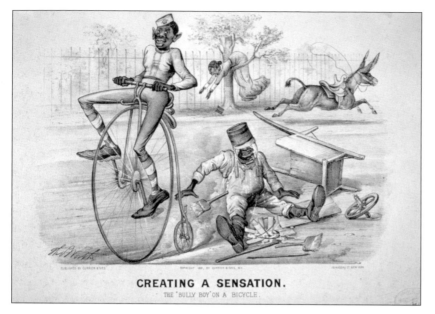

CREATING A SENSATION.

THE "BULLY BOY" ON A BICYCLE.

Racist caricatures, like this 1881 "Darktown" print by Currier and Ives, reinforced beliefs held by white Americans that blacks were incapable of becoming skilled cyclists.

Library of Congress, Prints & Photographs Division, LC-USZC2-2152

As support for better roads deepened within the ranks of the LAW and Wisconsin's early cycling clubs, engineers and designers brought forward a number of new designs to improve the high-wheel. This resulted in a period of turbulence for the small but growing number of domestic manufacturers. Wheelmen like Pratt, who played a key role in shaping the direction of the sport, cherished the high speeds and long distances that the high-wheel made possible. But many continued to fret over the reports of serious injuries that filled local papers when riders fell from the machines. By the early 1880s, there seemed to be a growing consensus that the high-wheel had peaked in terms of design; very few innovations seemed to offer meaningful improvement. Stagnation on the design front also drove increasing numbers of women from the sport, both because it was impractical to ride when wearing a skirt and because of the machine's continued instability. Few things were seen as "unwomanly" as stumbling around in the mud and filth of a public street after crashing one's bike. "Daredevil" cycling men were expected and encouraged to take those kinds of public risks. Women were not.[11]

Race was also a factor; in the 1880s cycling was seen as a primarily "white man's" sport. In Milwaukee, the advantages of race were made clear when "Arizona Indians," who according to newspaper reports could run "ten miles per hour," were pitted in a race against white cyclists. When the white rider inevitably overcame his Indian challenger, white participants returned home convinced not only of their cultural superiority but also of the bicycle's rightful place in the road of American progress.[12] Wisconsin's early cycling clubs were also routinely segregated by gender, and not just because the high-wheel design favored male riders. In January 1881, a year after the first organized ride in the city took place, the *Milwaukee Daily Sentinel* detailed a meeting involving area cyclists hoping to create a Milwaukee Bicycle Club. The gathering was for men only. The members gathered at the office of Angus S. Hibbard in the Chamber of Commerce building, and after electing officers discussed the design of new club uniforms. Hibbard suggested the uniforms "should be England corduroy, drab in color," with a "Polo cap and helmet," and a coat that would button "up to the throat." This, the men believed,

A young Franz Theodor "Terry" Andrae, ca. 1883, before his days as a high-wheel racer and bicycle industrialist.

Milwaukee County Historical Society

would ensure that the riders would gain the public's admiration and respect wherever they appeared.[13]

Acceptance into the LAW would make Wisconsin's riding clubs even more legitimate. In January 1881, a Milwaukee man named L. M. Richardson announced his intentions to broaden the wheelmen's infrastructure in the city by creating an office, bicycle sales room, and riding school.[14] Around the same time, Wisconsin's wheelmen moved more formally toward joining the national LAW, even though there was still some debate as to how official LAW membership would take shape in Wisconsin. To help gain clarity on the question, two local riders, D. G. Rogers Jr. and W. C. Reed, left for Boston to take part in an LAW meeting in May 1881, the same month that a riding group from Chicago traveled up to Wisconsin to ride from Milwaukee to Waukesha.[15] As 1881 progressed, it became clear that wheelmen had made significant progress in establishing the gentlemanly respectability of the sport, drawing clear boundaries around whom cycling was for and whom it aimed to benefit. "The Man on the Bicycle," reprinted in the *Milwaukee Daily Sentinel* in July 1881, illustrated just how well the strategy had worked:

Whatever emotion may be surging at his heart, whatever tempestuous yearning at riot in the soul within, the stoic face goes glimmering by us, betraying nothing but the grave content of one whose clear convictions have never failed him yet. He knows his purpose and his destination. That is enough for us.[16]

Knowing the public's respect was crucial to winning their upcoming political battles, wheelmen drew upon notions of martial honor and manly virtue to gain the public's admiration. Like soldiers dutifully answering the call, wheelmen rode into battle.

The fight to establish cycling's legitimacy in Wisconsin also borrowed a few tricks from the velocipede era. Riding rinks were still popular venues for experimenting with new high-wheel technologies, particularly in the snowy winter months. In November 1881, Richardson opened a rink reminiscent of the old velocipede halls in Milwaukee that again catered to white middle-class notions of respectability. Nightly events included brass band concerts, various trick performances, and "fancy skating." Newspapers noted that Richardson relied on "Chinese lanterns" to light the scene, giving the rink an exotic, otherworldly atmosphere. Richardson's rink also invited celebrities such as L. W. Conkling of the Chicago Bicycle Club, famous for his "60 inch wheel, the largest in the Northwest," to boost sales.[17] The limited popularity of indoor events hinted, however, that a dramatic change loomed in the area's cycling culture. Within the span of just a couple months, bicycling had moved almost fully out of doors. Cycling's renaissance would take place in the streets.

As wheelmen continued to take advantage of their social privilege, women also worked to define their place in the sport. Wisconsin's women riders led the effort to make the sport more inclusive by demanding improvements to high-wheel design, particularly changes that would make the machine more gender equitable. In the late 1870s, elite eastern women could be glimpsed cycling through city streets on a two-seated machine called the "tricycle." The new design offered greater stability with three wheels instead of two, and it enabled women to tour cities and towns with a companion, a clear benefit at a moment when women were often greeted with suspicion when traveling alone. The "Salvo Sociable," introduced by James Starley, was especially popular with couples as leisurely touring of area parks and walkways became a favorite recreational activity among the urban elite.

Tricycles became popular machines for women because they allowed riders to wear skirts. This tricycle-built-for-two, ca. 1885, included steering and pedaling mechanisms for the front and rear riders.

Milwaukee County Historical Society

The persistent presence of female riders suggested that women might also organize themselves into clubs. Threatened by the possibility, men reacted by making their sport both more exclusive and more manly. In fact, early Milwaukee wheelmen cultivated a militaristic culture within the cycling clubs to strengthen their claims to legitimacy and power. Clubs often met in public locales to practice their riding throughout Milwaukee, as the Milwaukee Cycling Club did for a series of rides throughout 1882. At the events, often described in newspaper accounts as "drills," the wheelmen would ride around town following the directions of a leader, referred to as a "Captain," who would direct the men "through a series of evolutions" that echoed a military unit's maneuvers. To further the military appearance, the 1882 club adopted uniforms that included a "bottle-green" helmet and coat, "yellowish-gray" knee breeches and stockings, a belt with a silver buckle, and a white flannel shirt. The helmet, patterned on the German cavalry, was trimmed with gold silk and cost each rider a fairly hefty sum of $2.25. Other local club uniforms were described as having a "dark navy" polo cap, shorter jackets, corduroy pants, and "stockings to match." Club badges often rounded out the ensemble, giving the men the look of decorated officers and generals.[18]

Men's conformity to their club's expectations became crucial to cycling's early perception, and Wisconsin's club riders reinforced it in a variety of ways. One important strategy involved the bicycling songs, which were sung in unison as the parades and bi-

Early LAW clubs mimicked military structure with ranking officers, buglers to signal maneuvers, dress uniforms, and formal review ceremonies.

Harper's Weekly, June 18, 1881

cycle columns made their way through the streets. Before the riders took their positions, club leaders dispersed the most recent sheet version of the club's "songs," which the riders quickly memorized. The sound of dozens or even hundreds of men singing certainly added to the spectacle of the early club rides. Wheelmen continued to sing the songs even as they returned home after a ride, often over the club dinners that usually capped off a long afternoon or nighttime lantern ride.[19] Another way to establish club unity was to gather members to support local events. One especially popular venue was Decoration Day, the annual patriotic commemoration for those who had been killed in the Civil War. When a major Decoration Day parade was scheduled in Chicago in 1882, area wheelmen jumped at the chance to participate. "Unless they desire to bring up the rear," the *Milwaukee Sentinel* cautioned, local riders had better sign up fast.[20]

For all the bicycling enthusiasm on display throughout Milwaukee during this period, both Milwaukee and the state of Wisconsin faced serious challenges in broadening cycling's presence. "The greatest drawback to cycling in Milwaukee is the rotten and uneven pavements," the *Milwaukee Sentinel* observed bluntly in April 1882.[21] The desire to seek new and innovative solutions to this problem became a key dynamic of local bicycling manufacturing. In 1882, for example, Milwaukee newspapers reported on the creation of a new "marine bicycle" that allowed a bike rider to travel across water. Perfect for the abundance of lakes and rivers in the Badger State, this early "paddle boat" hit speeds of eight to twelve miles per hour and included an awning with the pontoons so that the rider could have a "sail when the wind is favorable" without having to fear a sunburn. An 1884 article in the *Milwaukee Sentinel* indicated that at least some state residents adopted the design. "A marine bicycle in Pewaukee Lake is the latest attraction astonishing the natives," it reported.[22] Winter presented the biggest obstacle of all for area riders. According to the *Milwaukee Sentinel*, roughly one hundred bicycles routinely traveled the city in November 1882. By the end of the month, however, reports indicated, "Wheelmen have generally pulled their property up for the winter, so but little riding will be done until next season." As a result, bicycling in Wisconsin became synonymous with the appearance of spring, as the excitement of taking the season's first ride in March or April usually provided a capstone to a long, cold winter.[23]

Improved weather encouraged riders in other cities to take up cycling as well. Oshkosh's bicycle scene was also growing quickly by the early 1880s, led by bicycle sales agent Benjamin Hooper, who also tried to organize a club.[24] Formed in 1882 at the

Benjamin Foss Hooper served as the first president of the Oshkosh Cycling Club and is shown here wearing the club's official uniform. He was later married to noted reformer and suffragist Jessie Annette Jack Hooper.

Courtesy of Oshkosh Public Museum

Phoenix engine house, the "Oshkosh Bicycle Club" became the city's first LAW club. Among the early members were club President Benjamin Hooper and Jay A. Hinman, who emerged alongside Hooper as a leader in the city's cycling community. They went to work selecting a uniform and colors, but also organized a number of amateur races at the city fairgrounds where they finished first and second respectively in a race of one-mile heats.[25] Hinman also opened the Oshkosh Bicycle Agency, a shop that specialized in "new and second hand bicycles, bicycles supplies, and sundries."[26] By 1883, Hinman's shop carried Henry Pope's Columbia bicycles and women's models.[27] Oshkosh residents also experimented and tried to improve upon the high-wheel design. Blacksmith H. A. McKenzie designed a machine he claimed could travel a mile a minute with ease. The *Oshkosh Daily Northwestern* debated whether to call the machine a unicycle or bicycle, as it was comprised of several wheels within a larger wheel and was operated with hand pumps instead of pedals. Those who viewed the machine seemed skeptical that McKenzie's improvements would actually work.[28]

The height of the 1883 spring cycling season was marked by one notable event: the appearance of a female bicycle racer in Milwaukee. Identified only as "Louisa" in local papers, likely a reference to the noted female racer Louise Armaindo, the woman was profiled in the *Milwaukee Daily Journal* in an article called "Louisa and Her Legs."[29] The reporters seemed to focus more on her body type and were clearly dismissive of her racing talents. The article detailed how the twenty-two-year-old had managed to break into the professional racing circuit, but in ways that stressed her dependency on men. "The men are awful jealous of me for winning the championship," Louisa admitted. "I have a man, of course, that is an agent to go among the men and transact my business," she went on, "but its [sic] hard work, and not very healthy when carried on as I am carrying on." By assuring fans that she "had a man" to manage her burgeoning career, Louisa cleverly carved out a space for women racers in the sport, even as her presence clearly caused discomfort. Doors into the sport remained open to women, even if only narrowly so.[30]

Influential figures from the eastern cycling scene also made a visit to Milwaukee that summer. In June 1883, Bostonian J. F. McClure, managing editor of *The Wheelmen*, visited the Cream City. He told local journalists that Milwaukee ranked "high as a good riding place," and noted that the area bicycle clubs were of the "highest character." Commenting how far ahead Milwaukee was in comparison to cities such as Saint Louis and Kansas City, McClure nonetheless stated that in comparison to Boston or New York, Wisconsin still had a ways to go. When further compared with Europe, McClure acknowledged, the United States in general still lagged far behind. "In England, the machine is much more used, and there must be fully 250,000 being daily ridden," he said. "There are over 5,000 bicycles used in the English mail service." McClure was especially troubled by the condition of American roads. "In this country a Wheelman can travel fifty miles a day with ease, while in England, where the roads are better, seventy-five and even a hundred are possible." Finally, he noted, "The ladies are also coming to use the tricycle, and hold it with as much favor as the men do the two-wheeler."[31] McClure's comments helped deepen Wisconsin's desire to one day be seen as a frontrunner in the national cycling scene.

Early cycling leaders in Wisconsin also recognized that bicycling industries had slowly gained a foothold in the Upper Midwest, particularly in Chicago, which emerged after the Civil War as one of the great North American industrial centers. There, new high-end producers Gormully and Jeffrey appeared, making machines under the Rambler brand available from Detroit to Minneapolis.[32] These developments also suggested that the demand for high-wheels was, at long last, becoming more stable. Manufacturing

Tournaments held by the Springfield Cycling Club in Massachusetts became iconic sporting events in the United States. In 1883, high-wheel racing was still a fledgling sport in Wisconsin, but it was already a major attraction out east.

Library of Congress, Prints & Photographs Division, LC-USZC2-1405

growth also increased interest in the exploits of bicycle riders all over the world. Stories about long-distance rides became especially popular as the 1880s went on, deepening the fascination for long-distance riding that stretched back to the earliest days of velocipede mania. With solid rubber tires and improving roads, long-distance riders gained new visibility. Lyman Hotchkiss Bagg, for example, a Yale graduate who began a two-year cross-country odyssey in the spring of 1884, detailed his adventures for an admiring American audience in *Ten Thousand Miles on a Bicycle*. The same year, the Englishman Thomas Stevens rode his Pope-produced Columbia bicycle from San Francisco to New York. Upon reaching the East Coast, Stevens set sail for Europe, and for the next two and a half years continued to pedal around the globe. His travels were chronicled in the pages of *Outing* magazine and later in a book, *Around the World on a Bicycle*.[33]

Fueled by these tales of long-distance riders, Wisconsin's men rallied for the creation of better roads. European races, in particular, helped build a case for improving US roads, as European cycling exploits, Wisconsinites recognized, were entirely the result of wide boulevards paved to accommodate bicycling traffic. Slowly but surely, Wisconsin residents were drawn to the challenge of matching Europe's "civilized" events. Wisconsinites saw these possibilities firsthand at area racetracks, often originally used for horse events at county fairs. In Janesville, Francis Cornelia Norton Tallman, "Nellie" to friends and family and the wife of Edgar Tallman, noted in her 1883 diary that she had taken her sons to the Rock County fairgrounds to witness a high-wheel race featuring champion riders from Ireland and Canada. They were racing against a horse, Ohio Maid. The race was five miles long, and the horse easily won. Despite the defeat, the English and Irish cyclists had created a new sense of wonder around the high-wheelers. In fact, Nellie Tallman's decision to take her sons to the race stirred what would become a longstanding family love affair with the sport. By the early 1890s, her son Stanley had established himself as a locally famous bicycle racer.[34]

Racing's grueling competitions, intense rivalries, and close finishes drew many spectators. Wisconsin would not get a competitor at Springfield until Walter C. Sanger in the 1890s.

Harper's Weekly, September 25, 1886

As the decade wore on, more and more Wisconsin cities were touched by the spread of Milwaukee's rapidly expanding bicycling culture. *The Milwaukee Sentinel* ran news in 1883 of a massive ride sponsored by the Milwaukee Bicycle Club, which planned an excursion through nearby Waukesha as part of its planning for June 30 to July 4. "Arrange your vacation for time, as you are assured a hearty welcome, splendid wheeling and a good time socially and bicycularly," the article noted. Bicycling clubs from within

Tensions grew between cyclists and those who wanted to limit where they could ride. In 1888, members of the North Side Victor Cycling Club rolled calmly down the rut-filled Whitefish Bay Plank Road, but George Fry (far right) was arrested later that day for riding down a smoother and safer wooden sidewalk.

Milwaukee Public Museum Photography Collection

a 300-mile radius were invited, and editors made sure to note the bicycle's popularity was skyrocketing.[35]

At the same time, Milwaukee men secured new clubhouses to host and provide social spaces for membership. Little is known about the particular dynamics of the early clubhouses in Wisconsin, but there is plenty of evidence documenting these spaces in other locales. David Herlihy, for example, has chronicled the clubhouse of the Massachusetts Bicycle Club, which opened in 1885. It was an elegant three-story clubhouse on Newbury Street, near the heart of Boston's Back Bay. The ornate façade had a large window, and the top of the building was home to a large sign announcing the name of the club. Members even installed a small ramp with access to the front door that could accommodate tricycles, meaning that the club may have welcomed women riders.[36]

By 1885, Wisconsin had enough members to support a formal alliance with the LAW. Although the decision to join the national LAW did not ultimately occur that year, it was clear by the middle of the decade that Wisconsin's riders were playing a more active role in building the national cycling culture. One of the most important examples of how Wisconsin's early riders made an imprint on the developing national scene was through wheelmen's club songs. Milwaukee's connections to wheelmen songwriting ran deep, as Milwaukee's Angus S. Hibbard wrote a majority of the songs for the 1885 edition of "Club Songs for Wheelmen," a pamphlet published in Chicago for distribution to wheelmen clubs nationwide. With songs such as "Big, Big Wheels," "Rolling through the Woodland," and "Over the Handles," Hibbard's songs illuminated the spirit of brotherhood popular in LAW clubhouses and League publications. In "The League of American Wheelmen," Hibbard illuminated the dimensions of the wheelmen community:

> Now I am a bold Bicycler
> And I ride a great big wheel
> I'm a member of the brotherhood,
> That binds us firm as steel;
> Whichever way you call it,
> 'Tis a band of brothers true,
> It is the League of American Wheelmen,
> Or the L.A.W.[37]

Unable to contain the enthusiasm for cycling that these and other songs helped spread throughout the state, reports soon indicated that communities throughout Wisconsin had developed their own local cycling cultures.[38]

A wonderful front-row seat into these events appeared in the *Milwaukee Sentinel* on June 26, 1885. Under a headline describing the "gay cavalcade of bicycle riders," the article noted that at a little past five o'clock on a warm summer evening in Milwaukee, roughly twenty-three cyclists lined up in a row at the lakefront. With the sun shining high and warm over the city, the young cyclists stood watch "with a cigarette" in their mouths, posed by their bicycles with an "earnest expression" and outfits made of flannel. Nearby, reports said, a number of admiring ladies stood by, gawking as the riders slowly made their start just before six o'clock. Riding two abreast, the riders snaked their way up the lakefront and into Whitefish Bay, singing songs as they slowly approached the residence of their club captain. There, the men ate "an inviting supper" and then turned homeward. By that time, the sun had vanished behind the rolling hills to the west of the city, cloaking the road in darkness. The *Milwaukee Sentinel* reported that the return ride took place "in the silvery gleam of the moonlight," as the cyclists glided quietly by, silhouetted against the backdrop of a glittering Lake Michigan. Milwaukee was slowly earning a reputation as a great place to ride.[39]

CHAPTER 4

The Safety Model and the Beginning of Wisconsin's Bicycling Boom

"It is safe to say that no sport of the present century has
grown so rapidly in popular favor as bicycling. . . . Ten years
ago the wheel was a rarity in Wisconsin, there being only
three or four of them in regular use. . . . To-day [*sic*] there are
upwards of 1,000."

Milwaukee Sentinel, 1890[1]

For many of the Wisconsinites excluded from cycling clubs, the state's emergence as a biking destination seemed both unfair and undeserved. For women, the real benefits of the sport remained largely out of reach. But beginning in 1885, the walls drawn around early cycling clubs started to crumble. These changes not only challenged the dominance of the all-male, all-white clubs but also expanded the popular understanding of who a cyclist could be. Several improvements to high-wheel design helped initiate a full-blown bicycling boom by 1890. In 1885, bicycle manufacturers in England debuted what was called a "safety" model. The safety, as its name suggests, introduced features that made the new machines both safer and easier to operate. Distinguished by the use of a new chain drive along with a much smaller front tire, these models allowed for direct steering by using a handlebar placed within easy reach of the rider. The improved center of balance helped increase the stability of the machine, and the seat, lower to the ground, also made it easier to mount and dismount.

Late in the 1880s, safety models would also come to feature pneumatic tires, which cushioned the riding experience and greatly expanded the distance average riders were able to ride. Though this innovation was not developed at the same time as the safety model—it didn't, in fact, reach American shores until 1892—the addition of pneumatic tires accelerated the safety's appeal with the public into the early years of the boom. Pneumatic tires got their unlikely start with the experimentation of a Scottish veterinarian living in Belfast around 1888 or 1889. As the story goes, John Dunlop was tinkering with his son's tricycle in his shop when he discovered that lining the wheel with an inner tube filled with compressed air would not only cushion the ride but also increase its speed. The following year, a bicycle racer gave Dunlop's new technology a try on the racetrack, and he won several contests in Belfast. When Dunlop finally found an investor for his design, they partnered to form the Pneumatic Tyre Company. It would eventually supply tires to vast sections of the British cycling trade. After they developed a process to harden the

New safety bicycles had a chain drive, smaller front wheels, and improved balance. These modern machines began to appear in downtown Green Bay around 1890.

WHi Image ID 2001

tires with canvas in order to prevent flats, new speed records made it clear that the pneumatic tire would revolutionize cycling. An explosion in sales quickly followed. Between the appearance of the first popular safety models in the United States in 1887 and the beginning of the bicycle boom in the United States three years later in 1890, the number of firms making or importing bicycles rose dramatically, from roughly twelve to almost seventy-five. By 1890, it seemed possible that the high-wheel would be supplanted by the new safety bicycles.[2]

From the vantage point of 1885, however, all that future growth was impossible to see. In the United States, many manufacturers dismissed the safety model and its smaller tires. With its "safe" features and less imposing design, producers believed the "bicyclette," as they called it, would never catch on in the rough-and-tumble United States. Pope and others may have been jealous that the new model had British origins; American mechanics had again been out-paced by foreign engineers. John Kemp Starley, nephew to

Cycling clubs, such as this one from Florence, Wisconsin, ca. 1892, gradually saw safety models replace the increasingly obsolete high-wheel.

WHi Image ID 97179

the great British designer famous for his tricycle designs, James Starley, was one of the first to capitalize on the new machine. One of John Kemp Starley's most popular new rides was the Rover. Weighing a hefty forty-five pounds, it lowered the front wheel to a much more reasonable thirty-six inches and incorporated a central chain drive to ease acceleration and cruising. The chain drive was comprised of what we would describe today as a large forward gear, two pedals, and a bike chain connecting the gear to the rear wheel. Though its initial asking price was high, the Rover would eventually be one of the more affordable models. American producers did not see it coming, but the birth of modern cycling was at hand.[3]

In the United States, women helped generate the call for more egalitarian bicycle design, calling for a model that would work for all genders. Pope finally gave in to the growing consumer demand and released his own safety model, the Veloce Columbia.[4] Once again Wisconsin's riders took their lead from the Northeast, where safety models became a ubiquitous feature of the city landscape during the last part of the decade. As one female rider put it, "A sudden desire awoke in the feminine mind to ascertain for itself, by personal experience, those joys of the two-wheeler which they had so often heard vaunted as superior, a thousand times, to the more sober delights of the staid tricycle."[5] Meanwhile, women continued to experiment with various bicycle designs at area indoor rinks. In October 1885, the *Milwaukee Sentinel* reported that the South Side Palace Rink hosted a "lady bicycle rider," who gave lessons to women on how to use the new machines.[6]

Despite its beginnings as a "white" sport, Wisconsin's still-small population of African Americans took a strong interest in the bicycling boom. Several black newspapers covered the rise of the safety model throughout the late 1880s and early 1900s: La Crosse's *Wisconsin Labor Advocate* and Milwaukee's *Weekly Wisconsin Advocate, Wisconsin Afro-American,* and *Northwest Recorder.* As the boom deepened, black papers followed market trends and provided space for local business to advertise their bicycling products. The papers echoed many of the same frustrations and anxieties as white editors.[7] George Edwin Taylor, the editor of the *Wisconsin Labor Advocate*, was an African American born in Arkansas in 1857. A black business owner and publisher located in La Crosse between 1886 and 1887, Taylor's time in Wisconsin was ultimately short lived, but he would go on to pursue a storied political career. In 1904, he became the first-ever candidate of a national African American party for the US presidency, representing the National Liberty Party. As a man with wide political ambitions and an interest in local affairs, Taylor provided coverage of

Hy Sandham's watercolor print, published around 1887, depicts the pageantry and excitement of a wheelmen club touring the countryside.

Library of Congress, Prints & Photographs Division, LC-USZC4-3043

the increasing bicycle boom. In an article called "Inventor of the 'Wheel,'" the *Advocate* argued that Pierre Lallement, one of the men who worked in Michaux's velocipede shop, deserved more credit for the invention than the public seemed ready to acknowledge.[8] In another article, reprinted from the *Boston Herald*, Taylor included an article that poked fun at church members who lamented that their pastor "does not ride a bicycle." This was a common complaint in black and white communities, as pastors who did not ride were often ridiculed as being behind the times.[9] Taylor also included news about long-distance cycling trips, including the story of a man who rode from Omaha, Nebraska, to Buffalo, New York, over the span of six weeks.[10] Taylor received advertising support for his newspaper from bicycle retailers across the state line in Minneapolis who marketed "second hand" bicycles in his columns, indicating a growing market among African Americans.[11]

African Americans won increasing acceptance to a number of sporting venues in the last half of the 1880s, making names for themselves as baseball players, boxers, jockeys, and bicyclists. Moses Fleetwood Walker, for example, became one of the first professional black baseball players in 1884. Isaac Murphy won widespread recognition as a black horse jockey. By the mid-1890s, the first major black superstar of the cycling scene would emerge in the name of Marshall Walter "Major" Taylor (unrelated to George Edwin Taylor). As scholars have pointed out, evolving notions of manhood common in the 1880s had not yet settled on a distinct manly ideal, meaning the color line had not yet closed its doors to blacks. Yet the flowering of interracial sports was brief. Starting in the last half of the 1890s, civilized manhood became synonymous with whiteness, and black men were no longer welcome to participate in the same way.[12]

With so many kinds of new riders expressing interest in the sport, Milwaukee-area cyclists called a meeting at the Plankinton House in February 1887 to form a League

Parker H. Sercombe raced his new safety bicyclette against Terry Andrae on his trusty high-wheel in 1887. Sercombe lost the race, but the safety would eventually surpass the older machine. Sercombe later became a bicycle manufacturer in Milwaukee.

Pneumatic, vol. 1, no. 5 , 1892

of American Wheelmen chapter. It was largely made up of the men who had participated in earlier wheelmen activities, and not surprisingly, was an all-white venture. "Wisconsin is probably the only state in the union with so large a number of wheelmen where a state division does not exist," the *Milwaukee Sentinel* lamented.[13] Milwaukee's wheelmen were encouraged to organize by the victories gained by wheelmen in New York, who gathered ten thousand signatures that spring to petition the city to change cycling regulations. Even though many New Yorkers continued to insist that bicyclists posed a threat to pedestrians and horses, the protests were outmuscled by the growing power of the bicycle lobby. On June 25, 1887, New York Governor David B. Hill signed the "Liberty Bill," which made all of New York's city parks open to riders, so long as cyclists followed basic rules of traffic and safety. The law provided an important precedent for bicycling laws across the country, including Wisconsin. Such victories encouraged Wisconsin's wheelmen to increase their influence over local city and county governments.[14]

New forms of bicycle racing also gave energy to the movement. In August 1887, just two months after the Liberty Bill took hold in New York, two of Wisconsin's more notable local riders agreed to race in a daring head-to-head contest pitting the old high-wheel technology against the new safety model. Parker H. Sercombe rode what papers described as the "bicyclette," while Franz Theodor (Terry) Andrae rode a massive fifty-four-inch high-wheel. They raced twenty-one miles that day to see, once and for all, which of the models was fastest. Observers of the race instantly recognized that the bicyclette offered better stability and a smoother ride, while the high-wheel had the clear advantage of a much higher top speed. In the end, the high-wheel claimed victory in this early battle, winning by nearly six minutes. Even so it seemed clear that the high-wheel's days were numbered. The safety, which some observers called a "sawed-off" high-wheel, simply presented too many design advantages not to be taken seriously.[15]

The growing popularity of the safety machines also led to public demonstrations of their use. Thirty-six bicyclists participated in a "lantern parade" in September 1887 through Milwaukee. "The effect of the procession was both striking and pleasing and applause was not infrequently bestowed upon the riders," the *Sentinel* reported.[16] The riders were "decked out with colored lanterns" and "in some instances were covered with colored cloth" illuminated from inside. The article also noted that although a "few headers were taken," only a few minor crashes occurred. It is likely that these parades employed a mix of old-style high-wheels and new-style safety models.[17] All over the state, bicycles were becoming more ubiquitous.[18]

Early Bicycling Lingo

EARLY BICYCLISTS USED a wealth of slang terms to describe their sport. After the safety model helped bring thousands of new riders to bicycling in the late 1880s and early 1890s, these terms became increasingly popular in the culture through venues such as the bicycling press, including publications like the *Pneumatic* and the nationally recognized *Outing*.

bloomer girl: a young woman who wore a tailored bloomer suit consisting of baggy Turkish trousers and short jacket as athletic wear for bicycling

boneshaker: the rigid primitive bicycles and velocipedes that "shook your bones"; later, applied to high-wheels with bumpy rides

centurion: honorary title for a man or woman who completed a century ride

century: a ride of one hundred or more miles; the term is still used today as an important riding milestone for dedicated bicycle tourists

coasting: taking one's feet off the pedals and placing them on the handlebars or small pegs attached to the fork, usually when going downhill

commander: elected leader of a local or state LAW chapter; commanders often wore military badges that identified their rank

consul: the local LAW member tasked with welcoming visiting bicyclists and providing housing, entertainment, and food for travelers

header: a headlong crash over the front of a high-wheel

ordinary: another name for a high-wheel bicycle

park-bikists: riders who meandered from side to side down a path without consideration for others

penny-farthing: a name used for high-wheels after the high-wheel era, popularized in

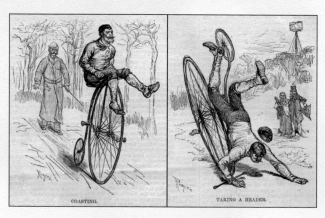

COASTING.   TAKING A HEADER.

Harper's Weekly, December 20, 1879

Early Bicycling Lingo

England; it is often, though erroneously, assumed to be historically correct

run: fast-paced short ride, usually between two cities; the most popular Wisconsin run went from Milwaukee to Waukesha

safety: bicycle design with two similarly-sized wheels that replaced the high-wheel and kept the rider closer to the ground, making it safer for the rider; the same basic design is still used today

scorcher: a reckless wheelman who sped down city streets, alarming pedestrians and horses

steed and mare: early names for bicycles

tour: long, slower-paced ride outside the city that included stops in multiple towns and cities

As more and more cyclists took to the streets, accidents became more common between cyclists, pedestrians, and carriages. In October 1887, for example, a "peculiar accident" took place at Cass Street and Juneau Avenue in Milwaukee. William Breckenridge, a high school student, was riding down Juneau Avenue on the sidewalk when a man identified in newspaper reports as Dr. Jacob Mendel rounded the corner in a carriage just as Breckenridge left the sidewalk and entered the street. The two collided. Breckenridge was knocked down from his tall perch atop his high-wheel, suffering bruises to his head and hip. Mendel's horses were frightened in the collision and bolted upon contact. Their speedy departure threw their driver out of his buggy, and Dr. Mendel fell to the ground, cutting open his scalp in what must have made for a terrifying scene. Police reports indicated that Breckenridge liked to practice "riding his wheel" over his school's lunch hour and was probably speeding to make it back to class when the accident occurred.[19] Another story from 1888 told how one of Milwaukee's YMCA directors fell off of his bicycle. "Both hands are terribly lacerated," the report read, a common occurrence for those who continued to risk high-wheel riding at a time when urban streets were frequently littered with broken glass, sharp rocks, and other debris.[20] Area newspapers occasionally shared information on especially dangerous intersections, advising readers to avoid them at all costs.[21]

THE "NEW WOMAN."

Conservative white men feared the growing class of educated women who demanded equal suffrage and tested gender boundaries. Many male cyclists were suspicious of the "new woman," as in this cartoon, and were skeptical that she could master the bicycle.

Puck magazine, June 19, 1895, courtesy of University of Wisconsin–Stevens Point

Meanwhile, women continued the work of organizing themselves into cycling clubs. Out east, the nation's first women's bicycling club appeared in Baltimore in the spring of 1888. It attracted some fifty members and made regular excursions covering up to forty miles at a time. Later that summer, several members rode in the LAW parade in Baltimore.[22] It was the first time women appeared on bicycles as part of the LAW's annual meet. Their presence helped spur a growing nationwide interest in women's cycling organizations throughout the country. As club members, women did not relegate themselves to casual rides in the park but instead sought to secure many of the same privileges as white men. Though not on par with the LAW, Milwaukee's female clubs aroused suspicion—and curiosity. In an article called "How She Mounts a Bicycle," writers at the *Milwaukee Sentinel* were especially fascinated by the fact that new innovations in bicycle design made it possible for women to straddle the bicycle without fear of lifting their skirts, an occurrence that was "easily done" in all corners of the city, and by women of all kinds. "Every day a lady . . . cuts graceful capers on her machines and skims about like a swallow," it said. Area men seemed utterly baffled that women found cycling as appealing as they did.[23]

Some wheelmen clearly resented women's increased presence in the sport. The wheelmen were, of course, consciously cultivating a respectable male bicycling culture, but they often insisted their motives were not political and should not be perceived as such. Under the headline, "Not a Political Parade," the *Milwaukee Sentinel* described an October 1888 bike parade being "taken by many for some sort of a political demonstration, but it was not such in any sense." However, wheelmen adopted many of the traditional signs of a political parade during the ride. They wore patriotic red, white, and blue uniforms and decorations. They rode to the accompaniment of brass bands playing patriotic songs. They used brightly colored lanterns to emphasize their spirit of unity. The men also rode with large, gaudy banners proclaiming their club names, much like a political party would in an election season. Perhaps most telling, one rider even stole his sister's dress and had hoisted it on a pole above his head for the duration of the parade. Around the base of the dress, the man painted the words "Milwaukee Wheelwomen"—a signal that the Wheelmen felt unease at the idea that women could join their ranks. It is also worth pointing out that this particular parade featured an even split between high-wheel machines and safety machines, suggesting the safety model was coming into fashion among the city's elite club riders.[24]

The uptick in safety model production and use encouraged state residents to examine how these bicycles might be used in more professional and practical capacities. A

Tours organized by wheelmen clubs often took the form of spectacle. The Oshkosh Wheelmen carried banners and flags and wore their club uniforms while on a tour along Lake Winnebago, ca. 1885.

Courtesy of Oshkosh Public Museum

remarkable article from the May 1889 *Milwaukee Sentinel* described how Milwaukee's physicians organized sometime during the spring of that year—following the wishes of "some of the younger members of the profession"—to use bicycles in making their nighttime calls around the city. Doctors recognized that with a bicycle, a physician could more easily reach patients in an emergency. The only problem, they noted, was that not every physician knew how to ride or even how to pack the gear required for a medical visit into panniers. Nor were many physicians—particularly older physicians who "did not look kindly upon this innovation"—willing to risk the embarrassment that might come from crashing in the streets while on a call.[25]

To help allay the doctors' fears, a bizarre midnight meeting was called at the base of the Solomon Juneau monument near the Lake Michigan waterfront in downtown Milwaukee. According to the account in the *Milwaukee Sentinel*, "Midnight came and in the dim light a number of dusky forms could be seen moving about the place of rendezvous." Then, a man stepped forward and asked who would be the first to give the bicycle a try. Several men spent some time practicing on the machines as their colleagues offered encouragement, support, and probably also a few catcalls. "Only the stars might witness their undignified antics," the paper reported. Although many doctors of the older generation remained suspicious, the *Milwaukee Sentinel* predicted that bicycle riding would become a standard part of the curriculum in area medical schools. It seemed clear that lives might be saved thanks to the efficiency of the bicycle.[26]

Undeterred by the negative reaction of their male peers, Wisconsin women continued to organize club activities, some of which included both men and women. In May 1889, one Milwaukee report said,

Milwaukee's physicians would rendezvous at midnight under the Solomon Juneau monument on the bluffs above the Lake Michigan shoreline, pictured here in 1889. The darkness hid their embarrassment as they learned how to ride.

WHi Image ID 53655

The first ladies' bicycle party was given on the east side one day last week, consisting of a party of nine; five ladies and four gentlemen. Three of the ladies rode safeties, and two rode tandem cycles. It is only a question of time when bicycle riding for ladies will be quite the rage and before the season is over, many who have never given the subject a thought will become quite the expert on the wheel.[27]

While it is difficult to say with certainty why these particular women chose a gender-integrated club, the presence of men offered a range of strategic benefits for women interested in increasing the sport's accessibility, more than an all-women club might offer. It is also likely the women were offering a response to the exclusive practices of the men's cycling clubs. In any case, by July 1889, newspapers noted that the new female-friendly safety bike designs had fully caught on among women riders in the state. A woman named Maggie McGill made one of the first purchases, and the *Milwaukee Sentinel* noted she started a trend: "A number of other young ladies are negotiating for similar machines, and it is soon expected that a ladies' bicycle club will soon be organized here." Soon, these women would forge an important new dynamic in Wisconsin's cycling scene.[28]

Women's increasing presence in the sport did not come easy. It generated fierce debates and unleashed a wide range of cultural anxieties. Many women, including a few early feminists, insisted that bicycling posed physical and moral dangers that women ought to avoid. Other warnings were decidedly more sexist. A bishop in Buffalo, New York, for example, likened female cyclists to "witches astride of broomsticks." Others disagreed. As Lucy M. Hall explained to the readers of the Boston *Congregationalist*, the bicycle "offers positive advantages over almost any other form of exercise," noting that while being outside was bound to attract men's attention, as "the pastime [bicycling] becomes more common [their] objection will lose its force altogether."[29] One of the emerging fears of the late 1880s was that women would use the bicycle to escape the sight of their male companions, who were understood to be guardians of female civility. As women adopted some of the sensibilities common in men's cycling circles, however, they found that they were increasingly greeted with smiles and admiration on their daily rides, and many of the fears slowly started giving way. Describing the scene in New York's Central Park, Florence Finch Kelley remarked for the *Milwaukee Sentinel* that "on a recent fine day a wheelman counted thirteen women on bicycles," a presence she and others interpreted as the beginning of a key social transformation.[30]

Kelley's description again suggests that Wisconsin's women were somewhat behind their eastern counterparts in their adoption of the bicycle, in large part because new bicycle designs took a longer time to reach the Midwest. In her article, she seemed optimistic that the sweeping changes in New York would soon be seen in Wisconsin. "The tricycle is about to become a thing of the past," she wrote. "The ladies' bicycle, which was introduced last season, is already superseding the clumsy three-wheeled machine and is winning its way into general favor at a rapid rate." Slowly but surely, the increasing number of women riders in the boom cities of the Midwest lent validity to bicycling's changing geography. Kelley noted, "New York and the Western cities . . . monopolize the women's bicycle. . . . New England will have none of it, and the South looks at it askance." More and more female riders made Milwaukee, Chicago, Detroit, and Toledo seem akin to the great cities of the East Coast. In this way, women can be understood as key diplomats for the bicycling boom of the 1890s, helping to generate the early enthusiasm that eventually transformed Wisconsin into a state known for cycling.[31]

Women's keen interest initiated a number of changes, including the way cycling was marketed and branded in Wisconsin. One of the most telling examples took place in 1889, when Milwaukee hosted the Grand Army of the Republic's twenty-third annual national encampment in August. It is hard to think of a more expressive display of late-century honorable manhood than a gathering of aging Civil War veterans. The huge veteran's reunion, easily the largest gathering of Civil War old-timers to take place anywhere in the country that year, guaranteed that Milwaukee would be flooded with men (and their sons) looking to have a good time. Area cycling manufacturers capitalized on their presence by encouraging the veterans to use a bicycle to tour the city while they were in town. One notice placed by the Milwaukee Bicycle Agency showed that times were changing: "It will pay you to call at the Milwaukee bicycle agency during your stay. . . . We have wheels of all makes and at all prices, including Safeties for ladies, gentleman and children."[32] By tapping into a market that appeared, at least on the surface, to be overwhelmingly male, the ad demonstrated that even the most manly of gatherings might also draw several thousand women and children. Marketers opened the door to their participation, asking them to also partake in the advantages of cycling during their visit. This would not have been the case a few years before, when cycling was still a firmly male-dominated sport.

By the end of 1889, it became clear that women were beginning to embrace cycling throughout the city. "Lacy bicycle riders are becoming numerous," the *Milwaukee Sentinel* noted. "There are about twenty-five ladies of this city who ride the wheel, and it is said that the number will be increased very largely next year." It added, "The growing craze among women to ride bicycles is due to the appearance of a machine especially made for them." As local papers asserted, "The young lady of Milwaukee has been just a trifle envious of the boys gliding by on their glistening wheels." The *Sentinel* writers were sure to note that the bicycle offered plenty of romantic opportunities for young men and women who suddenly found themselves mobile in new ways. "There is no knowing what the future of bicycling has in store for Milwaukee," it said, "but the city already has its bicycle romance." Wonderfully suggestive of the suspicions these female riders unleashed, the coverage highlighted one of the most important developments of the early safety era in Wisconsin's bicycling story.[33]

Milwaukee's North Side Victor Cycling Club joined a growing number of bicycling advocacy groups during the high-wheel era. This studio portrait taken in 1889 shows members (left to right) Arthur Zochert, George Fry, Harry Riesen, George Riesen, and Walter Zochert.

Milwaukee Public Museum Photography Collection

Although the city itself became more accepting of women riders, their growing participation in the sport did not put a halt to the boy's club mentality. Men's racing continued to offer an exclusive venue to showcase male competition. Terry Andrae won a notable early race in October 1889. After the race ended, the Milwaukee wheelmen opened their clubhouse on West Water Street, where an informal reception greeted members and invited guests.[34] Clubhouse events such as these became an important space for cultivating male camaraderie in Milwaukee's early cycling years. Milwaukee riders gathered there in December for a "book party" hosted by Andrae. Each man brought "at least

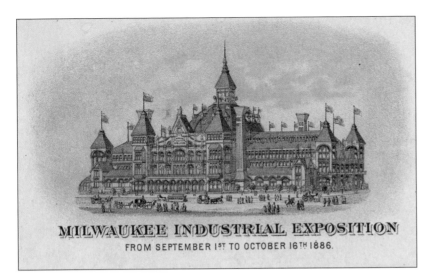

MILWAUKEE INDUSTRIAL EXPOSITION
FROM SEPTEMBER 1ST TO OCTOBER 16TH 1886.

From 1880 to 1900, the Industrial Exposition Building in Milwaukee was the frequent site of indoor bicycle races and a popular starting point for century rides.

WHi Image ID 53326

one book to form a nucleus for a large library," newspapers noted. Speeches celebrating the club library followed. By forming a library and engaging in some "higher learning," the cyclists also ensured that their presence in the city and state would be seen as cultivated, gentlemanly, and civilized. As they hoped, this gave them an increased political legitimacy, though they of course never used those terms precisely.[35]

While old-style club riding remained fairly segregated, other bicycling venues showed more promise for integration. In December 1889, for example, male and female riders in Milwaukee hosted an indoor "Winter Bicycling Tournament" at the Industrial Exposition Building downtown. Nearly one hundred bicyclists—male and female—rode laps inside the building as a brass band played. An audience that included friends of the cyclists watched from the grandstand as the riders circled. As a great way to get some exercise during a long Wisconsin winter, it is easy to understand why the event proved so popular. That popularity waned as the weather improved, however. Increasingly, cycling became a seasonal sport in Wisconsin.[36]

Warming weather throughout the early part of 1890 brought new stories of cycling triumph and adversity. In June 1890, three women completed a century ride (100 miles) between Newark, New Jersey, and Philadelphia, Pennsylvania, outdistancing many of their male challengers.[37] Meanwhile, complaints poured in to local police in Milwaukee claiming that cyclists who rode on sidewalks were putting foot pedestrians at risk. "Chief Janssen has issued an order to the patrolmen to arrest every one that is found riding a bicycle or 'safety' on a sidewalk," the Milwaukee Sentinel noted in June 1890.[38] Concerned about the stereotypes of unsafe riding these reports were generating, Milwaukee riders wrote editorials in response. Cyclists argued that bike riders ought not be the "scapegoat" for sidewalk misuse. After all, they pointed out, merchants in the city routinely blocked the sidewalks during deliveries, and many people parked their horses or carriages on the sidewalks while running errands.[39]

With the sight of cyclists more common than ever, the year 1890 marked an important turning point in the imagination of local riders. That summer, as bicycling's popularity soared to new heights throughout Milwaukee and the state of Wisconsin, the Milwaukee Sentinel ran a retrospective on the sport's unlikely rise:

Members of the Wisconsin division of the LAW took a break from their cycling to rest along Lake Winnebago, ca. 1885.

Courtesy of Oshkosh Public Museum

It is safe to say that no sport of the present century has grown so rapidly in popular favor as bicycling. Ten years ago the wheel was a rarity in Wisconsin, there being only three or four of them in regular use, and there was such a prejudice against them that the riders were often threatened with bodily harm for simply appearing on the street. Public sentiment, however, has changed very much during the last decade, and to-day [*sic*] there are upwards of 1,000 bicyclers in Milwaukee, and public opinion not only tolerates, but seeks to increase and perpetuate the sport.

Tellingly, the article downplayed women's contributions. Though it did chronicle women's influence on the sport further down the page, the article made clear in its analysis who deserved credit for the boom. "This remarkable transition is due largely to . . . the efforts which the Milwaukee wheelmen have made to develop and make popular the sport." In particular, the article highlighted the efforts of William L. Simonds, who later became chief consul of the Wisconsin LAW. Simonds had been one of the original high-wheel riders in the city, making his first appearance alongside the small handful of riders back in 1880. Two other notable names mentioned by the *Sentinel* were Henry P. and Terry Andrae. "H. P. Andrae is among the pioneer cyclers, having commenced to pedal a wheel in 1880," it noted. The Andrae brothers formed part of Wisconsin's bicycling manufacturing front. Along with the Andrae factories and a few others by 1890, several sales agencies called Milwaukee home.[40]

Just as it had happened with Pope's factories on the East Coast, a deep connection had been established between bicycle manufacturers and the bicycling community—a bond that remains strong within the sport today. But the connections between bicycle

Milwaukee Wheelmen officers of 1891: (back, left to right) C. F. Kilby, Andrew Steel (treasurer and director), Martin C. Rotier, Henry P. Andrae, William L. Simonds, Henry J. Rotier (captain), Frederick Mayer Jr., and August Rutz; (front, left to right) T. E. Hutchings, Abraham Cressy Morrison (president), and Oscar E. Binner (vice president).

Milwaukee County Historical Society

Milwaukeeans nicknamed Terry Andrae's brother Henry P. Andrae "the colonel" because of his similar bicycling leadership and manufacturing experience to Colonel Albert Pope, ca. 1898.

Pneumatic, vol. 8, no. XX, 1898

manufacturers and local wheelmen chapters can also be seen at a smaller and more localized scale in the example of the Andrae family. In 1855, the young entrepreneur Julius Andrae emigrated from Meissen, Saxony, to Milwaukee. Trained as a machine-shop worker, Andrae opened a blacksmith shop that made iron parts for boxes used by the US Army in the Civil War, but after the war, turned to more lucrative ventures, gaining wealth as a manufacturer and supplier for electronic doorbells, incandescent lights, and telephones.[41] Meanwhile, his two sons, Henry and Terry, became enamored with the bicycle craze. Although Henry was an active bicyclist, Terry was the athlete in the family and became a proficient racer. As the boom progressed, Terry's success in high-wheel racing built a reputation that earned him the nickname the Flying Badger.[42] The rising influence of the Andrae family helped speed their move into the local bicycling industry and community. Julius used his successes as an area contractor to eventually fund a new bicycle factory and repair shop that were managed by Terry.[43] Meanwhile, his brother Henry, a lesser-known racer who was nicknamed the Colonel, became an active member in a variety of Milwaukee wheelmen clubs, serving as secretary, chief centurion, vice president, and racing board chairperson.[44] Club members like Henry used their growing financial influence to urge legislators to support bike-friendly initiatives throughout the city and state. In this way, the Julius Andrae and Sons Bicycle Shop became a primary gathering place for wheelmen and bicycle enthusiasts.

It did not take long for the Andraes to enter the wider world of bicycle manufacturing. By the late 1880s, their company was manufacturing "bicycles, tricycles, and safeties."[45] Their later models included the Light Roadster for touring, the Road Racer, the Lady Andrae, which featured a drop frame, and the Racer for track racing.[46] In Milwaukee, local racers seemed to prefer Andrae bicycles. The 1896 Annual Milwaukee Road Race featured an Andrae bicycle as the top prize, valued at one hundred dollars.[47] The Andrae family also opened a bicycle riding school at the Broadway Armory, similar to the early velocipede rinks, where novice bicyclists could learn how to ride the company's new safety models.[48] The bicycle boom of the 1890s also introduced other manufacturers to the scene. As illustrated in later chapters, the Andrae Company was joined by other companies as well as parts factories that made every piece from pedals to spokes and hired hundreds of workers, including young children. These efforts made Milwaukee one of the Midwest's top centers for the manufacture of bicycle parts, components, and other items such as lanterns and racing gear. Bicycles rapidly grew into a million-dollar local industry in Milwaukee.[49]

Franz Theodor "Terry" Andrae was Milwaukee's first decorated amateur cyclist. His many victories on the racetrack earned him the nickname the "Flying Badger."

WHi Image ID 100820

The *Milwaukee Sentinel* acknowledged that women had also played a role in popularizing the sport during the 1880s, but it seemed reluctant to offer the credit they deserved. "While bicycling has grown wonderfully with the men, its progress as a recreative sport for ladies has been no less remarkable, considering the objections which were urged against females as bicyclists." The report, which presented an overly rosy view, concluded, "A few years ago a woman would have risked her reputation by appearing in public on a wheel, but the prejudice has been rapidly overcome." It included many names of the leading female riders in the city, although many were only partially identified by their first initials. The list included such long-lost Wisconsin women's names as Misses E. Anderson, M. E. Bowse, Laura Smith, E. Wood, A. Schiess, May Mooers, Lou Bird, and many others. For good measure, the article also reminded readers that married women also liked to ride bikes.[50]

The role of women in early cycling was not simply restricted to improved access to cycling clubs, increased buying power, and appeals to mobility. Some women presented new designs and solicited new patents, leaving a clear mark on the production side of cycling. Kate Parke of Chicago came forward with a new design for a bicycle lock in 1890, while Alice A. Bennitt, also of Chicago, presented plans for a bicycle canopy. "My invention relates to that class of canopies or sunshades which are adapted for use on bicycles," Bennitt wrote, adding that it "may be readily adjusted to shade either side of a rider and which may be readily detached from a bicycle or attached thereto." She recommended the contraption be made out of aluminum or a lighter wood so that it would not add extra weight to the bicycle. Together, the efforts of women like Parke and

Julius Andrae and Sons began their bicycle manufacturing operations by making high-wheels at their plant in Milwaukee. "Colonel" Henry P. Andrae owned this Andrae high-wheel on which he likely participated in wheelmen activities.

Milwaukee County Historical Society, photo by John Urban

Bennitt demonstrated the investment women had in the sport and the long-overlooked ways that women's efforts helped shape the rise of the bicycling industry.[51]

By 1890, then, there was what bicycling historian David Herlihy has described as a "new king of the road" edging out the still-popular high-wheel: the safety. For the first time in American history, bikes (both high-wheel and safety) stood on the verge of fulfilling the original promise of providing a practical and efficient machine

Tricycles came in all shapes and sizes, and their stability made them popular children's toys. This tricycle was used by Howell David and Ivor Hugh Davies of Oshkosh, ca. 1890.

Courtesy of Oshkosh Public Museum

that any able-bodied person could use—a true "poor man's horse."[52] Women increasingly demonstrated that the poor man's horse could also have a lady rider, and together men and women pushed bicycle sales to new heights. By 1891, Americans were purchasing an estimated 150,000 bicycles annually.[53] At the same time, Edouard Michelin of France made further improvements on the inflatable tire, giving riders the ability to change flats while out on the road with a minimal set of tools. These developments foretold the coming of America's first great bicycling boom.

Its arrival made many people nervous. In 1890, just as the boom deepened across the Upper Midwest, black riders worked to carve out for themselves a place in the sport. That spring, Saint Louis hosted the first "World Bicycle Tournament for Colored Riders," and James Milton Turner, a highly respected member of the African American community, worked as the event's master of ceremonies. Later in August, perhaps cheered by the successes of the World Tournament, a group of black Saint Louis cyclists moved to purchase a new bicycle clubhouse. The fierce antagonisms they met from area whites foreshadowed the battle over black exclusion that would polarize the LAW community in the coming years, severely limiting its powers as a national lobby.[54]

CHAPTER 5

The Troubled Beginnings of Wheel Fever

"Therefore I say, if the LAW passes a law against the colored man and against him only, be it to the everlasting shame and disgrace of the LAW."

Letter to the Editor, *Bearings*, 1894[1]

Inequality shaped the direction of bicycling in the Badger State throughout the early 1890s. At a time of widespread gaps between rich and poor, Wisconsinites struggled with what the new bicycling fever meant and who ought to benefit from it. Since the late 1880s, safety-model bicycles had opened a whole new range of transportation options to state residents, but not everyone welcomed the changes. Nor did everyone believe that access to bicycling should be equally shared. With sales skyrocketing and bicycling's popularity on the rise, Wisconsinites were asked again to answer some basic questions about the sport: Who should be allowed to ride? Where should that riding take place? And who should benefit from cycling? Was Milwaukee open only to white gentleman riders? Or would the boundaries drawn around and within the sport continue to change? Between 1890 and 1894, in the midst of growing unrest, these questions became more and more fraught for Wisconsin's diverse residents. Sorting out the sport's proper boundaries would lead to decisions that ultimately undermined cycling's future. Wisconsin was on its way to becoming a great cycling state, but it would ultimately fall far short in offering the sport's benefits to the widest audience.

Many sensed that 1891 would be the greatest bicycling season yet in the Upper Midwest. Milwaukee newspapers, for example, seized upon the buzz and filled their columns with wild speculation about how widespread the boom might be in the coming year. In March, the *Weekly Wisconsin* said that the "coming summer promises to be a most active one in cycling circles." It went on to point out the ever-growing demand for new bikes in area stores, estimating that roughly five hundred riders filled Milwaukee's streets at any given time. Indeed, the rolls of the Milwaukee Wheelman's Club swelled with the warming weather, claiming by the end of March a membership of 114. "It is likely that this number will be greatly increased before the middle of summer," the *Weekly Wisconsin* assured readers.[2] Reports also indicated that a large number of women were purchasing new bikes. "Dealers report a brisk demand for the best class of wheels, many ladies among the purchasers." Further, "It is estimated that there are forty-five ladies in Milwaukee who are devoted to the wheel. Most of them use the Ramblers," one of the earliest and most popular safety models available in the state.[3] As the safety supplanted the high-wheel, a new feeling of possibility and adventure, often vaguely inclusive of women riders but not of riders of color, started to grow.

New reports of military and police applications for the bicycle also made it more legitimate in the eyes of consumers. In January 1890, the *Chicago Herald* ran a story on how Waukesha, Wisconsin, police were using the new safety bicycles to combat local crime. In one account, the *Herald* detailed how a Waukesha deputy chased down Josie Ellia on a bicycle after she escaped from prison, where she was being held for stealing a watch.[4] Waukesha's 1890 decision to use bicycle cops anticipated a growing number of

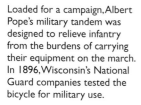

Loaded for a campaign, Albert Pope's military tandem was designed to relieve infantry from the burdens of carrying their equipment on the march. In 1896, Wisconsin's National Guard companies tested the bicycle for military use.

Pneumatic, vol. 6, no. 11, 1896

POPE'S ARMY TANDEM.

In lieu of the horse, the United States Army envisioned the bicycle as a new steed to conquer the Wild West in the late 1890s. Several countries did use the bicycle in combat during the early fighting in World War I.

Library of Congress, Prints & Photographs Division, LC-DIG-pga-01798

distribution agreements with police and the military throughout the country. In the summer of 1891, bike manufacturer Albert Pope encouraged the army to adopt bicycles by giving forty bikes to the First Signal Corps of the Connecticut National Guard. Wisconsin's National Guard tested bicycles during a series of "military relay runs" through eastern Wisconsin. On August 29, 1896, two members of Company I from Marinette raced south to deliver a message in Milwaukee. Wearing their "regular military uniforms with knapsack, canteen, haversack, leggings, and rifle," the soldiers journeyed to Appleton and Oshkosh, where they passed their messages to two new racers. Similar races were organized by other companies, most notably by Company E in Fond du Lac, whose collision-filled race in 1897 was won by Oscar Huelsman.[5] The army would consider several bicycling contracts during the last part of the nineteenth and early twentieth centuries, but few ultimately won renewal. Nonetheless, that the army even considered the use of bicycles for combat and logistical operations shows just how important cycling had become and how deep the optimism surrounding the sport ran as consumers in Wisconsin and elsewhere turned to the bicycle.[6] No longer the plaything of daredevils, the bicycle was slowly becoming "respectable" in the eyes of mainstream society.

Racing offered yet another venue for the expansion of bicycling. Wisconsin residents were fascinated by stories celebrating new records set around the world. In 1891, for instance, at London's Herne Hill Velodrome, Montague A. Holbein set a twenty-four-hour track record by covering a whopping 326 miles in a single ride. Three years later at the same venue, Frank Shorland topped the mark by almost a full hundred miles. These two examples suggest not only how rapidly technology had improved the safety model, but also how important a growing sense of male celebrity remained in the sport. New six-day races between the day's top male racers generated tremendous fanfare and became a particularly noteworthy feature at New York's Madison Square Garden. There, in 1893, Albert Schock rode almost 1,600 miles in less than one week. The proven reliability of the safety model in these races helped convince skeptics that the high-wheel would soon be a relic. The feats also demonstrated, for many whites,

Chicago's World Columbian Exposition in 1893 exhibited an exciting array of new technologies but also underscored inequalities that defined life in the United States.

WHi Image ID 82871

the steady ascension of western technological progress, a theme that found its fullest expression at the World's Fair in Chicago.[7]

Chicago would play an important role in shaping Wisconsin's bicycling boom of the early 1890s, particularly in its model of the "White City." In 1893, the city hosted the World's Columbian Exposition, also called the World's Fair, a massive festival from May 1 to October 30 that the US Congress proclaimed "an exhibition of the progress of civilization in the New World." Cyclists and visitors from all over the world made their way to the Windy City to take in the sights. Chicago's cycling community worked with fair organizers and developers to ensure that the bicycle, one of the many technologies celebrated in fair displays, would have a prominent place in the story of "progress" told at the exposition. But as thousands of visitors made their way to the city, it became clear that fair planners had a very limited idea of "civilization" in mind when they designed the exposition grounds and events. As historian Gail Bederman has shown, organizers split the fair into two racially distinct areas. The White City—replete with majestic fountains, sprawling courtyards, and grand plazas—represented the progress of white civilization. The other part of the fair, the Midway, showed the supposed barbarism of uncivilized, and usually dark-skinned, races. Organizers also excluded women's products and displays from most of the exposition showcases and downplayed women's roles in humankind's forward march.[8]

As a result, women and people of color joined together to protest the exposition. Noted activists Ida B. Wells and Frederick Douglass stood outside the White City and alerted incoming guests, many of whom arrived on their bicycles, to the injustices they would see. Wells, a writer widely known for her anti-lynching advocacy, and Douglass, the legendary ex-slave and social reformer, handed incoming guests a pamphlet titled *The Reason Why the Colored American is Not in the World's Columbian Exposition*. The pamphlet argued that any civilization willing to degrade its own people was not as civilized as it claimed to be.[9] In response to the efforts of Douglass, Wells, and other protesters, the exposition's directors, all male and white, finally agreed to make room for black people—as long as proposals put forward by blacks were approved by all-white state governing committees. Not surprisingly, none were approved. Sensing that Chicago's nonwhite communities might feel embittered by the exclusion, exposition managers set aside a special "colored American" day, which was included among a range of special white ethnic days. But the fair had already helped pave the way for the separate-but-equal treatment, which would become the law of the land with the Supreme Court's *Plessy v. Ferguson* decision in 1896. This policy, which the early cycling commu-

The Crab Tree Special was built by a twenty-year-old man from Ellenboro, Wisconsin, known only as "Atkinson." Because he was too poor to buy a bicycle, he built this machine using only a jack knife, an old saw, wood, and other scraps. The machine was displayed as a "curio" at the Columbian Exposition in 1893.

WHS Museum F1998.91.3, photo by Joel Heiman

Bicycle exhibits and races were popular at Chicago's Columbian Exposition in 1893. The central monument at the fair was an enormous "Statue of the Republic," which the Gormully and Jeffery Manufacturing Company of Chicago used in their advertisements to promote their Rambler bicycles.

Pneumatic, vol. 4, no. 3, 1893

nity helped foster in the decades following the Civil War, arose out of a culture of racial exclusion and white privilege.[10]

Clearly, by the early 1890s middle- and upper-class whites had firm ideas of who the "civilized" were and what benefits those inside the circle deserved. Cyclists at the fair, including the nearly 700 riders who participated in the massive bike "lantern parade" in August 1893, were often the ones expressing those ideas most clearly. Made up of members of Chicago's "Lincoln" club, they rode dressed as "Chinamen."[11] In this way, bicycling's proponents continued to see cycling as a "white" sport.

FOR visitors who came to Chicago from places like Wisconsin, the efforts of the exhibition symbolized the hope that better infrastructure might spread civilization into the country's rural hinterlands. For most of the nineteenth century, locals cared for rural roads in the United States without any help from the government. Loose organizations of neighborhood men performed maintenance and instituted fees for roads only when it was deemed necessary. This arrangement often resulted in remarkable inefficiency and terrible roads. Travelers to the Old Northwest during the 1830s and 1840s filled their accounts with descriptions of crumbled bridges, muddy quagmires, and bumpy rides. The experiences of the Civil War and the decades after 1865 expanded the role of local and federal governments, but even strong postwar development failed to improve roads. When velocipede mania hit in 1869, it quickly became clear that anyone who wanted to ride a bike would have to do so indoors at rinks or on city sidewalks, because those were the only places not littered with piles of horse manure, tree branches, mud, and shattered glass. The problems remained largely unsolved into the last decades of the century. Wheelmen who traveled to Europe through the late 1880s could not help but draw comparisons between the roads at home and the wide and expansive boulevards of Europe, and published their astonished accounts in local newspapers. As one rider put it, "I did not know how bad the roads in this state were until I began to ride a wheel myself."[12]

The growing disparity between America's roads and the "civilized" roads of Europe encouraged American wheelmen to take more drastic steps in their cycling politics. One of their first steps was to transform the League of American Wheelmen. Racing, long an important element of cycling subculture, became increasingly professionalized throughout the early 1890s with the use of safety models in racing events. But many in the league did not see themselves as racers. The majority of members came to believe that the league should be promoting cycling for the everyday rider. So as bike racing be-

The high-wheel came early to Racine, but like many cities and rural townships, poor weather quickly deteriorated its dirt roads.

WHi Image ID 40120

came more and more popular in comparison to LAW-sponsored club riding, the LAW voted to modify its constitution in June 1888, ending what some LAW leaders saw as the undue influence of the Racing and Rights and Privileges Committees. Instead of racing, the LAW would focus its political efforts on "good roads." While racing remained important to the league's overall goals, this decision marked a clear turning point in the wheelmen's identity. The dream of expansive boulevards lured the LAW forward.[13]

The wheelmen, of course, were not the only ones advocating for better roads, but LAW activity spurred other groups concerned with improvement. Across the Midwest, good roads advocates stepped forward in the first part of the 1890s. Iowa became one of the first states to hold a statewide roads convention, while Lewis J. Bates of Michigan was one of the first American wheelmen to call for national road reform.[14] Between 1888 and 1892, wheelmen also prepared the groundwork for the Office of Road Inquiry in the Department of Agriculture, which was eventually created in 1893. Roy Stone, the office's first director, lauded the cyclists' involvement over the preceding years, saying that "every wheelman is a preacher, a worker, and a fighter for good roads."[15] Whether the wheelmen's new efforts would create better infrastructure, however, remained to be seen.

The bicycle's increasing prominence also gave more power to the wheelmen in their efforts to fight laws curtailing bike riding. Wisconsin's wheelmen leveraged their influence on government to secure new rights for cycling in public. They also became

The LAW was masterful with their good roads advocacy. In 1898, the organization held a photography contest for bicyclists to document the worst roads in the United States, including this photograph by J. I. Phillips, a resident of West Virginia.

WHi Image ID 91851

more competent in bringing bicycle-based litigation to court, organizing legal defense teams to represent riders who faced fines and protecting cyclists against antibicycling actions.[16] This led to stiffer local "anti-tack" and "anti-glass" laws to punish those who tried to sabotage bike riders by placing debris in the streets—apparently a fairly common problem in the late nineteenth century. LAW members also negotiated for laws to protect against bike theft. In nearby Michigan, for example, important laws were passed to encourage people who might have information on a bike theft to approach police.[17] And wheelmen worked to get bike access aboard regional trains and boats, ensuring that riders in Wisconsin who wanted to visit an out-of-state destination, such as the World's Fair in Chicago, could easily do so. Railroad companies ultimately agreed to accommodate bikes for a small fee. As the *Pneumatic* reported, "Bicycles and baggage have no further relation to each other than that they begin with the same letter, and a wheelmen is no more entitled to have his wheel carried free than he would his horse and buggy."[18] Since this was the case, wheelmen made sure that prices were regulated and fairly applied. They even had membership cards made so riders could travel to Canada without "hindrance or import duty." League members also lobbied for street signs that were "completely" installed and clearly marked.[19]

Paying for better infrastructure, everyone seemed to recognize, would be expensive. To help cover the cost of new roads, many early advocates suggested creating new taxes. Some moderates said that bicycles should be taxed and regulated like carriages, while others, including many Democrats, advocated for no new taxes whatsoever. Local municipalities also increased fines for bicycling infractions to generate more revenue. In Fond du Lac, for example, police were instructed to arrest members of the Winnebago Wheelmen if they continued parading through the community. Police cited local disturbances caused by their frequent bell ringing and pounding on brass kettles.[20] In Oshkosh, meanwhile, when the city review board tried to impose a tax on bicycles, wheelmen responded by streaming into City Hall to individually meet with the clerk. Described as having "their fighting clothes on," possibly in reference to their league uniforms, they took turns arguing their case against the tax.[21]

The Oshkosh wheelmen were willing to compromise. They simply asked that if they were regulated through new taxes and legislation, then all of Wisconsin's sporting communities should be, too. If the law were applied to other outdoor sportsmen, such as a tax on deer hunters' guns, then the bicyclists would have no problem paying their fair share into city and state coffers. Wheelmen also argued that their bicycles quickly depreciated with use. A bicycle worth $150 when it was purchased new, they often said, quickly dropped in value to just $25, making it unfair to impose a fixed rate on those who rode older machines or who rode only infrequently. If the proposed taxes in Oshkosh were not overturned, the wheelmen threatened "some trouble" and vowed to bring the case to the attention of the national LAW.[22]

Pharmacies, hardware stores, and department stores profited from the boom by selling bicycles, sundries, and athletic clothing. Frank Percey's Guns, Ammunition, and Cutlery in Oshkosh, ca. 1892, sold bicycles as well as other sporting goods.

Courtesy of Oshkosh Public Museum

LAW members were in positions to advocate with local government on account of privileges marked by both their race and gender. The exclusivity of that privilege was nowhere clearer than in the activities of their cycling clubs, which sometimes bore clear markers of their identities. Perhaps the most intimidating uniform belonged to the "13 Club," whose members wore black sweaters with a white skull and crossbones, the skull having the number 13 etched on its forehead. Membership was limited to the thirteen male riders who participated in the most sponsored runs for the year. 13 Clubs were also seen in other parts of the United States, including the Quaker City Wheelmen of Philadelphia, who used the elite designation to increase interest in their chapter's activities.[23] Scattered details collected from the *Pneumatic*, Milwaukee's cycling magazine, indicate that the 13 Club held its monthly meetings at 8:13 p.m. and that its leaders earned a yearly salary of thirteen cents. As part of the official LAW chapter in Milwaukee, the 13 Club hosted its own social events, such as a "select" dance party *Pneumatic* writers called a real "winner," and apparently employed a young black mascot. Whites-only cycling clubs gave the White City's ideals a tangible expression.[24]

Elite members of the LAW could join the 13 Club, allowing them to wear the skull-and-crossbones coat of arms on their wool jerseys.

Milwaukee County Historical Society

Echoing some of the "uncivilized" spectacle that was a key feature of the World's Fair midway, early white cyclists in Wisconsin put on garish minstrel shows to further mark the boundaries of their sport. Infamous for their racist caricatures of black and immigrant cultures, minstrel performances were a popular form of entertainment for the nation's white men during this era and had a wide following in Wisconsin. One minstrel show hosted by the Milwaukee Wheelmen on April 28, 1892, was titled *Hard Times*. Images of the event show men wearing blackface and others dressed down to parody the poverty of working-class and perhaps immigrant groups. Such costumes reinforced the middle-class, native, white, and masculine identities of the participants and gave clear signals about who wheelmen believed was a respectable cyclist and who was not. The *Pneumatic* predicted that *Hard Times* would help the Milwaukee Wheelmen celebrate their eighth anniversary. "'Hard times' socials are the most unique and entertaining amusements yet invented," it reported.[25] In 1893, the Mercury Club in Milwaukee also held a minstrel show, what it called its "hard time smoker." According to the write-up the event received in the *Bearings*, a Chicago-based cycling magazine, sixty-five members attended. "The first prize, for the toughest 'mug,' was awarded to Otto Thieme, who apparently went dressed as a 'tramp.'" The Bay View Wheelmen and the Milwaukee Wheelmen hosted similar performances.[26]

Minstrel shows sent clear messages about who was invited to be a wheelman in Milwaukee and elsewhere, but the national organization of the LAW took the additional step of formally banning black riders in early 1894. Although the national leadership initially voted in 1892 supporting a racially integrated membership, two years later it

Minstrel shows were a popular fundraising activity for the Milwaukee Wheelmen. Cast members from the "Smoker" show on October 15, 1893, dressed in costumes that mocked the poor, vagrants, immigrants, and blacks.

Milwaukee County Historical Society

came to a much different conclusion about who a cyclist was.[27] Southern wheelmen, it appears, were bitterly opposed to an integrated LAW, and worked to ban black riders from southern clubs in the early 1890s. This kind of racial antagonism was not, however, unique to the South and was not solely about relations between blacks and whites. California's wheelmen, for example, expressed hostility toward a perceived influx of Chinese riders in the late 1880s and early 1890s.

In the eyes of many scholars, the 1894 ban on black membership in the LAW has been understood as a southern coup over the national leadership, led by wheelman William W. Watts of Louisville, Kentucky, at the meeting of the national assembly of the LAW at Louisville in 1894. Watts used the strong showing among southern members to push through a ban on blacks even as most northern members lamented the move. In fact, as David Herlihy has suggested, there was much more to the debate.[28] Through the early 1890s, clubs generally allowed black riders. The Association of American Cyclists even voted to reverse an earlier decision on black exclusion in 1892, opening its doors to what one critic described as "Mongolians, Turks, Ethiopians, Bulgarians, Swedes, Hollanders, Ninth Ward Men, and many others."[29] Beginning in 1893, however, a fresh round of rising racial antagonisms against the increased presence of nonwhites in the sport led to a renewed round of racial restrictions.

Throughout the fall of 1893, it became clear to the LAW's national leadership that southern chapters were going to push for black exclusion at the February 1894 meeting in Louisville—a ban many northern members were complicit in effecting. As rumors about the coming Louisville assembly meeting filtered through the wheelmen's ranks, many northern white riders simply wished the racial tension would disappear. Chicago's *Bearings* appeared ready to fight the southern chapters if they moved for formal black exclusion. "The negro question in the League, like the negro himself, refuses to be downed," its editors wrote. After dismissing southern appeals to LAW secession as foolish and potentially devastating to the nation's bike riders, it made its position clear. "Come, come, you Southern Knights of the Wheel, make your fight bravely . . . but do not try to carry the day by threats which you do not intend to carry out, and much less make threats with the foolish idea of carrying them out just because you can not have your own way."[30] By the end of December 1893, the *Bearings* had changed its position, this time endorsing the idea of black exclusion. The switch seemed to be justified by white riders on the grounds that there were very few black riders, a recognition that was quite cynical given the overtly racist culture cultivated for years within the LAW. "The number of negroes that there are in the League or that ever will be, is not enough to worry even the most fastidious person," its editors explained. Sensing the deepening resolve of the southern chapters, *Bearings* editors saw no hope for a peaceful resolution, and thus decided that it was best to save the LAW's good name and not initiate a potentially brutal internal struggle. In the end, the *Bearings'* editors said they would back the ban.[31]

It is hard to say how all of this played out in nearby Wisconsin, but there is evidence to indicate that throughout 1893 racial antagonisms did stiffen within the state's wheelmen clubs and chapters. Back in May, bicyclists in Milwaukee had debated imposing a harsher color line in the Milwaukee-to-Waukesha road race, but Democrat Frederick J. Schroeder, chairman of the Racing Board, paid them no attention. In an attempt to downplay racial tension, the *Milwaukee Journal* suggested that the appeals had mostly originated from weaker riders who knew black riders might defeat them. Citing "anonymous letters" written to Schroeder, the *Journal* indicated that the Milwaukee Wheelmen unanimously voted to accept black riders, but said little about how many blacks might have participated in the League, or what their experience was ultimately like.[32]

There are few records that document evidence of black riders in Wisconsin, but such records do exist. A photograph of Milwaukee Wheelmen from the August 1893 meet reprinted in the *Bearings* clearly shows an unidentified black rider in the center of the frame, a man we can only assume rode with the club at the event. The image also shows how the club apparently used a black boy as a mascot. The youngster lounges in the grass before the group, and wears one of the distinctive 13 Club jerseys. Young black mascots were a fairly common part of the bicycling landscape at the time. One famous bike racer had a mascot nicknamed the "Dark Secret," and he was sometimes called upon to race other black mascots as a way to warm up crowds before the main event. Such races were often a highlight for white audiences. The *Bearings'* editors liked

A young black mascot wearing a fez cap and a 13 Club jersey is shown lounging in front of participants at a Milwaukee Wheelmen meet on August 14–15, 1893. Another black man stands in the back row, center.

Bearings, vol. 7, no. 3, 1893

to joke that the mascots could even eat their prizes, as an August 1893 article suggested watermelons were the appropriate prize for their efforts.[33]

The LAW's decision to ban black riders in 1894 marked a low point for the sport's history. Almost immediately, northern whites went to work to distance themselves from the decision. "The much mooted question of excluding the negro from the ranks of the L.A.W. . . . will come very near being adopted at the next National Assembly meeting," the *Pneumatic* reported late in 1893. Two years later, in 1895, as racial animosities deepened even further throughout the country, the *Pneumatic* tried to isolate the ban as a southern problem: "The antagonistic feeling against the colored man originated in the southern states and now the agitators will be able to fight in their stronghold." Such comments allowed northern chapters like those in Wisconsin to begin the work of denying or silencing the depth of racial prejudice at home. Yet by accepting the new rule, Wisconsin's wheelmen showed they were complicit with its racism.[34]

Unable to rely on the privileges of a widespread readership and advertising base common in white newspapers, Wisconsin's black newspapers nevertheless tried to gain access to the bicycling boom. For example, Milwaukee's *Wisconsin Afro-American* echoed many popular opinions in August 1892 when it said better roads for bicycling would lead to improvements throughout the state. In discussing these improvements, however, an opportunity arose to highlight the inequalities blacks faced. "With good roads," one article joked, "perhaps the country doctor would cease, as years rolled on, to become obese from too much sitting in his wagon."[35] At a time when blacks were denied equal access to professional health care and state medical schools and colleges, poking fun at the laziness of the area doctor was one way to show how the bicycle might improve society by spreading access to health care, regardless of skin color. In contrast to their white peers, black Wisconsinites also seemed to welcome what the bicycle offered women. "Every lady in our age should have the good judgment to invest in a wheel and judge for herself of the real pleasure she is missing," the *Wisconsin Afro-American* reported in August 1892. "It lightens the trials and cares of life, sustains health and beauty, and saves time and money." This was a compelling rebuttal to the sexist anxieties of women's bicycling coverage in the white press.[36]

The popularity of Chicago as a destination for Wisconsin's white riders also gave rise to racial tensions. Area blacks blasted the pretensions of white cycling by calling attention to the moral shortcomings of white riders. In 1893, the year the World's Fair opened, Chicago's *Daily Inter Ocean* ran a story that mocked white Wisconsin riders. "The foolishness of some of the crack riders who come here to participate . . . may make the sport unpopular and unprofitable," it said. "Two of the fast riders who appeared yesterday had been drinking so heavily the night before that they were unable to ride in all the races, and were unable to make time creditable to themselves." Under the headline "Rapid Bicycle Riders Get Drunk at Milwaukee and Disgust Spectators," the article went on to detail the embarrassment the Wisconsin men caused for the Milwaukee Wheelmen, who apparently felt "rather sore" that they had to deal with their members' excesses. Besides providing an opportunity for blacks to mock the excesses of all-white clubs, it also pinpoints the tension between the sober respect of the old-style wheelmen's culture and the masculinized culture of racing that would dominate riding in the 1890s.[37]

Nonwhite riders generated a mixture of fear and distrust wherever they appeared in Wisconsin. Clear racial animosity marks a newspaper article on Kanegro Nagaye, for example. Described in the *Pneumatic* as a "Jap who rides a wheel in this city," Nagaye made his appearance on Milwaukee streets in the spring of 1893. "He is quite a novelty in Milwaukee and the boys make much of him," the paper noted. In an issue later that summer, editors of the *Pneumatic* also poked fun at Chinese coverage of cycling. "A Chinese newspaper," it wrote, had described bicycling as "each man [riding] a chariot . . . advanced by the aid of the feet and not drawn by an animal." To hammer their assumptions of white American superiority home, the *Pneumatic*'s editors followed the report with comforting statements about white Americans' cultural superiority. "It is not surprising that America turns out such good cyclists. They are a progressive people." Bicycles were fast becoming the sign of a "superior" American culture.[38]

Suspicion of new riders was not limited only to race. White women riders also remained a persistent anxiety. Because women riders might threaten male control of the sport, men downplayed women's challenges in column after column of area newspapers and magazines. "The pretty girl rider likes to show her escort that she can keep up with

First Grand ....Fair, arranged by the Ladies Auxiliary, of the North Side Cycling Club. October 21 to 24. 1896. At the Club House, Reservoir Ave. & First St. ....Admission 25 Cents.

As bicycle clubs grew, some organizations, including the North Side Cycling Club, created women's auxiliaries mostly composed of wives and girlfriends. Their primary duties were to raise funds and support the male riders.

Milwaukee County Historical Society

him at a fair pace," a story in the *Pneumatic* said. "No girl was ever induced to mount a wheel except by the persuasion of some male enthusiast, and they simply can't do without them." By characterizing women as completely helpless without the aid of male riders, such stories reinforced male control and explicitly threatened women with exclusion from the sport. "At any rate, if the girls flock together by themselves to the extent of organizing clubs, the boys will probably retaliate by ostracizing them," one article read.[39] In another, the *Pneumatic*'s editors suggested to women that cycling was best pursued as a way to make their men happy. "The woman who can ride a bicycle well, is pretty sure to have in her the making of a good wife," the article concluded.[40] With unmasked condescension, the cycling press undermined those who held a bolder vision of cycling equality and discouraged women and minorities from enjoying the benefits of the sport.

In the end, however, largely on account of their race and relative wealth, white women were more successful at establishing a foothold in the mainstream cycling world than nonwhite male and female riders. After all, white women were sometimes admitted to the LAW, though usually only as "auxiliary" members. For full membership, white women created their own bicycling clubs. In Milwaukee, the *Pneumatic* revealed the suspicions that plagued these women's riding groups. "So woman is completing her conquest of the planet," the author wrote. "She rows. She smokes. She preaches . . . she shoots. She rides. And now she has lassoed the iron grasshopper and has fearlessly mounted it."[41] Other articles were more supportive: "In some of the large cities many a working girl has purchased a wheel with her own earnings. A better bargain she has never done. The health, the pleasure, the strength and the happiness she buys with it will prove the worth of ten times the price."[42] Despite resistance, women increasingly took part in the ideal of the White City as the bicycling boom expanded between 1890 and 1893.

THE *Pneumatic*, published and edited by long-time Milwaukee rider Martin C. Rotier, became the most popular and most influential cycling magazine in the state during the early boom. Riders could subscribe for fifty cents a year by sending their money to the *Pneumatic*'s offices at 418 East Water Street.[43] As editor, Rotier worked tirelessly with illustrator G. Liebscher to serve Milwaukee's wheelmen with a variety of bicycling news shorts, brilliantly illustrated cartoons, stunning advertisements, and official notices concerning the cycling community around the state. The *Pneumatic* also offered updates on legislative efforts to improve roads. During the last half of the 1890s, it also provided information about the state's premier racers and the broader racing community. Simply indispensable to anyone interested in Wisconsin's bicycling history, it even featured a "Ladies' Department," where news unique to women could be found. Subscriptions to the *Pneumatic* grew rapidly throughout the boom years. In 1893, just as the Chicago Fair opened, *Pneumatic* editors boasted that their circulation "increased the past two months by the addition of three hundred new subscribers." By servicing the growing cycling community, the paper helped frame the expectations many people brought to the White City.[44]

Subscribers to Milwaukee's *Pneumatic* magazine learned about upcoming races, minstrel show fundraisers, new bicycle models, repair shops, and political opportunities to expand the rights of cyclists.

Pneumatic, vol. 6, no. 11, 1896

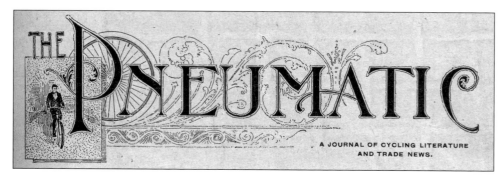

The *Pneumatic* quickly became the go-to venue for the biggest stories in cycling, including news of round-the-world trips. The summer the fair opened, the *Pneumatic* mentioned how three years after setting out from Saint Louis, recent Washington University graduates Thomas G. Allen Jr. and William Sachtleben successfully completed their celebrated world tour on bicycles.[45] The *Pneumatic* also told the story of a young man named Frank Lenz, originally from Pittsburgh, who set off on his Victor safety for an exotic trip around the world. Riding solo, Lenz carried little more than a camera and a knapsack as he started out across the United States. Unlike the hostility female and nonwhite long-distance riders often encountered on America's roads, men like Lenz could easily make money by striking out on these heroic and manly voyages alone. Lenz secured his sponsorship from *Outing* magazine, which also published stories about his progress. He also received help securing diplomatic papers from former Republican Wisconsin Governor Jeremiah McLain Rusk, who in 1893 was in Washington serving as the Secretary of Agriculture under President Benjamin Harrison.[46]

Passing through the Upper Midwest at the same time as the World's Fair, Lenz's journey took him through Waukesha, Wisconsin, as a photograph from the collections at the Milwaukee County Historical Society documents. Once his itinerary moved abroad, the *Pneumatic* started to link his ride to white culture's fascination with more

Pittsburgh's Frank Lenz posed for this snapshot in Waukesha during his world tour in 1892. Some of the Milwaukee Wheelmen joined Lenz on his route from Milwaukee to Waukesha.

Milwaukee County Historical Society

"primitive" and "uncivilized" societies. The paper ran a number of stories updating Wisconsin's readers on his whereabouts. As early as August 1893, during the final months of the exposition, *Pneumatic* editors expressed a sincere concern over his safety after he fell out of touch with his contacts in Pittsburgh. Lenz reappeared, however, with a letter later that fall that spelled out some of his troubles while riding through China. By the middle of 1894, having ridden through Calcutta and the Middle East, riders in Wisconsin learned from the *Pneumatic* that Lenz was leaving Tehran.[47]

By December 1894, citing yet another breakdown in communication, international outcry compelled *Outing Magazine* to send a team of riders to find him, a decision that was also mentioned in Milwaukee's *Pneumatic*. Tragically, Lenz never turned up; the consensus is that he was likely murdered in Armenia.[48] Although his body was never found, in May 1895, the *Pneumatic* carried the sad news confirming Lenz's death. "At last the fate of poor Frank Lenz has been settled," it said. American investigators rushed to the scene. The *Pneumatic* later published sources further confirming and elaborating upon Lenz's death, including the testimony of detectives.[49] In many ways, his brutal murder fed turn-of-the-century beliefs about the savagery and incivility of peoples abroad.

Meanwhile, businesses throughout Wisconsin, lured by the vision of the White City, started adding the bicycle to their everyday routines. Many of Wisconsin's newspaper editors, for example, saw that the bicycle enabled deliverymen to reach a new range of subscribers. Since an intelligent and informed reading public was seen as crucial to any truly civilized society, the bicycle offered a chance for cities and towns to achieve some of the White City's highest ideals. Young delivery people soon carried papers to new clients and subscriber lists in Milwaukee, Appleton, Janesville, and other cities and towns. In fact, newspaper companies around Milwaukee started equipping their offices and facilities to make cycling an essential part of modern journalism. A good example is the *Milwaukee Sentinel*, which constructed "a special apartment" in its new building for the storage of bicycles. "More than a dozen" bicycles were in use by the *Sentinel*'s staff by the middle of 1893.[50]

Memorial Day bicycle parades also demonstrated the virtues of white civility and society. Few holidays of the late nineteenth century were as highly regarded as Memorial Day, particularly as the much-revered generation of Civil War veterans began dying. The *Pneumatic* reminded readers that riders showed "little respect" when they rode casually and individually on Memorial Day, without taking part in a formal parade on their bikes. "The 30th of May," it proclaimed early in 1893, "has been set aside in honor of those men who fought and died for our country," and no self-respecting "true American wheelmen" would dare insult the pride and honor of the Civil War generation by not taking part in this expression of patriotism. Riders decorated themselves and their machines in flags, and a common parade route through Milwaukee took riders from the George Washington monument on Wisconsin Avenue over to the Soldiers' Home, where the cyclists deposited flowers on the graves of the Union dead. The June 1894 issue of the *Pneumatic* noted that over three hundred wheelmen attended the Decoration Day parade, and "each one carried a wreath or bunch of flowers to be laid" on the graves. Originally a holiday led by blacks in Charleston, South Carolina, to celebrate the end of the Civil War and the destruction of slavery, Memorial Day became an expression of white patriotic duty.[51]

High-profile patriotic events such as these helped cyclists gain political respect. Politicians of the time coveted wheelmen support because league riders were often young, wealthy, influential, and well educated. They could also easily access large numbers of voters on Election Day. As historian Michael Taylor shows, the bicycle made it possible for door-to-door canvassing on a scale unprecedented in US history. Since the bicycle had also become a fashionable accessory for women and men of leisure, its incorporation in political buttons and pamphlets often translated into electoral gains,

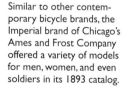

Similar to other contemporary bicycle brands, the Imperial brand of Chicago's Ames and Frost Company offered a variety of models for men, women, and even soldiers in its 1893 catalog.

Milwaukee Public Museum Photography Collection

"Imperial Wheels"

Many cycling organizations had large clubhouses where members socialized, gathered for group rides, and conducted business. This clubhouse for the North Side Cycling Club was located on Reservoir Avenue in Milwaukee, ca. 1895.

Milwaukee Public Museum Photography Collection

making candidates who used them successfully appear younger and more progressive in their politics.[52]

Building the metaphorical White City throughout Wisconsin during the early 1890s would take a tremendous grassroots effort. First, the wheelmen needed to continue adding to their numbers, and one way to increase interest was by fostering a sense of community among riders. As we have seen, riding clubs did this by providing a space for members to meet and get to know one another. Annual wheelmen meetings became lavish affairs. Clubs purchased real estate in a variety of locales. Founded in 1884, and originally named the Flat Foot Bicycle Club, the Milwaukee Wheelmen first met in the open air on Court House Square, but they opened a new clubhouse in 1888 on the corner of Wells and Second Streets. The club's growing membership required frequent relocation into larger quarters, first into a flat at 225 West Water Street above the Julius Andrae and Sons Bicycle Company. The clubrooms were tastefully furnished and included a pool and billiard table. In 1891, the club again moved into larger, more elegant quarters inside the Loan and Trust Building.[53] Just two years later, photographs in the *Pneumatic* announced the Milwaukee Wheelmen had upgraded their facilities

As a Falling . . . . .
Snowflake

Is the beautiful Lady Andrae Bicycle—the ideal wheel for ladies.
Made especially for the use of ladies. Finished in exquisite style. Enameled in Black or Maroon.
You can ride it a year, or two years, and it is still the beautiful Lady Andrae Bicycle.

If We Don't . . . . .
Know You

You had better write us for terms on 1896 agency.
During the past season we have not dared to ask for more agents, but with our increased facilities, we can take care of your business.
Better get ready to sell the Cycle that never disappoints. Your customers will ask for it.

Julius Andrae and Sons produced the state's most popular bicycle model. The company's "Andrae Never Disappoints" branding appeared in cycling newsletters, on billboards, and on buttons.

Pneumatic, vol. 7, no. 1, 1897

again. The latest clubhouse featured "large, handsome parlors and reception rooms," a "pool and billiard hall, a smoking room," and a large dance hall. The club also had a large rear building exclusively for the storage of bicycles.[54]

In addition to building the reputation and presence of wheelmen through clubhouses, some wheelmen became increasingly cozy with a number of area industrial elites. In the early 1890s, Milwaukee's Andrae family, though not on par with the nation's greatest manufacturers, was fast becoming the most famous and influential cycling producer in Wisconsin. As makers of high-quality but affordable bicycles, the Andrae family answered a key local-market demand by producing reliable machines for a community that lacked the deep pockets more common in other parts of the country. Local boosters in Milwaukee's *Pneumatic* went so far as to proclaim "Colonel" Henry P. Andrae the "Colonel Pope of Milwaukee," comparing him to the great bicycling tycoon Albert Pope of Massachusetts. Of Andrae the *Pneumatic* said, "He is not only the most popular wheelman by actual vote," but "is virtually the father of everything pertaining to cycling in Milwaukee."[55] In addition to bicycles, the Andrae plant and others like it helped stock area bike stores with tools, bicycle parts, and other gadgets. In the end, the bicycle boom of the early 1890s helped create a new industry of bicycle manufacturers and repair shops throughout the state, shifting the culture and landscape of Wisconsin from farming toward industry.

The bicycle industry played a large role at the Chicago World's Fair. As the White City offered its case for what modern America would look like in the twentieth century, bicycles became a key element. The fair's opening ceremonies in the fall of 1892 featured uniformed military cadets from Toledo, Ohio, who paraded the grounds on their bicycles. The following spring, closer to the fair's formal opening, newspapers organized a stunt to showcase how the bicycle might one day be used to revolutionize life in the country. General Nelson A. Miles, famous for his exploits during the Civil War and

The Milwaukee Wheelmen was the state's largest and most influential cycling club. Members proudly wore this logo during the 1890s on their cycling costumes and racing jerseys.

WHi Image ID 99216

Logo of the North Side Cycling Club, the state rival of the Milwaukee Wheelmen. Led by Louis Pierron and Emil Koehn during the 1890s, the club was known for organizing major bicycle meets at Milwaukee's National Park and road races.

Milwaukee Public Museum Photography Collection

Indian Wars (and soon to become even more famous for suppressing the Pullman labor strike in Chicago a year later), sent a message by bicycle from the Chicago fairgrounds to New York. Wheelmen, riding at breakneck speeds, got the message to New York within five days, almost as quickly as a railroad car would have. The LAW, sensing that the fair would draw thousands of cyclists, held its eleventh annual meeting just a short distance from the fairgrounds. The grand Transportation Building, meanwhile, featured hundreds of bicycles from the top American and European firms. Albert Pope, always further plotting his domination of the domestic cycling scene, set up a display lauding the bicycle's history. Pope encouraged his guests to compare the new models to an old Lallement velocipede, part of Pope's private collection of "historic" bikes.[56]

Yet not all was rosy for wheelmen who attended the fair. They were especially distraught when a disgruntled office-seeker assassinated popular Chicago mayor Carter H. Harrison just a couple days before the World's Fair ended. As a "particularly good friend to the wheelmen," the *Pneumatic* noted, "he was one of the first executives to issue orders, some eight to ten years ago, to the effect that a wheelmen be permitted the same rights on public thoroughfares as horsemen." Harrison's assassination did not put an end to cooperation between the LAW and local governments, however. In Detroit, Mayor Hazen S. Pingree sent a letter to the LAW calling attention to his efforts on behalf of Michigan's bicycle lobby. "Their . . . power is an excellent example of what organization will do," the *Pneumatic* noted.[57] Wheelmen were also encouraged in their lobbying by several Wisconsin newspapers. The *Milwaukee Sentinel* became a particularly strong ally of Milwaukee wheelmen. The *Pneumatic* referred to the paper as the "wheelmen's friend" and often said it appreciated the good relationship it enjoyed with *Sentinel* editors, particularly on matters related to the good roads movement.[58]

The World's Fair ultimately brought hundreds of thousands of visitors to Chicago, but local and county fairs held throughout Wisconsin also promoted cycling's benefits wherever and whenever possible. "County fairs have introduced an innovation in setting aside one or two afternoons for bicycle racing, and horsemen look with jealous eyes upon its popularity," the *Pneumatic* reported in 1893. By effectively supplanting the very popular pastime of horse racing, bicycle racing generated a devoted fan base throughout the state willing to spend valuable leisure time watching famous riders make a name for themselves on the racing circuit. It is easy to imagine the excitement these early racers caused around the state, especially in the more rural counties where cyclists were just beginning to make regular appearances on local roads.[59]

Together, the great fairs and expositions of the early 1890s helped increase the number of men's cycling clubs throughout the state. *Wright's Directory of Milwaukee for 1894* lists a

Another popular club in Milwaukee was the Badger Wheelmen, whose logo cleverly placed the state mascot on top of a bicycle wheel.

WHi Image ID 99219

number of the new clubs, including the Mercury Cycling Club, which met at the corner of National and First on the south side; the Milwaukee Wheelmen, which met at 537 Milwaukee downtown; and the North Side Cycling Club, which met biweekly on Reservoir Avenue. Other Milwaukee clubs in the directory were the Associated Cycling Club of Milwaukee, the Junior Cycling Club, the Bay View Cycling Club, and the Comet Cycling Club.[60] The Milwaukee County Historical Society, the Milwaukee Public Museum, and the Wisconsin Historical Society each have materials documenting these organizations, particularly the North Side Cycling Club and the Milwaukee Wheelmen, but less is known about smaller clubs such as the Mercury and Comet Cycling Clubs. The 1894 directory also lists a dozen bicycle manufacturers and dealers in the city, including the Julius Andrae and Sons shop on Water Street; the Fry-Zerbel Cycle Company on Kinnikinic Avenue; the Hansen-Huennekens Cycle Company on Ferry; the Milwaukee Bicycle Company on Third; and the Telegram Cycle Manufacturing Company on Water. Manufacturers and dealers also had their addresses printed alongside the locations of several bicycle repair shops. Taken together, the directory entries show how widespread the city's cycling economy had become.[61]

THE boom that characterized the beginning of 1893 soon gave way to fears of a serious market crash. Early in the year, area bicycle manufacturers and retailers were nothing but optimistic. "The Julius Andrae Cycle Works are not simply busy," the *Pneumatic* noted that April. "H.P. Andrae states that at this rate of increase in business the firm will have to largely increase their room and force for next year's trade."[62] Shortly afterward, a financial panic in the nation's markets unleashed tremendous volatility. The panic started with a series of bank failures in February 1893 caused by the overexpansion of rail networks, declining agricultural commodity prices, and the mining industry's overproduction of silver. Effects were wide ranging. In Chicago, for example, workers at the Pullman Palace Car Company experienced drastic cuts to their wages and launched a strike that virtually halted, for a time, all rail transportation west of Chicago. These examples of unease soon spread to Wisconsin, where financial woes not only deepened the agricultural frustrations taking hold in the state but also threatened the growing bicycle industry at the end of 1893 and the beginning of 1894. In Milwaukee, the *Pneumatic*'s reporting changed from sunny tales of booming business to depressing stories of area bicycle shop closings, worker unrest, and slow bike sales.

Bicycle shops like Frank Sladek's in Manitowoc, ca. 1895, were gathering places for cyclists and offered the latest machines, athletic clothing, and a variety of sundries.

WHi Image ID 98961

Riders in 1893 increasingly noted evidence of regional economic decline wherever they went. Cyclists in the midst of the panic filled regional cycling magazines and newspapers with reports of shuttered storefronts, factory closings, and fears of a market collapse. The panic hit one of the Upper Midwest's great cycling destinations, Chicago's famous Cycle Row on Wabash Avenue, especially hard. The *Pneumatic* reported that there were once twenty-three bicycle stores on Cycle Row, arranged along two urban blocks. Only eight remained in business by the end of 1893. These drastic reversals dampened the hopes and ambitions of the bicycle boom, marking the beginning of bicycling's coming decline.[63]

In May 1893, hoping to kick-start some new sources of revenue, the city of Milwaukee announced a new tax on bicycles. The city's bicycling establishment reacted positively to the news. "If this comes to pass," the *Pneumatic* said, "it will be a good thing. . . . It will be a point gained for the bicycle to attain recognition and secure more rights." The middle- and upper-class white men who constituted the majority of the state's cycling community saw new taxes as a perfectly legitimate means for the city to create economic growth. They also came to see tax paying as a way to generate support for cycling from local governments, including funds for new trails, new roads, and new regulations to make the riding experience better. Increased taxes, they routinely suggested, might lead to improvements that would forestall some of the economic volatility unleashed by the panic.[64] For wheelmen, government became a legitimate ally in moving America forward. When Ohio governor and future Republican Party presidential candidate William McKinley visited Cleveland in 1893, the *Pneumatic* reported that an estimated three hundred Ohio wheelmen escorted him through town. When the governor's carriage reached a bad stretch of road, the wheelmen promptly turned off, stopped, saluted, and shouted "Good roads!" to highlight to McKinley the need for reform. These and other bold acts by cyclists deepened the call for improved highways.[65]

With financial panic creating new stresses on the middle class, the affordability of new bikes encouraged converts to take up cycling not as a way to express leisure and gentlemanly refinement but more simply as a way to save money. Declining wages and market volatility renewed working-class interest in the bicycle, as few transportation options could match the low cost and reliability of a bike. At first, this enthusiasm found a coherent expression outside of the United States and Wisconsin. Working people in London encouraged the donation of cycles to workingwomen and "working girl's" clubs, while the Clarion, a small British socialist organization, encouraged the use of bicycles for everyday transportation. This deepened the call for an expansion of cycling in Wisconsin, as many of state's residents sympathized with the growing international call for more reliable and economically feasible transportation options. English socialists even planned to have revolutionary "scouts" tour London on bicycles to rally workers to their cause.[66]

Not surprisingly, members of the English upper class did not appreciate what they described as "intrusions" into their world. Many worried that their safety in rural areas would be threatened if working-class cyclists managed to move beyond the slums and industrial centers. While these fears were overblown, the threat to the bicycle's position as a fixture of upper-class privilege was clear. In England, the bicycle became a symbol of a rising class consciousness. "There was a real democracy in the cult of the wheel," one worker remembered a decade after the boom. This "comradeship born of the road" brought people together, riders said, teaching them to rely on one another for repairs and community news. The democratic potentials of the bicycle continued to capture the fancy of many early riders as the economy got worse, but it remained unclear how far bicycling would reach into the lower classes.[67]

Slowly but surely, Americans began to regard the bicycle as a legitimate vehicle for street use, and in Wisconsin massive numbers of white working-class residents adopted the cycle into their everyday routines. Many white working-class residents even joined the LAW, further undermining, though not overthrowing, its early elitist culture. Flushed with an emerging working-class consciousness, the league slowly became more economically inclusive, largely on account of the availability of cheaper bicycles throughout the 1890s. Wheelmen began publishing road books and maps to help everyday people plan long-distance rides. These and other materials helped spread important information to

Cyclists widely believed the sport offered a relaxing alternative to the stress of daily life. Participating in long tours into the countryside offered an opportunity to contemplate nature and enjoy a healthier lifestyle.

Puck magazine, July 1, 1896, courtesy of University of Wisconsin–Stevens Point

August Beduhn of Oshkosh posed next to his early-model safety bicycle, ca. 1895. Mass production eventually made bicycles affordable to working-class people such as Beduhn, who was employed as a filer.

Courtesy of Oshkosh Public Museum

new groups of cyclists and local industries, including names of hotels and restaurants where wheelmen could find special rates. Citing fifty new additions to its hotel list, the *Pneumatic* reported in May 1894 that the Wisconsin division of the LAW planned to have a League-sponsored hotel in every town in the state. But the League's officers expressed disappointment when area wheelmen behaved badly, particularly when its working-class membership brought a crasser culture to league events. As hotel owners complained about the "slovenly" appearance of some of the riders who came in off the dusty roads, the *Pneumatic* reminded readers that true LAW riders showed respect by wearing their formal dining coats when eating at League-affiliated hotel restaurants. In this way, the League continued to police its growing working-class membership through its strict adherence to upper-class fashions.[68]

While the wheelmen intended these efforts to broaden the respectability and legitimacy of the white middle-class men who dominated cycling at the time, women worked to put these strategies to their own use, using the working-class influx to expand calls to broaden access for women. Women used their husbands' and male relatives' hotel and road maps to make themselves more mobile, putting more female riders on the streets. Pamphlets also listed LAW-accredited repair shops, as well as the names of local LAW officials. This information further encouraged women and other groups to venture farther from home on their rides, and again expanded the popular opinion of who belonged on the streets as a cyclist.[69]

To those who were able to partake in long rides outside the city, the *Pneumatic* offered an abundance of articles that illuminated a pastoral vision of riding, one that was still seen as a gentleman's pursuit. An August 1893 issue ran the following:

> The bicycle rider who "scorches" over the country intent on making the most miles in the shortest time, or with keeping up with the heedless leader of his party, misses more than half of the delight of his ride. What does he know of the country he rides through, of the wild flower by the roadside, the blue sky over him, the fields around him, or the blue mountains in the distance. His eyes are glued to the road or path, and his mind is on his handlebars or his pedals, or his hurrying companions.[70]

Here, as in many early wheelmen writings, the rural landscape is something to commune with and reflect upon—not work with. "Cyclists, of all persons, should have a gospel; and their glad message to a conservative world should be the redemption from conventionality; for the very essence of our sport is its freedom," the *Pneumatic* not-

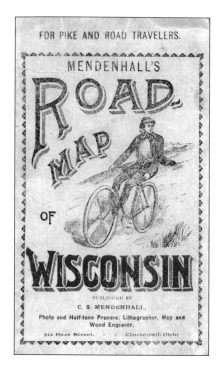

FOR PIKE AND ROAD TRAVELERS.

MENDENHALL'S

ROAD-
MAP
OF
WISCONSIN

PUBLISHED BY
C. S. MENDENHALL,
Photo and Half-tone Process; Lithographer, Map and
Wood Engraver.
512 Race Street. - Cincinnati, Ohio

By the mid-1890s, several Wisconsin touring maps and guidebooks were published that indicated road quality and distances between communities.

Milwaukee Public Museum Photography Collection

ed.[71] It was freedom *from* labor that captivated the wheelmen, who clearly assumed that work degraded the farmer and other rural workers; the dainty country visitor, by contrast, had a respectable air of city refinement. Here again the White City's ideals loomed large.

Sensing that the cyclists represented the very industries and lifestyle that had eroded agricultural life in the last part of the century, rural working-class residents looked upon men's cycling culture with a remarkable level of disdain. When reformers within the LAW called for "civilized" changes—improved grades, improved surfaces, and better signage, for example—in 1893, farmers across Wisconsin voiced their discontent because many of them took these calls to mean the end of rural traditions and lifestyles in the state, effectively blaming cyclists for the broader cultural changes they were experiencing and were suspicious of. These protests did not win many friends among the more urban and cultured wheelmen, who turned to the *Pneumatic* to respond. "Many of the farmers . . . those incorrigible, brain-lacking human specimens . . . are vigorously protesting, in a loud ungovernable voice, Senator Apple's road bill which has recently been enacted in the state legislature." Unsurprisingly, given the tenor of this and many other statements by the wheelmen leadership in Wisconsin, it would prove difficult for cyclists to forge any sense of solidarity with farmers. Wheelmen attempts to court rural and small-town folk across Wisconsin ultimately proved unconvincing. "Everyone has the utmost respect for the earnest and hard working tillers of the soil," *Pneumatic* editors wrote, "but soon they must lose this if they [the farmers] persist in working against the improvement of highways, and the advancement of civilization." Clearly, at least for the wheelmen, the "civilized" LAW had no place for rural people.[72]

In the end, the exclusionary culture of the early 1890s, which reached a peak during the 1893 World's Fair, put on full display the cultural limitations that would plague early cycling in the Badger State. These limitations were both products of the nation's early cycling culture and reflective of that culture at the same time. Nonetheless, cycling's proponents also recognized that for their sport to have a future, the state's roads had to be improved everywhere, and not just in the wealthiest communities or near the biggest cities. If Wisconsin was to become a great bicycling state, the sport would have to broaden its appeal to groups well beyond its historical bases of support in Chicago and Milwaukee. The success or failure of these efforts would be determined in the last half of the coming decade.

CHAPTER 6

The Leading Division of the West

> "Good roads help to build up thriving market towns and
> other small communities. . . . They are the people's roads."
>
> *Pneumatic*, 1894[1]

For bike riders of the late 1890s, New York City came closest to delivering on the White City's dreams of a landscape transformed for the benefit of white society. Writing for the *New York Sun* in July 1896, twenty-four-year-old Stephen Crane, author of *The Red Badge of Courage*, described New York's bicycling scene:

On fine days [bicyclists] appear in thousands. All mankind is a-wheel apparently and a person on nothing but legs feels like a strange animal. A mighty army of wheels streams from the brick wilderness below Central Park and speeds over the asphalt. In the cool of the evening it returns with the swaying and flashing of myriad lamps. The bicycle crowd has completely subjugated the street. The glittering wheels dominate it from end to end. The cafés and dining rooms of the apartment hotels are occupied mainly by people in bicycle clothes. Even the billboards have surrendered. They advertise wheels and lamps and tires and patent saddles with all the flaming vehemence of circus art. . . . Down at the Circle where stands the patient Columbus, the stores are crowded with bicycle goods. There are innumerable repair shops. Everything is bicycle. In the afternoon the parade begins. The great discoverer, erect on his tall grey shaft, must feel his stone head whirl when the battalions come swinging and shining around the curve.[2]

ON THE BOULEVARD

...By..

JOSEPH E.

HOWARD

Of the
Travesty
Team

Howard
&
Emerson.

5

——— PUBLISHED BY ———

CHAS. K. HARRIS, author of "After the Ball"

Alhambra Theatre Building, MILWAUKEE, WIS.

CHAS. SHEARD & CO., London, England.   WHALEY, ROYCE & CO., Toronto, Canada.

Music became a popular aspect of wheelmen meetings and social events. Composed by Joseph E. Howard in 1897, "On the Boulevard" became a sensation among the LAW and was played in many clubhouses.

Wisconsin Music Archives, Mills Music Library, University of Wisconsin–Madison

Crane's description of New York, where "everything is bicycle," contrasts with the stark images of ruin that filled Wisconsin newspapers two years earlier in 1894. In the midst of bitter labor strikes and economic woe, Chicago's White City burned down the July following the World's Columbian Exhibition. Never intended to survive the fair, many of the White City's temporary buildings were already crumbling by 1894. Radicals nationwide saw the ruins as a metaphor for American inequality—the White City was, after all, glittering and expansive on the outside, but thoroughly shoddy and rotting from within. When fires broke out, Chicago's elites suspected arson at the hands of the city's working class, even though it was clear most of the fires had no political origin. The charges of arson reflect the political dynamics of the moment: the wealthy fearing they would soon lose their property and their privileged position to a working-class movement dedicated to bringing it all down.[3]

Nonetheless, the economy, at least for some, did expand between its near meltdown in 1893 and the "heyday" of the bicycle boom of 1895–1896. Yet divides between rich and poor grew deeper and more entrenched as a result. With relative stability came a return to manufacturing, even as working conditions continued to worsen. More products flooded the marketplace. At the same time, declining wages for factory workers and a general sense of political frustration were pervasive.

As Chicago fitfully regained its industrial swagger, bicycle manufacturing in the region also rebounded to meet growing demand. By 1895, bike production and sales had returned to and even exceeded pre-panic levels. In the Badger State, dozens of new hardware and department stores offered fresh lines of safety bicycles, luggage, tools, tires, and all manner of bike components. Scores of new repair shops popped up along state roads, ensuring a strong network of bicycling infrastructure to support new riders. Membership in bicycling organizations soared, pushing the League of American Wheelmen to more than one hundred thousand registered riders nationwide for the first time in its history. An unparalleled number of riders were on Wisconsin's streets, making the period from

The work of bicycle mechanics became vital as more riders took to the streets. Leorr O. Chase is seated at his workbench building a wheel at the Hoaglin and Chase Bicycle Shop in Oshkosh, ca. 1898.

Courtesy of Oshkosh Public Museum

1894 to 1898 the true high point for bicycling in state history, a mark that even today's cycling enthusiasm would be hard pressed to match. By 1896, Crane's description of New York was almost as true of Wisconsin: everything truly was bicycle.[4]

As we have already seen, the growth of Wisconsin's bicycling community had many sources. Tremendous homegrown enthusiasm surrounded cycling from the start, and a strong economic and manufacturing base spread the bicycle to new consumers. While the state's imposing natural environment presented challenges for a number of years, by the 1890s wheelmen had effectively pushed local governments to improve the sorry condition of the state's rural roads and pathways. In addition, Wisconsin's historical ties to influential bicycling centers such as Boston and New York helped drive the state's cycling reputation and provided a steady flow of goods, materials, and bike-friendly migrants. Nearby Chicago's solidification as an industrial powerhouse after the Civil War also strengthened cycling's hold on the Badger State.

The consolidation of manufacturing power in the last half of the century played probably the biggest role in expanding Wisconsin's bicycle boom. Bostonian Albert Pope's personal influence helped finance the wheelmen's spread across the country. In fact, his Columbia bicycle brand was at the forefront of the league's expansion in Wisconsin. In places such as Appleton, Columbia agents moved in and started laying the groundwork for a league chapter. Taking up residence at an Appleton boarding house, Pope's agent, William Ganong, received samples of safety bicycles from Pope's factory that doubled as mobile advertisements when Ganong himself, or purchasers, rode them. Slowly but surely, these efforts helped foster a small group of riders in the town. Reporters from the *Appleton Crescent* played their part by describing Ganong's machines as "very handsome and serviceable."[5] Soon a chapter formed with Ganong serving as its captain. Nine members quickly joined him, and before long the chapter had a president in Clarence F. Rose and a treasurer and secretary in Dudley Ryan.[6] A month later, a dozen area women joined some of the men in forming the Appleton Cycling Club.[7]

College Bicycle Clubs

Most of Wisconsin's colleges and normal schools formed competitive cycling teams. Like most teams, Ripon College's team dissolved when the boom faded and cycling became a track-and-field event.

Ripon College Archives

BY THE 1890s, the bicycle fad had spread to the campuses of Wisconsin's public and private colleges. Bicycle advertisements were common as early as 1890 in the University of Wisconsin's yearbook, the *Badger*. National brands like Albert Pope's Columbia Bicycle Company used prominent advertisements to lure more students, already a key cycling demographic, to the sport. Wisconsin-based manufacturers like Julius Andrae and Sons, Warner Cycle Company (Madison), Badger Bicycle Company (Oregon), and Sterling Bicycle Company (Kenosha) also placed regular ads in college publications. Bicycles provided co-eds with a simple means of transportation and a fun extracurricular activity.

Students soon organized themselves into cycling clubs. Formed around 1894, the University of Wisconsin Cyclers adopted elements of the League of American Wheelmen's structure by electing officers, expanding their general membership, and forming a racing team. With six officers, twenty-five members, and six racers, the "U.W. Team" had a strong campus presence throughout the decade. By 1900, nearly every state campus and private college in Wisconsin had an organized cycling team.[1]

Professor George M. Browne led student members of the Bonnie Botanical Cycling Club on educational tours of the region's flora and fauna.

Courtesy of UW–Oshkosh Archives and Area Research Center

Not all clubs were competitive. Many used bicycling to promote a sense of campus life. At the Oshkosh Normal School, for example, male and female students formed the Bonnie Botanical

College Bicycle Clubs

Cycling Club (BBCC) in 1897 as a way for biology students to visit the countryside. Honorary club member Professor George M. Browne occasionally led their jaunts and helped locate seasonal blooming plants. Officer positions and the structure of the BBCC also mimicked the LAW.[2]

Bicycle clubs at Lawrence University were segregated by gender, although male and female bicyclists often enjoyed tours together. The Lawrence Women's S. B. Bicycle Club had over twenty members when the organization formed by 1894.[3] Recognizing

Women formed their own bicycle clubs because LAW chapters sometimes barred their formal membership. The women who started Lawrence University's S. B. Cycling Club posed for this photograph in 1897.

History Museum at the Castle, Appleton, WI

that many of these students also used bicycles to travel to and from school, the Appleton Cycling Club helped the university build special three-foot-wide bicycle paths.[4]

Wisconsin's bicycling boom was also the result of early political progressivism, particularly the notion that white men's oversight of the public sphere, supported by an expanded tax base, could and should benefit society—even as that society was narrowly defined. While racism, sexism, and class-based exclusions limited who counted on Wisconsin's political stage, these animosities actually strengthened white men's commitment to bicycling. As the majority in the state, they drove the construction of a political cycling coalition that by 1894 made Wisconsin a destination for other riders from around the country. It was not *the* great bicycling destination in the United States, as commentators like Crane make clear, but by the mid-1890s Wisconsin was an emerging player on the nation's cycling scene.

Whether Wisconsin was to remain so could only be determined in the realm of politics. As historian Michael Taylor has argued, the wheelmen's ability to organize blocs of voters in places like Wisconsin, Indiana, and Ohio enabled them to advance a very effective agenda for better roads and bicycling rights during the last quarter of

What the President's
hand-shaking receptions
will soon develop into, at the rate
the bicycle craze is growing.

America's bicycle lobby became an important factor in presidential elections supporting William McKinley in 1897. Although a racist caricature, the presence of the black rider indicates the growing significance of people of color in politics and bicycling.

Puck magazine, April 28, 1897, courtesy of University of Wisconsin–Stevens Point

the nineteenth century. Speaking in New York in 1883, an early wheelman noted, "We are a strong body. Take us consolidated together, and we command a great many votes. I think that if we make a little deal with the politicians it wouldn't be very long . . . before you will have both the Republicans and Democrats running after the 'wheel' votes."[8] Though the wheelmen's partisan support varied from city to city and election to election—the LAW supposedly represented "no particular section of the country, but all sections; no particular occupation, but all occupations; no particular interests, but all interests; no particular rank in life, but all ranks"[9]—the New York wheelman was correct. Few politicians, regardless of their party, could afford to overlook the bicyclist. By virtue of his race and sex, he was already a key player in national politics, but as a bicyclist he embodied an increasingly powerful vision for America's future.

In electoral politics, wheelmen after 1894 generally supported the Republican Party, spurring the rise of moderate party leaders like William McKinley in Ohio. Despite the wheelmen's claim to represent "no particular interest," their goodwill rarely extended across party lines to the working-class and populist constituents of the era's Democratic Party. In the midst of Democrat Grover Cleveland's second presidential term in 1894, for example, the *Pneumatic* discouraged area wheelmen from voicing support. "He has slighted the good roads movement and altogether does not sympathize with

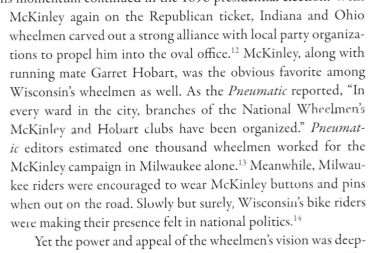

bicycle riders," the *Pneumatic* glowered. "Grover will realize to his sorrow the serious effect this discourtesy may have on his re-nomination and election."[10]

Wisconsin wheelmen mobilized their greatest energy in October 1894 behind Major William H. Upham, the Republican candidate for governor and a Civil War veteran from the legendary 2nd Wisconsin Volunteer Infantry. The old soldier certainly resonated with the wheelmen's patriotic appearances at Memorial Day parades and veteran's reunions. *Pneumatic* writers declared Upham a "friend of the wheelmen," pointing out that the major's son was a bicycling enthusiast and strong advocate for improved roads.[11] When Upham won the election and became Wisconsin's eighteenth governor, his victory proved that wheelmen support could yield results at the ballot box for the Republican Party. This momentum continued in the 1896 presidential election. With McKinley again on the Republican ticket, Indiana and Ohio wheelmen carved out a strong alliance with local party organizations to propel him into the oval office.[12] McKinley, along with running mate Garret Hobart, was the obvious favorite among Wisconsin's wheelmen as well. As the *Pneumatic* reported, "In every ward in the city, branches of the National Wheelmen's McKinley and Hobart clubs have been organized." *Pneumatic* editors estimated one thousand wheelmen worked for the McKinley campaign in Milwaukee alone.[13] Meanwhile, Milwaukee riders were encouraged to wear McKinley buttons and pins when out on the road. Slowly but surely, Wisconsin's bike riders were making their presence felt in national politics.[14]

Yet the power and appeal of the wheelmen's vision was deeply entangled with implied appeals to white male supremacy. The overwhelming power of white racial demographics in the North, including in Wisconsin, encouraged both parties to adopt racially dismissive attitudes that deepened the nation's inequality. In February 1894, for example, *Pneumatic* editors reacted strongly to the LAW's decision to ban nonwhites, arguing that segregation of the sport should be left for each state to decide. This position was in line with the racist legal reversals that followed the Supreme Court's 1896 decision in *Plessy v. Ferguson*, which upheld the constitutionality of state laws requiring racial segregation of public facilities under the doctrine of "separate but equal." *Pneumatic* editors were painfully naive in their assessment that the rollback of federal protections would not change the status of black bike riders in the North. As one article put it, "The colored men who ride are comparatively few, and in many cases their intellectual and social standing is fully equal to many of their white brethren. Therefore, why should a hue and cry be raised against them in these states? We repeat, let each state battle with this question

William H. Upham was elected Wisconsin's eighteenth governor in 1895, in part due to his promise of improved roads and the support of the bicycling lobby.

WHi Image ID 64410

African American cyclists also took advantage of the deepening bicycle boom. This group stops for a photograph atop the Alameda Bridge in Denver, Colorado, ca. 1905. Wisconsin passed Colorado to become the leading wheelmen division of the West in 1895.

History Colorado, Lillybridge Collection, 20000294

as it will." Obviously, *Pneumatic* writers felt that some states were overstating the significance of the race issue. In April, the *Pneumatic* wrote, "Now that the smoke of the contest on the negro question has rolled away," only twenty-three "colahed gen'men"—a thinly veiled slur—were listed as league members. By believing states could be trusted to protect black access to facilities, Wisconsin's wheelmen had implicitly endorsed black exclusion.[15]

Indeed, suspicions about blacks continued to undermine hopes for racial equality throughout the Badger State. As the 1890s progressed, and as reports of southern lynchings became more commonplace in Wisconsin newspapers, whites in the state seemed to prefer there be no black presence at all—either as bike riders or as citizens. In February 1895, the *Pneumatic* reported that the Oshkosh Wheelmen had adopted a resolution "not opposed to the exclusion of the negro from League membership."[16] By leaving the decision to club members, the white majority effectively decided not to protect the rights of its black neighbors. This is true even though black inclusion would have benefited the all-white owners of local bike factories, repair shops, and stores. Indeed, Oshkosh's example shows that whites willingly restricted access to the cycling community even though doing so was against their economic interests.

Wisconsin's tiny black population resisted these moves by forming their own organizations outside the white mainstream. Blacks, Indians, and other nonwhite groups rode bicycles in Wisconsin during the last half of the nineteenth century. But the organization of nonwhite groups into informal, non-LAW-affiliated clubs likely remained small in scale since no surviving records document their existence. Black riding clubs did appear in a number of other US towns and cities. In Milwaukee, the *Pneumatic* noted their appearance with a typically dismissive entry in April 1894: "It is understood that the wheelmen of the dusky color will retaliate on their fair-skinned brothers by organizing a league from which white men, in general, and Kentuckians in particular, shall forever be barred." Since it was at the LAW meeting in Louisville shortly before this that blacks were banned from the league, the black community targeted Kentucky in particular in its protests against exclusion in the cycling world.[17]

For white men, however, being a member of the LAW offered the very tangible benefit of belonging, of feeling like they were part of an important and respected group. This helps explain why cycling rose so quickly as a preferred mode of white recreation. White riders often celebrated how cycling instilled a sense of pride and community. "The bicycle has . . . long since been recognized as a new social force," the *Pneumatic* reported in March 1894, one which broke "down the barriers and prejudices of caste and exclusiveness." The *Pneumatic* went on to say that a wheelman in the countryside "finds his wheel an aid to a social reception and kindly recognition among fellow-cyclers." Clearly, being a member of the LAW helped the era's white men feel a much-coveted sense of communal belonging wherever they went. "A wheelman on his travels never feels lonely and unfriendliness in a strange town," read one summary in the *Pneumatic*. "There is an unwritten law, known to the fraternity of the wheel, by virtue of which the latchstrings of the local bicycle clubs hang out for him to pull, and, entering, count himself at home."[18] Such statements offer a window into the state's early culture, which denied minorities inclusion even as it encouraged full participation by white males. The bicycling trend, which became so popular and important to a massive white majority, simultaneously celebrated itself as progressive and free while denying these benefits to blacks, Indians, and "others" outside the mainstream.

To further create a sense of community among Wisconsin's white male cyclists, the Wisconsin Division of the LAW published a series of maps and guidebooks to encourage their use of the growing bicycle network. Created in 1896, Martin C. Rotier's *Bicycle Road Map of Wisconsin* featured a series of twelve maps that were folded together into a

A group of cyclists rest on a tour of Washington Island, ca. 1895. Cyclists from Wisconsin and out-of-state visitors took advantage of Wisconsin's country roads and detailed bicycle maps, which directed tourists along ideal routes.

Racine Heritage Museum Archival Collection

small cardboard box that could easily be transported by tourists. As one of the state's first and most comprehensive roadway maps, it differentiated the "best cycling roads" from "ordinary roads" and created a numbering system to indicate road conditions and flat or hilly terrains.[19] A year later, Samuel J. Ryan compiled the *Wisconsin Tour and Handbook*. This pocket-sized book provided cyclists with a comprehensive guide that listed the distances between towns, described road conditions, and recommended safe and scenic routes for travelers. Most importantly, the book outlined a system of local consuls in each town who were expected to greet and entertain visiting wheelmen. In Appleton, Mayor Herman Erb Jr. served as the local consul—an important signal to visiting cyclists that the city was committed to supporting bike riders. Hotels used the handbook to lure bicyclists with advertisements for discounted rates.[20] Despite these benefits, the state's poor roadways would ultimately delay the full realization of Rotier's and Ryan's visions for a landscape crisscrossed by bike-friendly amenities.

Still, wheelmen hoped to expand the benefits of the sport into other regions of the state. Because they knew road reform would be both labor intensive and expensive, wheelmen grew particularly interested in using convicts to build roads. Since they had already alienated rural workers in the state by assuming they were incapable of unity or reform, many believed coerced labor might offer the best chance for change. "Convict labor on public roads is the question of the day," the *Pneumatic* noted in October 1893. "Whether or not it is advisable to utilize prison inhabitants for the improvement of our highways would be a good subject of debate among the wheelmen." Convict labor also provided entertainment in the state's clubhouses, where members gathered to sing songs about the issue as a way to audition for the wheelmen's popular minstrel shows. By 1894, wheelmen in Wisconsin were openly asking the government to use convict labor to construct highways, noting that Minnesota had already begun the practice. It also pointed to Alabama, where convict labor, mostly black, had constructed new modern highways near Birmingham. "People living on these roads ride their wheels the year around, rain or shine," the *Pneumatic* said. By taking Alabama as their model, some of Wisconsin's wheelmen accepted that state's racist and exploitative practices rather than developing a solution that would have promoted jobs, instilled local pride, and deepened a sense of community investment in public works for the long term. This was precisely the critique leveled by Milwaukee wheelmen in November 1894 who said that the jobs for highway construction should go to men already in the state and in need of work.[21]

Members of the Appleton Cycling Club took a break along the shoreline of Lake Winnebago, ca. 1896. (Left to right) Harry Pope, Hugh Pomeroy, George Peerenboom, Samuel J. Ryan, and Charlie Green helped Appleton become a leader in the state's bicycle community.

History Museum at the Castle, Appleton, WI

These appeals undermined the wheelmen's attractiveness among poor, nonwhite, immigrant, and working-class Wisconsinites. But whatever the wheelmen lost by failing to build a broad movement they gained, at least temporarily, through enthusiasm. Wheelmen continued to lobby hard for better roads throughout the state. They printed maps and travel guides to help the public better understand which roads most needed help. Not surprisingly, these roads were often near wheelmen's clubhouses. The Milwaukee wheelmen also sponsored century rides and hosted a number of speaking tours where local experts, not all of them cyclists, lectured on the political and logistical questions facing good roads supporters.

Two Milwaukee wheelmen, both from the upper ranks of society, led these efforts. The first was Abraham Cressy Morrison, a Milwaukee businessman and a chief consul to the national LAW in the middle 1890s who also served as the president of the Milwaukee Wheelmen in 1891.[22] The other was Otto Dorner, a Milwaukee attorney who served as a league officer in Wisconsin and as a representative to the national LAW. Dorner would emerge as an especially influential leader in the state's good roads movement.[23] When he got involved in 1895, he was just twenty-six years old. Before becoming the state's leading advocate for road reform, he studied law at the University of Wisconsin–Madison and was admitted to the bar in 1889. At the high point of his bicycling activism, he worked in advertising for the Pabst Brewing Company.[24] Dorner gained the wheelmen's respect by being a dedicated rider. In September 1895, the *Pneumatic* noted him as being especially "fond of touring," particularly long, leisurely rides through the countryside. In other words, he was the perfect man for the LAW's good roads efforts: moneyed, educated, cultured, and employed by one of the city's most powerful companies.[25]

In addition to road advocacy, Morrison and Dorner were precisely the kind of men the national LAW leaders preferred for state-level leadership, joining bike industry leaders such as Albert Pope. Wisconsin's increased presence on the national LAW stage gave the state more recognition as a cycling destination. With their newfound leverage, Dorner and Morrison became involved in Wisconsin's bicycle manufacturing, as ties between the LAW and the business community were common. These ties were especially important to men like Pope, who developed and then used wheelmen's publications like the *Pneumatic* to advertise their brands.[26]

Maggie Bruehl of Oshkosh, ca. 1897, stopped for a photograph alongside a terribly muddy and impassable road.

Courtesy of Oshkosh Public Museum

The *Pneumatic* relished all of these developments and was optimistic about the progress of road improvement at the beginning of 1894. As the recent economic panic receded and the spectacle of the 1893 World's Fair faded into the background, the publication explained, "The country is slowly but surely arising to the occasion and the press, generally, seems awake and generous to assist this reform which must become as popular as it is necessary."[27] Many challenges still lingered, however. Articles in the *Pneumatic* continued to discuss unimproved roads in rural parts of the state. "One defect of the railway

Touring grew in popularity with improved maps and roads. Herbert Gaytes (right), a member of the Beloit College Bicycle Club and Cyclist's Touring Club of London, and T. P. Gaylord loaded their tandem for a tour in 1896. Herbert's membership card is also pictured.

Beloit College Archives, Herbert Gaytes Collection

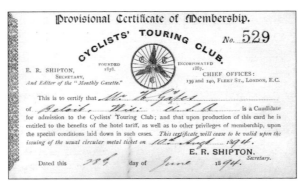

system is its tendency to build up large cities at the expense of small towns and villages," one article in February 1894 argued. "Good roads help to build up thriving market towns and other small communities. Then they cannot be monopolized like railways. . . . They are the people's roads."[28] Sounding surprisingly egalitarian and idealistic, wheelmen hoped to turn their message into statewide support in the mid-1890s.

To build the coalition they needed, Wisconsin's wheelmen created the Wisconsin League for Good Roads in 1895, the state's first highway improvement association. The Wisconsin League had to overcome not only the wheelmen's elitist outlook, but also Wisconsinites who questioned whether improving the roads was necessary in the first place. One persistent argument emerged from the state's farmers, who said that a new roads administration would only lead to unnecessary spending and require new taxes. Though the wheelmen quickly dismissed these worries, the farmers had a good point given the small number of taxpayers in many rural areas. Road reforms would be expensive, and many rural people felt they could not afford to support new infrastructure spending.

Further, it was not clear to many rural people that improved roads and highways would better their lives. Farmers argued that many of the places roads were slated to go lacked the resources required to construct them. In other words, city and county governments would have to work with outside companies to have materials brought in. Many saw this situation as ripe for corruption and scandal, and others worried that handing over local authority of roads would harm rural life, a common worry as Wisconsin's rural landscape became more industrial in the last decades of the century. There was also a profound cultural distrust of the wheelmen, rooted in the days of the velocipede mania, as "city dudes" and "lazy fellows." The wheelmen themselves may not have fully deserved these labels, but they surely helped cultivate ill will through their exclusive rules. Farmers remained anxious about the number of young people who were leaving the rural enclaves of the state for cities, which were often viewed as dangerous and corrupt. In the eyes of many farmers, few embodied the urban, well-heeled industrial United States better than the wheelmen "dudes" and their fancy bicycles.[29]

Wheelmen answered these critiques with numbers. New roads would spread wealth into the countryside, they said, being careful to deemphasize their own self-interest in spreading that wealth through their ties to Milwaukee banks and investors. One common argument held that farmers would be able to transport their goods to nearby markets more easily if they had improved roads, and that this ease of transport would translate into savings. Another argument said that farm animals would be less prone to injury if roads were improved, since a smoother surface would keep them from falling, tripping, or losing shoes on caked mud, rocks, and other debris. Because good roads would also increase the speed of rural transport, wheelmen claimed that farm commodities, whose prices had dropped due to the 1893 panic, would make it to markets in Minneapolis, Chicago, and Milwaukee faster and in better quality, fetching a higher price as a result. Wheelmen added that better roads would improve rural mail service and speed the flow of vital information between rural producers and consumers. In the end, however, the wheelmen seemed most fond of saying that "civilization" itself depended on the development of roads. Not surprising, this comment only deepened perceptions that they were out of touch with the real challenges facing rural people.[30]

With the good roads movement bogged down in a heated public debate, wheelmen worked privately to create new biking paths. These paths were cheaper to install, smaller in scale than roads, and did not require government oversight. As a result, the mid-1890s gave rise to a handful of city bike paths in Wisconsin. One of the first of these was in Appleton, where grassroots efforts by area wheelmen raised several hundred dollars for a path linking the city fair grounds to College Avenue. "This is the first bicycle path

The good roads movement helped transform the Wisconsin landscape. By the middle 1890s, new maps documented area roads, paths, and trails. This one, produced in 1896 by the Wisconsin Division of the LAW, also illuminated changes in terrain—"level," "hilly," and "very hilly"—on routes through several counties.

WHi Image ID 68728

that has been built in Wisconsin," the *Pneumatic* noted with approval in August 1895.[31] Soon many other cities had efforts underway to build paths, including La Crosse, Sparta, Ripon, and Black River Falls, with the *Pneumatic* providing frequent coverage of the projects. These paths further distanced urban lifestyles and experiences from rural ones, even as they expanded access for urban riders.[32]

In addition to creating urban bike paths, wheelmen also pursued opportunities to spread the cycling gospel with renewed energy after 1894. They pedaled around Wisconsin to meet with rural residents and used a variety of tactics to approach rural communities. Again, they appealed to "civilization." Writers for the *Pneumatic* liked to point out that North Milwaukee, a factory town situated around the large A. D. Meiselbach Company bicycle plant just north of downtown, lacked good roads, undermining the town's livability. What was the use, editors asked, of having bike factories if roads were so impassable that workers couldn't even ride their bikes to their job? Though the *Pneumatic* praised the community for its beautiful homes, well-equipped general store, and modern electric system, along with "a goodly number of high minded citizens," wheelmen feared North Milwaukee would never become a great city without better roads. Stung by these charges, North Milwaukee residents turned to the wheelmen for advice on how to improve their situation. They invited Otto Dorner and LAW chief consul Frank P. Van Valkenburgh, also a Milwaukee lawyer, to advise them on how to build better roads. After a short bike ride to the community meeting, the "good roads apostles," as they were called, demonstrated the need for improved streets by shaking the dust from their clothing. Dorner, who was not well known outside the wheelmen community, brought newspaper clippings praising his good roads credentials and made the meeting chairperson read them aloud to the crowd. For three hours, "the apostles" spoke about roads and shared their stories to an enthralled crowd of fifty residents. Part of the presentation undoubtedly included photographs Dorner had collected for the LAW's yearly competition for the most deplorable road conditions in America.[33]

The apostles who rode into town on their fancy bikes and used the dust in their clothes to demonstrate the poor condition of roads made for great political theater, but the wheelmen often failed to win rural support. They were impatient and condescending in their negotiations with rural people. One of the best examples of this is Isaac B. Potter's *Gospel of Good Roads: A Letter to the American Farmer* (1891), which outlined a detailed case for road improvement by talking down to the farmer at every turn.[34] In depicting the state's farmers as ignorant rubes hostile to all forms of change, Potter's book expanded the growing divide between city and country in Wisconsin. Eventually, seeing that their words had won them few friends, the wheelmen backed off.

A few bicyclists, however, sided with the farmers, saying that it was unfair for an already struggling rural class to be burdened with the additional expense of new infrastructure, especially in an increasingly volatile economy. Why not make those who could actually afford the new roads pay for them?[35] Publications like the *Pneumatic* could hardly endorse this view. Wheelmen were far more likely to shift the blame back onto rural people. As a typical entry in the *Pneumatic* put it:

> The mullenheaded farmer who happens to distinguish himself as a great crop raiser, or wins a prize at the county fair for having the best cabbage, usually is honored with an election to some office such as road supervisor, although his knowledge in the construction and proper maintenance of highways does not exceed that of his overgrown cabbage head.[36]

Needless to say, wheelmen had induced a profound distrust of rural people during the last half of the 1880s and early 1890s. By the middle 1890s, they began to suffer the more negative effects of their exclusionary ways, and rural road improvements stalled.

While its politics were anything but diplomatic, urban cycling in Wisconsin did undergo a massive expansion between 1894 and 1896. Milwaukee's city directories for the middle part of the 1890s help illuminate just how dramatic Wisconsin's "bicycle boom" was. All elements of Wisconsin's bicycling culture and manufacturing sectors underwent rapid growth. New clubs such as the Badger Wheelmen, the Century Cy-

Logo of Wisconsin's division of the LAW

WHi Image ID 99222

The growth of cycling infrastructure in Wisconsin was reflected in the number of bicyclists on city streets. White men, women, and children were encouraged to partake in the sport, as is evident in this group in Neenah, ca. 1897.

Neenah Historical Society

cling Club, the Nineteenth-Century Cycling Club, the Cream City Cycling Club, and the YMCA Wheelmen, for example, joined new manufacturers and dealers such as the William Pollitt Cycle Works, the Wagner Peter Cycle Works, Chief Cycle Manufacturing, Columbia Bicycles, Cream City Cycles, and the A. D. Meiselbach Company. These organizations joined a slew of new parts and components manufacturers, enamellers, riding schools, and department stores where consumers could easily find products and services. In just a few years, transportation in Wisconsin had radically changed, and out of these transformations grew the reputation that has made Wisconsin such a popular bicycling destination today.[37]

The boom became so widespread that it soon altered broader urban transportation patterns. An estimated five hundred employees in Milwaukee opted to bike to work each day in 1894 rather than ride the rails. "In nearly every case," the *Pneumatic* noted, "they are business men [sic] who are busy and hasty and want a quick mode of conveyance."[38] Rather than pay the streetcar fare, in other words, the city's working residents chose the bicycle as a cheaper and faster route to downtown. This became an especially attractive option as continued economic troubles in the wake of the 1893 panic made even basic transportation expenses a burden for some workers. Slowly but surely, bicycling became a mainstream option for working people, rolling away from its elitist roots.

Perhaps the greatest testament to the scope of the bicycle boom in Wisconsin arrived halfway through the decade. In 1895, Wisconsin boasted the highest LAW membership of all "western" states. "Michigan, Ohio, Colorado, Illinois, and other Western divisions which, in former years, have looked down on this state with contempt, because it was weak in numbers, now find the tables turned. . . . Now the membership list numbers over 800," the *Pneumatic* reported in June 1895. This was a remarkable triumph for the state's riders, who seemed stunned that Wisconsin was now home to a larger membership base than even nearby Illinois and its formidable Chicago clubs. It was a triumph Wisconsin riders bragged about openly and loudly in the pages of the *Pneumatic*. "The Wisconsin Division is no longer in the rear ranks of the League of American Wheelmen, but is now the leading division of the West," it reported. Everything was bicycle in the Badger State, but to really understand how this happened, it is necessary to look beyond the exclusive, all-male clubs and into the riding culture of everyday Wisconsinites. It is a story that has never been told until now.[39]

CHAPTER 7

Women and Labor During the Boom

"Let me tell you what I think of bicycling. I think it has done more to emancipate women than anything else in the world."

Susan B. Anthony, 1896[1]

"[S]eldom has any department of human industry taken on such proportions in so short a time as has the bicycle industry of this country."

Daily Northwestern, 1895[2]

A poster by Edward Penfield in 1896 captured the growing women's market for the Stearns brand, based in Syracuse, New York. Bicycle companies began marketing their latest models to women as their presence grew in the sport.

Library of Congress, Prints & Photographs Division, LC-USZC4-6645

Women riders were one of the great sights George F. Peabody of Appleton remembered of his visit to New York City in 1895. Peabody made yearly visits to New York in order to do purchasing for his small Appleton department store, and the sheer number of bicycles he saw during his visit stunned him. He seemed especially interested in how New York's women took "afternoon spins with great regularity." The entire place, he said, seemed gripped by "the fierceness of the wheel fever," with perhaps ten thousand riders at any giv-

Two young Ho-Chunk men, Henry Badsoldier Stacy and Will Stohegah Carriman, pose in a studio portrait for Charles Van Schaick, ca. 1905. People of color actively participated in the bicycle boom despite the efforts of many white men, who tried to control access to the sport.

WHi Image ID 61314

Women, such as the two pictured here in Racine in 1897, used the bicycle to push traditional domestic boundaries.

Racine Heritage Museum Archive Collection

en time gathered, as he put it, "along the boulevards and the drives."[3] Increasingly after 1895, women, but also nonwhites and working people, routinely challenged the terms of access to the sport. In both the factories and the streets, "wheel fever" made its presence felt.

The fever reached its breaking point in Wisconsin during the middle 1890s. When Wisconsin became home to the biggest LAW membership in the western states in 1895, the state's wheelmen rejoiced at their triumph. In important ways, however, the scale and scope of the boom far exceeded the growth in numbers. Because the league formally excluded vast sections of the public, and because its riders constituted an intense but otherwise small cycling community in the late 1880s and 1890s, it is possible to overstate its significance to the boom. Doing so would mean downplaying others who shaped Wisconsin's love for the bicycle, particularly those unaffiliated with the LAW. In fact, women, organized labor, and nonwhites would all play crucial roles in determining the scale of the bicycle boom.

Christina Dando argues that bicycling's popularity after the introduction of the safety led to a growing "network of new technologies" for women and men—bikes, maps, repair kits, and specialized tools, along with literature to help riders use them. These new technologies allowed women in particular to challenge their outsider position. Dando suggests that these items helped women explore new parts of cities with the certainty that they could find their way around and repair their machines in the event of a breakdown, leading to a greater appreciation for personal independence. As women learned more about their communities and surrounding landscapes, they also worked to transcend their limited roles in American society. Their efforts go a long way in explaining why men reacted so negatively to female cyclists on Wisconsin's streets as the boom deepened, and why these negative reactions ultimately helped bring the boom to an end.[4]

Indeed, as Ellen Garvey and other students of early cycling show, women's efforts to expand access to the sport often inspired intense animosity. Men commonly described women's "irrational" desire to bike instead of tending to domestic affairs. But as Garvey points out, while men in the 1890s were certainly sexist and often dismissive of

their female peers, they were also sometimes willing to ignore these concerns for financial reasons. After all, there was plenty of money to be made from women bicyclists. Moreover, having white women on the roads helped secure bicycling against the perceived intrusions into the sport by blacks and other nonwhites. Women, in other words, managed to expand bicycling, but only along racial lines. At the same time, deep class-based divisions between the working class and the era's industrial leaders after 1895 provoked other tensions that both expanded the sport into new arenas yet threatened to undermine its economic and democratic gains.[5]

Geographers Phillip Gordon Mackintosh and Glen Norcliffe push these points further, suggesting that white middle- and upper-class women often rode in public "free of care."[6] From the beginning cycling was seen as an elite enterprise, and therefore it symbolized the kind of modern and progressive vision that civilized white Americans, male and female, could endorse. In this way, women's cycling actually encouraged the view that American women, while still unable to vote, were nevertheless better off than women elsewhere. "Society women have taken to the wheel," the *Pneumatic* reported from Milwaukee in April 1895.[7] As the wives of leading bankers, business owners,

LADIES' BICYCLE LEGGINGS

KALT-ZIMMERS MFG. CO.
... Manufacturers of ...
Fine Overgaiters and Leggings
419 East Water Street

The Kalt-Zimmers Manufacturing Company of Milwaukee, ca. 1898, sold leggings to women to protect their legs and skirts from the bicycle's chain.

Milwaukee Public Museum Photography Collection

and physicians rode around the city, they showed off a new kind of "refined" white womanhood. Yet many women, particularly activists and suffragists, found this token status disheartening and worked against it. Bicycling would change dramatically as a result. Unable to obscure the deep economic divisions between the working poor and the elites, these gains by women were ultimately not enough to make the cycling boom a truly transformative moment.

With white women's presence in the sport resting on a beleaguered foundation, it is telling that men continued to frame the debate in new battles over just what these women should wear when out and about. New bicycling and outdoor fashions found their way into Wisconsin's storefronts. Many scandalized public tastes. One garment in particular, the short, baggy pants called bloomers, ignited a firestorm of derision and condescension. For much of the nineteenth century, reformers of all stripes had been on the search for an alternative to dresses and skirts, which remained the dominant ladies' fashion through the 1880s and 1890s. With increasing urgency, led by women's embrace of cycling, calls for clothing designs such as bloomers and new bike designs such as the drop frame, which enabled a bit more room for skirts, increased. Women were given three choices for cycling clothing, but none seemed all that promising: adopt straight-legged trousers similar to what men wore and risk endless public ridicule; wear bloomers, which were unpopular among both women and men; or wear a modified skirt that kept the legs free to move but would not blow up in heavy winds or bundle up over long distances. As women struggled to define what was respectable and what was not, they challenged the norms of fashion. It was unclear what this meant, at least at first, but nearly everyone recognized something profound was at stake in these early struggles over women's cycling attire.[8]

Cycling Fashion

AS WOMEN BECAME active cyclists, the question of what to wear become controversial. Long, flowing dresses and skirts constricted movement and also posed a safety problem as they were easily caught in the gears and torn. The invention of the "drop frame" safety bicycle and rear wheel netting helped accommodate full-length fashions to some degree, but many riders preferred newer styles of dress.[1] Photographic evidence suggests that Wisconsin's women typically wore a modified skirt, but bloomers made numerous appearances in Wisconsin throughout the 1890s, provoking fashion reform as the century came to a close.

Nineteenth-century reformers, including the eponymous Amelia Jenks Bloomer, had encouraged baggy "Turkish" pants or "bloomer" suits as early as the 1850s. Early loose-fitting bloomers, which required corsets, were replaced with a more relaxed and form-fitting version for bicycling by the 1890s. Despite the freedom offered by the bloomer suit, Wisconsin's women cyclists debated the virtues of adopting it. Madison's women cyclists and political leaders were initially opposed. Belle Case La Follette said it would be unfortunate to adopt clothing different than street dress, as did Mary Kelly Upham, who thought skirts were more sensible. Other women cited bloomers as unbecoming, immodest,

A woman's bloomer suit, ca. 1895.
WHS Museum 1947.1156,a, photo by Joel Heiman

and even unwomanly. Wheelwomen remained divided on the issue, as interviewees in Ashland opposed bloomers while Appleton women supported the dress reform, as did women in Green Bay and Eau Claire.[2] Rumors of ordinances prohibiting bloomers spread through the state,

Cycling Fashion

including Appleton, where a ban was ultimately deemed a hoax.[3]

To encourage the adoption of bloomer suits, women in Wisconsin promoted the fashion through clubs and public rides. In Green Bay, wheelwomen planned to form a special bloomers club to support the first woman in the city to wear them.[4] According to the *Pneumatic*, Louisa Roth was credited as the first "bloomer girl" in Milwaukee, but unfortunately the magazine did not identify when she made her appearance.[5] Neither were bloomers limited to larger urban and town centers, as Kaukauna boasted fifteen bloomer girls in 1895.[6] Appleton's progressive women cyclists brought fresh reinforcements of "gallant wheelwomen" into the debate to "lead the reform to victory."[7] Despite women's desire for reform, some men treated the bloomer girls as mere sex symbols, as suggested by the *Pneumatic* when bloomers were first popularized in 1894: "There is no pen powerful enough to describe the feelings of a man on the occasion when for the first time he goes out riding with his girl who is dressed in bloomers."[8]

According to the *Pneumatic*, the popularity of bloomer suits for bicycling began to fade after 1896. Although bloomers had become more acceptable on Wisconsin's boulevards, male cyclists continued to persuade women toward more conservative fashions. Editors of the *Pneumatic* criticized Chicago women who visited Milwaukee aboard the SS *Christopher Columbus* in 1895 for wearing bloomers that were too revealing and expensive.[9] Male wheelmen instead continued to promote the modified divided skirt and jacket, which remained the most popular athletic wear for female cyclists. Later issues of the *Pneumatic* provided directions for making "bicycling costumes," including prewashing fabric in case of shrinkage in a rainstorm, adopting zouave-style jackets, and wearing shorter skirts.[10] However, cyclists like Boston's Annie Londonderry continued to advocate for reform as she successfully cycled around

The American Bicycle Company of Kenosha made this women's safety bicycle after 1900. The machine incorporated designs to protect a woman's skirt, including the drop frame and rear-wheel netting.

WHS Museum 1977.247, photo by Joel Heiman

Cycling Fashion

the world in 1895 riding a men's "straight bar" frame while wearing pants.[11] Despite these limited gains, the wheelwomen's bloomer advocacy ultimately helped push reforms that challenged the oppressive constraints of Victorian fashion.

Men's fashions were also of great concern to cyclists. Before affiliating with the national LAW, each local chapter was responsible for designing and purchasing a club uniform. The distinctive uniforms often mimicked costumes worn by fraternal organizations like the Knights of Pythias. Also influenced by military uniforms, early club members sometimes wore pith helmets, kepis, wool sack coats, and military trousers. In the 1880s, members of the Milwaukee Bicycle Club adopted a militaristic costume that more resembled an army officer's dress uniform than athletic clothing.[12] Clubs even formed special committees and had members vote on uniforms. The Winnebago Wheelmen of Fond du Lac voted in 1896 on a uniform of a matching coat, trousers, and cap. Each club was also responsible for creating their club colors and logo, which were to be displayed on their chapter's buttons. The Winnebago Wheelmen used a white button with purple text representing their club colors, as well as a copper-colored profile of an American Indian.[13]

Men's fashion changed as the militaristic or aristocratic wool uniforms of the 1880s were

By 1900, men's cycling fashion had evolved from wool uniforms to lighter tweed jackets and trousers. The formal clothing preserved a man's gentlemanly appearance on short tours.

WHS Museum 1983.206.10,a, photo by Joel Heiman

Cycling Fashion

replaced with improved and modernized athletic clothing. Although the LAW liked to claim that nonmembers had copied their styles, the clothing worn by exclusive, upper-class outdoorsmen, especially golfers, was even more influential to the wheelmen. By 1899, matching club uniforms became less popular and clothing was left more to the discretion of the individual. Headgear gradually changed from kepis and pith helmets to narrow golf-style and silk scotch-plaid caps. Dealers in bicycle sundries also began offering men new tweed bicycle suits similar to those described by fashion writers in New York City. A typical tweed suit could cost ten to twenty dollars, and even more expensive nautical-themed outfits were also available. Men also wore outdoor negligee shirts on long summer country tours and switched to warmer flannel shirts in the fall. Neckties were still appropriate, but buttoned frock coats and vests were replaced with looser jackets worn open on warm days. To complete the costume, by the turn of the century, male cyclists wore checked trousers, and the entire ensemble was expected to match accordingly.[14]

Cyclists gathered at the Industrial Exposition Building for the national meet in 1900. These determined riders wore the newest cycling fashions, including tweed suits, riding skirts, century bars worn on long chains, and cycling medals.

Milwaukee County Historical Society

Wisconsin women indeed became heavily involved in cycling during the height of the boom, but one in particular became internationally known, at least in part, for her bicycle activism. By the time Frances Willard published *A Wheel Within a Wheel: How I Learned to Ride the Bicycle, with Some Reflections by the Way* in 1895, she was already a famous educator, women's rights advocate, and temperance leader. Born on September 28, 1839, near Rochester, New York, she moved with her family at a young age to Ohio, where both of Willard's parents attended Oberlin College. At the time, Oberlin was a bastion of reform politics that was taking a leading role in the antislavery movement. It would also pioneer higher education for blacks in the antebellum Old Northwest. In 1846, the restless Willard family moved to Wisconsin, where Frances spent much of her childhood roaming a large farm the family owned near Janesville. Tutored by her college-educated mother, Willard later studied for a year at the Milwaukee Female College (later Milwaukee-Downer College) and then at North Western Female College (later part of Northwestern University), receiving a Laureate of Science degree in 1859, just two years before the outbreak of the Civil War.[9]

Willard fit the description of many well-educated white Americans who were being drawn into cycling culture, but she did not convert to cycling until she was well into her adult years. After many years of travel and continued study at some of Europe's best schools, where she no doubt witnessed firsthand the bicycle's popularity, Willard instead became involved in the temperance movement. In 1874, she helped create the Woman's Christian Temperance Union (WCTU), one of the nation's first and largest organizations for women, devoted not only to temperance but also a variety of labor reforms, women's suffrage, a range of public health initiatives including urban sanitation, and even international peace. Over the next couple decades, she became one of the most visible women's leaders in the country as well as a respected national leader for the WCTU's highly influential and often well-received educational and moral reforms. She allied herself with the Knights of Labor in their struggle for the eight-hour workday and became an influential leader in the global feminist cause as she organized and then served as the first president of the World WCTU. It was during this time that she also learned how to ride a bicycle.[10]

In *A Wheel Within a Wheel*, Willard described how her love of cycling came about. She recalled the importance of her move to Janesville as a child, where her out-of-doors upbringing allowed her to run wild and carefree. As a teenager, however, she remembered things changed. Her life moved indoors as she devoted her time to study, reading

Progressive reformer Frances Willard, who lived in Janesville as a child, was an avid cyclist who believed more use of the bicycle could improve women's health and well-being.

Library of Congress, Prints & Photographs Division, LC-USZ61-790

anything she could get her hands on, and writing whenever she got the chance. Bicycles remained a constant presence in the cities where she lived and studied as an adult, but it was the death of her mother, when Willard was fifty-three, that prompted her to make a lifestyle change. "I determined that I would learn the bicycle," she said.[11]

Through her temperance advocacy Willard had early on expressed her support for the bicycle because it held so much promise for keeping young men away from the beer gardens and taverns where so many domestic disputes originated. "I have always held that a boy's heart is not set in him to do evil any more than a girl's," she wrote, "and that the reason our young men fall into evil ways is largely because we have not had the wit and wisdom to provide them with amusements suited to their joyous youth." Bicycling was the perfect kind of amusement. Willard could also speak from direct experience that cycling offered many benefits for women. In 1886, she received a tricycle as a gift from Albert Pope himself. She later described her joy at riding it around in the early evening after her long days of work. The tricycle, she said, gave her good exercise and a feeling of calm after spending her day studying and reading indoors.[12]

Like many of her peers, Willard acknowledged that her close friends and family met her embrace of the bicycle with skepticism. She probably shared some of their worries—learning how to ride a bike, after all, is not the easiest thing to do as an adult. Pope's tricycle was far more stable, but the allure of riding an actual bicycle pushed her forward and gave her the courage to try the new machine. As she described in her book, three men were at first necessary to help her climb into the saddle of a safety bicycle, while two women helped her keep her balance. In short time, Willard came to see the experience of learning to ride a bicycle as comparable to overcoming virtually any of life's challenges. Lingering doubts and insecurities haunt anyone who has ever tried to learn something new, she reasoned, and sometimes the best way to overcome those fears is to just tackle them head-on. "Indeed, I found a whole philosophy of life in the wooing and the winning of my bicycle," she said. Seeing what potential the bicycle held for women, she noted, "We saw that the physical development of humanity's mother-half would be wonderfully advanced by that universal introduction of the bicycle sure to come about within the next few years."[13]

Willard never ceased her tireless work for a better society based on fuller incorporation of bicycle transportation. "We saw with satisfaction the great advantage in good fellowship and mutual understanding between men and women who take the road together, sharing its hardships and rejoicing in the poetry of motion through landscapes," she explained. For the rest of her life, Willard remained proud that she "had made [herself] master of the most remarkable, ingenious, and inspiring motor ever yet devised upon this planet." Her efforts helped make cycling one of the most cherished female pursuits of the late nineteenth century, and her reach extended far beyond the state where she had spent so many fond years. Though she died in 1898, only a few years after the book was published, coverage of her death often listed *A Wheel Within a Wheel* among her great life accomplishments.[14]

Through the leadership of Willard and other women riders, artists, and writers such as Maria E. "Violet" Ward, Alice Austen, Belva Lockwood, Susan B. Anthony, and Annie Oakley, women's cycling skyrocketed after 1894.[15] Inequities in wealth and income, however, helped ensure that white men would still reap the greatest benefits from the sport as the century came to a close. They secured these benefits after 1895 in a variety of ways. One way was as bicycling entrepreneurs, particularly in securing publishing contracts for stories, photographs, and essays written "out on the road." Wisconsin became a popular destination for many celebrity and outdoor bike riders during the 1890s. One was travel writer Tom Winder, who set out to ride his bike around the entire edge of the United States in less than three hundred days in 1895. His epic round-the-country trek started in New Orleans on March 14, and in his writing, Winder recounted tales of the many dangers he encountered and overcame.

Harriet Weishoff, pictured ca. 1895, was prepared to ride day or night with her front bicycle lamp.

Courtesy of Oshkosh Public Museum

From Winder's account, it's clear that the ride, and the privileges his white male status afforded him, made him something of a local celebrity wherever he went. He filled his book with descriptions of curious locals who would ride with him in order to conduct impromptu interviews as he cycled through their towns. Along the way, Winder offered a number of exotic descriptions of southern blacks that enhanced white claims to cycling. Not far from New Orleans, for instance, just a few days out of the gate, Winder described how the "darky" kids he encountered would run up to his bike to ask him questions. Bikes were, of course, well beyond the purchasing capacity of most blacks in the time of Jim Crow, and the children's curiosity at a white man cycling through their community is not surprising. Instead of commenting on the obvious inequalities his presence exposed, however, Winder used the encounters as a narrative device for depicting the South as behind the times.[16]

White consumers, meanwhile, loved such stories, and spent many dollars reading his exotic tales. As he turned east and then south around Minnesota to cross into Wisconsin, Winder found the Badger State a welcome relief from the wilds of the West. "I am going to get some pleasure out of this trip after all," he wrote. "The country to the east of Lacrosse [sic] for 25 miles is great. The roads are good! Every farm house is a mansion. . . . If I ever go to farming I am going to Wisconsin . . . where the grass is the greenest, the fields the cleanest . . . just enough trees to make it pleasant, hills to relieve the monotony of a dead level, and where the soft rays of the setting sun cast a glint of happiness over all nature."[17]

Wisconsinites continued the practice of approaching Winder as he rolled through their towns, often asking him questions about his travels and the gear he was using.

He had friendly words for his white companions in the Badger State. "One thing that excites the curiosity of the people is the canteen I carry. Many do not even know what it is, let alone its purpose," he explained, without the condescension he showed toward blacks in the South. Other Wisconsin residents were more suspicious of Winder's presence, however. Some blamed him for the persisting rains that covered the state as he moved through. "In the north they had called me a hoodoo, 'a rain maker,'" he said, and indeed high winds and rain seemed to follow wherever he went. As he neared Chicago, a gale sent a number of wheelmen who had ridden out to join him back to their homes. "Our party of 20 or more for a few moments got tangled up in a blow of sand that would have done credit to Arizona. And then the rain came down." These descriptions hint at not only the state of road infrastructure around the nation but also how Wisconsin's landscape was coming to be seen as a great place for cycling. Winder's book offers a glimpse into what made Wisconsin a beloved locale for riders during the boom.[18]

Century rides were among the most popular aspects of cycling culture, but critics of the bicycle satirized distance riding, believing that pedaling hundreds of miles was unhealthy.

Puck magazine, January 15, 1896, courtesy of University of Wisconsin–Stevens Point

Still, while the state attracted celebrity riders from all over the globe, many residents recognized that significant improvements to local infrastructure were needed for Wisconsin to remain a great bicycling destination, accessible to an increasing number of cyclists on its roads. A rejuvenated bicycling market fueled calls for all kinds of new projects and cycling investments. Many of the projects sought simple solutions to simple problems, but some offered outrageous answers to the state's lack of rideable roads. For example, in July 1895, the *Pneumatic* reported that an investor named E. J. Pennington had organized a company with capital of one million dollars to build an elevated wooden bridge linking Chicago and Milwaukee. The bridge would offer riders a private road between the two cities, letting them travel without hindrance from horses, carriages, mud, animal waste, or other obstacles common in the 1890s. Planners said that riders would be charged a ten-cent toll to use the bridge, and Pennington hoped that a good cyclist could make the trip between the two cities in just four hours. The grand scheme never saw the light of day.[19]

As various other improvement projects were tossed around, the state became a frequent host to organized rides in the late 1890s. Bicyclists played a key role, for instance, in Milwaukee's Semi-Centennial Celebration for 1895. Over 2,500 wheelmen rode in the Semi-Centennial parade as thousands of people lined Grand Avenue. The huge event brought life in the city to a standstill. Dozens of "wheelwomen" also participated, though they had only marginal roles in the parade. The all-male Milwaukee Wheelmen organization was given the distinguished honor of leading, and roughly sixty of its members rode at the front of the column dressed in "white duck trousers" and white hats. Wheelmen also had a float, with the words "Time and Progress" written on it. Terry Andrae, Milwaukee's most iconic bicycle manufacturer, stood atop the float alongside an old-fashioned high-wheel bicycle. The Badger Wheelmen also wowed crowds with their bicycles "finished up in white," while the South Side Bicycling Club had a float painted with the words "1845, Progress, 1895." Near "1845" was placed an old velocipede, already a relic from what must have seemed like the ancient past.[20]

Married couple William and Josie Smith traveled alone down a countryside road on October 29, 1899.

Courtesy of Oshkosh Public Museum

Not everyone welcomed the vision of progress so eagerly espoused by Milwaukee's wheelmen. While instances of violence between bike riders and rural Wisconsin farmers were rare in the 1890s, occasional havoc did give ammunition to bicyclists and farmers who bitterly complained about one another. In November 1895, for example, the *Pneumatic* reported that a farmer had actually cracked his whip across the back of a Wisconsin bike rider who attempted to pass the farmer's wagon. The farmer claimed the rider had refused to share the road. The court disagreed. The farmer suffered an eleven-dollar fine for the offense, suggesting that by the mid-1890s cyclists could use litigation to protect their rights. This marked a notable turnaround from just ten years earlier.[21]

Progress was also mixed for riders of color, as white control of the sport made it difficult for minorities to be accepted as cyclists. As Greg Bond writes, "Many whites believed immigrants from China were beyond the pale and incapable of becoming Americanized."[22] A Chinese bicycle rider tested the troubled racial waters in 1896. "Sam

Wing" captured the attention of the *Green Bay Dispatch* when he took to the streets to learn how to bicycle. "Even Chinamen become imbued with the hustle and progress of modern civilization and find it necessary to take to the wheel in order to keep up with the procession," the paper noted. In an era of harsh anti-Chinese legislation, marked by such draconian measures as the 1882 Chinese Exclusion Act, which had severely limited Chinese immigration, many whites assumed Chinese men were effectively incompetent at everyday tasks. "Sam has selected an 1896 'Yellow Fever' for his mount," the writers joked, invoking a barbed racial slur. In terms that suggested simultaneous amusement and dread, the article makes clear that a special kind of suspicion was saved for riders who did not fit the racial norm.[23]

Groups of women cyclists, such as these tourists near Black River Falls, ca. 1895, became a common sight on Wisconsin's roads.

WHi Image ID 3662

At the same time, women were exercising their buying power to secure a growing market for female clothing, accessories, and bicycles in area stores. Worried about the increased presence of women in the sport, the editors at the *Pneumatic* questioned the feasibility of gender-integrated cycling and frequently suggested women take a back seat to men. In 1896, for example, the *Pneumatic* suggested that men use their wives as their personal bicycling secretaries, arguing that they could record mileage information in their husband's cycling journals. "Get your wife to keep a log for you. . . . This will keep her interested in your cycling. . . . If you have no wife, get one at once."[24] Viewed as accessories, white women worked all the harder to create a safe place for themselves in the sport, as it was obvious men were not going to help their efforts. To capitalize on the young men and women who used bicycling to socialize together, local dealers also upped their inventories of tandem bicycles, adding yet another dimension to the boom. To some degree, tandems offered something of a compromise for those concerned about the gender upheavals cycling suggested. Men and women could ride the bikes together, but usually men remained in the lead. This guaranteed that men would accompany women wherever they went and thereby circumvent the possibility that women might go off on their own.[25] On the other hand, tandems also encouraged young couples to canoodle about without parental supervision.

Few issues rankled the blood of white conservatives more than the status of marriage, which many felt was under attack in part because the bicycle redrew lines of traditional courtship and romantic encounter. The *Pneumatic*, for example, ran a story in the

Liesure cyclists Louis Harder, Henry Harder, Edward Schildhauer, and Annie Schildhaur rest on a short tour along Madison's Lake Mendota Drive, ca. 1898.

WHi Image ID 59895

summer of 1896 detailing how a Wausau judge blamed the slowdown in marriages that season on bicyclists. "Since these pesky bicycles have been rolling and slipping over the streets," the judge said, men and women have had no reason to marry. They routinely peddled away together at any time of the night or day for romantic get-togethers. "The young lady possessed of a wheel can never be found at home evenings," he went on. "I will tell you right here that the bicycle is a menace to marriageable young men."[26]

Women's embrace of the bicycle, however, changed the nature of the debate in key ways. In consistently insisting on greater mobility, women expanded the public conception of where it was possible—and acceptable—for women to operate in public. Their gains came alongside further racial restrictions in places like the Jim Crow South. Early mass magazines such as *Ladies' Home Journal*, *McClure's*, and *Cosmopolitan* were important in this effort, as they offered women not just advice and commentary but also practical information, including road maps of tourist destinations and historic landscapes. Such aids opened new possibilities for travel. As Maria Ward, the author of a women's bicycling text, put it in 1896,

> Riding the wheel, our own powers are revealed to us, a new sense is seemingly created. The unobserved are gradually awakened, and the keen observer is thrilled with quick and rare delight. . . . You have conquered a new world, and exultingly you take possession of it.

Her description reveals how the language of conquest and possession, so common in men's cycling circles, could justify new roles and opportunities for white women as well.[27]

Ward was one of a band of new women's writers who, like Frances Willard, helped broaden the call for reform by encouraging women to take up the bicycle. *Bicycling for Ladies* (1896) gave riders basic pointers on how to maintain their machines, dress comfortably and practically for riding, and handle flat tires, as well as some basic insights into the history of the sport. *Bicycling for Ladies* clearly embraced bicycling for women, opening with a chapter on "Possibilities" that charted not only the sport's physical benefits but also its connection with nature. Ward chronicled a long list of benefits offered by the bicycle, including better roads and greater mobility for women—an "absolute freedom" that only the cyclist could know. Ward also included a discussion on "women and tools." "I hold that any woman who is able to use a needle or scissors can use other tools equally well," she wrote, a clear affront to some of the gendered assumptions of the time, yet a positive challenge to women to take up practices they had been long excluded from.[28]

Wisconsin women also used LAW maps meant for men (and therefore not published in women's magazines) to broaden their understanding of the landscape. Christina Dando has examined how Wisconsin's LAW maps of 1896 helped initiate a broader understanding of the state's landscape which was then passed on to women, who adapted it to their unique needs. The maps, which distinguish between cycling roads and

Cyclists from Tomahawk are shown with their Kodak Brownie cameras. By the mid-1890s, cycling had become a leading leisure activity for women and was often coupled with photography to document scenes along a tour route.

WHi Image ID 98616

regular roads by their grades ("level," "hilly," "very hilly"), were also packaged alongside cycling advertisements, which became more inclusive as manufacturers and other producers learned to adapt their marketing to women. At the same time, as paved roads grew in number, male expertise over the local geography slowly gave way to the road map. Thus, women's embrace of the bicycle helped usurp in small but incremental ways the knowledge men exercised over the landscape of local towns, cities, and the countryside. Women came to understand more about their communities and how they might navigate them. This was a dramatic change for a society that so often understood mobile and independent women as prostitutes or tramps.[29]

As the safety bicycle's popularity soared in the United States and throughout Wisconsin with the help of so many women riders, the growing number of cyclists required a massive expansion of the bicycle manufacturing industry to keep up with demand. In Wisconsin, a relatively unestablished bicycle industry in the 1880s had become one of the state's fastest growing sectors by 1898, valued at what the state estimated to be nearly $1.9 million.[30] Milwaukee's wheelmen recognized this opportunity to expand their personal wealth by manufacturing or selling affordable models, components, and sundries to new cyclists. Joining the Andrae family in manufacturing were area wheelmen Parker H. Sercombe and Frank H. Bolte, who began manufacturing their Telegram brand bicycles in 1892.[31] Edward Roth, another key player on the Milwaukee wheelmen's scene, was later joined by Henry Kasten. Together they owned the Roth-Kasten Cycle Company, selling English-made bicycles and operating a sizeable repair facility.[32] Each year manufacturers routinely unveiled faster and lighter models of bicycles, exemplified by Milwaukee's Huseby Manufacturing Company's use of bamboo frames and Racine's Beebe Manufacturing Company's wooden frames.[33]

To keep the bicycles affordable and to maximize profits, manufacturers paid bicycle workers low wages and demanded long working hours, all the while bypassing factory safety and age requirements for its workforce. Just before the bicycle boom, Wisconsin had experienced a tragic period of confrontation between workers and employers. Following a financial panic in 1877, unionization escalated in Wisconsin as members of the Knights of Labor and Central Labor Union organized the Eight Hour League to fight for a shorter work week while maintaining their pay rate for ten-hour work days. Tensions had grown by the spring of 1886 as workers called for general strikes in major cities. In Milwaukee, demonstrations forced the closing of many shops, idling a large percentage of the workforce. The striking workers and their families paraded through Milwaukee to bolster support. Governor Jeremiah Rusk tried to regain control by mobilizing the National Guard, but on May 5 volunteer soldiers fired upon the strikers, killing and wounding several bystanders and marchers. Skilled workers reorganized in the new American Federation of Labor (AFL), but the Panic of 1893 delayed its organization and many unions disintegrated.[34] By the century's end, the state's new locals of the International Union of Bicycle Workers (IUBW) became active in the rejuvenated labor movement as the struggle for fair pay, shorter work hours, and improved factory safety remained unresolved.[35]

As in many industries in Wisconsin at the turn of the century, bicycle factories were organized by scientific management that used time and motion studies, microcosmic cost accounting, detailed job analyses, and micromotion techniques to maximize productivity and efficiency. Historian John Buenker has described scientific management "as a catchall term for measures designed to specialize and bureaucratize work and to centralize planning and decision making." In other words, production was divided among specialists who were each responsible for a single aspect of production.[36] According to wage scales for the IUBW, this meant skilled union men spent their work hours filing frames, operating drill presses, assembling wheels, cutting frame tubes, and making forks. Meanwhile, nonunion adult employees and young boys performed duties typical of unskilled workers in late nineteenth century plants, like fetching parts,

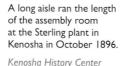

A long aisle ran the length of the assembly room at the Sterling plant in Kenosha in October 1896.

Kenosha History Center

hauling fuel, and assisting unionized men by holding tools or sweeping floors to keep work areas clean. Other young boys did intricate work such as polishing and basic installation of small parts.[37]

Regular inspection reports by Wisconsin's Bureau of Labor and Industrial Statistics provide important glimpses into the work performed at the state's bicycle plants. Men dominated the industry's labor force. At Julius Andrae and Sons in Milwaukee, for example, the workforce included 104 men and eleven boys under sixteen. The state's largest bicycle employers were Kenosha's Charles H. Steig Company, with a workforce of 260 men and twelve children under the age of sixteen, and A. D. Meiselbach, with 570 men and forty children under the age of sixteen.[38] However, most operations were much smaller. Huseby Manufacturing Company, Layton Park Manufacturing, League Cycle Works, Maxim Manufacturing, and Milwaukee Cycle Company all employed less than thirty men at a time. Only Maxim hired one woman.[39] The inspection reports also provide other important details about the work routines and pay in the state's bicycle plants. Since bicycling's popularity often depended on seasonal variations in the weather, manufacturing was primarily conducted in the months leading up to spring. Employment, therefore, was cyclical. By 1898, during the peak month of May, 1,067 people were employed at seven establishments. Starting in November of the prior year, factories nearly tripled their employment to produce the next year's models. During

These young boys, holding bicycle spokes, worked at the A. D. Meiselbach factory in North Milwaukee, ca. 1896. Manufacturers hired children to help assemble bicycles and haul parts through the factory.

Milwaukee County Historical Society

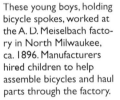

summer, after the peak sales season ended, factories would again collectively trim their workforce to a skeleton crew of just 297 people.[40]

Bicycle manufacturers also depended on child labor as an inexpensive workforce. In an 1898 and 1899 study of child labor in Wisconsin, three bicycle plants were inspected that together showed twenty-four children employed, averaging 14.3 years old. At the time, the legal working age was fourteen, and three children were identified beneath that limit.[41] Rarely were the manufacturers reprimanded for illegal hiring practices, but inspectors did force Julius Andrae and Sons to discharge four underage children.[42] Depending on the age, gender, or the protections offered by unionized status, workers were paid hourly, by the day, or by the piece, with most union men earning $7.00 to $20.00 per week while children earned, on average, $2.92 per week.[43] In this way, prominent wheelmen controlled yet another aspect of bicycling as they, in their capacity as industry leaders in the state, determined who would profit from the bicycle boom.

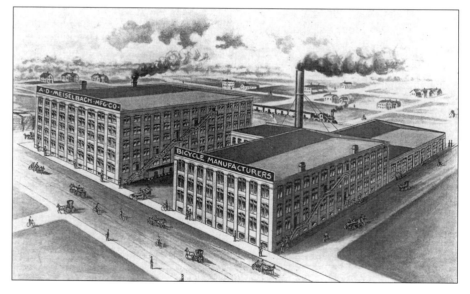

In the 1890s, A. D. Meiselbach was the largest bicycle manufacturer in Wisconsin. The company's enormous plant in North Milwaukee employed hundreds of workers and included a factory town for its employees.

Milwaukee: A Half Century's Progress, 1846–1896

Under these circumstances, some bicycle manufacturers prospered and expanded their operations to increase their profits. First located in Chicago, A. D. Meiselbach relocated to Milwaukee and renewed operations in 1895 at a small plant located on the corner of 19th and Saint Paul Avenue. Immediate orders for new bicycles flooded the business, requiring a hasty move into a larger plant in North Milwaukee. The new five-acre facility included a test track and two large, multistory brick buildings. Powered entirely by steam, the plant was fully equipped with modern machines to assemble frames and wheels. First staffed by 180 workers, continued demand enlarged the operation to over four hundred men and boys in just one year.[44] Despite the growth and success of companies like A. D. Meiselbach's, factory inspections indicated that many of these businesses placed workers in unsafe conditions as inspectors found a large number of violations. In Kenosha, for example, the Badger Brass Manufacturing Company, makers of acetylene bicycle lamps, was issued warnings to improve safety in most workrooms, reinstall doors to swing outward instead of inward for fear of fire entrapment, and install guards on machines. Inspections at the Charles

H. Steig Company turned up similar violations, requiring the owners to install guards and suction devices on buffing and polishing machines.[45]

Unsafe working conditions, low pay, and a general hostility between owners and employees forced bicycle workers to advocate for their rights. In Toledo, Ohio, the IUBW announced organized labor's formal entry into the bicycle industry. The union was formed on December 15, 1896. Wisconsin organized several local chapters of the IUBW during the height of the bicycle boom. These included Local 1 of Racine, Local 15 of Kenosha, and Local 300 of Milwaukee. When Racine's Local 1 formally organized in 1896, its Articles of Incorporation outlined the goals of the union: "To protect the interests and promote the local welfare of its members, and also for social, charitable, and benevolent purposes." Just three years later, union founders faced a difficult fight when they tried to expand their rights as workers.[46]

Bicycle Sundries

WISCONSIN'S BICYCLE BOOM created not only a sizable manufacturing base but also a demand for specialized components and accessories. Not every large firm made their own tires, tubes, and pedals, or specialty parts such as lamps, cyclometers, and repair kits. Sundries manufacturers filled this gap by providing inexpensive components and accessories. Typically these businesses were undersized, but they hired highly skilled artisans who wove baskets or sewed leather panniers as well as unskilled laborers, accounting for an estimated fifty thousand workers in the United States.[1] By 1897 purchasers could customize by selecting specific paint schemes, tires, and accessories.[2]

Using specialized repair kits, bicyclists became efficient at changing flat tires or fixing other basic damage.

Courtesy of Oshkosh Public Museum

Bicycle Sundries

Most of the sundry businesses in Wisconsin were clustered around the existing bicycle manufacturing centers in the state's southeast corner. A good example was the Brandt Weins Company of Milwaukee. Established in 1897, the company made braided-cane grips thought to be more comfortable and hygienic than rubber or cork. This small operation employed only four adult men and three teenagers, but the employees worked a grueling sixty-hour week to meet demand. Other accessory and parts companies in Milwaukee included Smith Manufacturing and Saveland Brothers, both of which crafted metal rims; Drake Manufacturing, which produced wooden rims; and adjustable handlebar manufacturers like Claus Manufacturing Company and Sanger Handle Bar and Plating Company. Most of the businesses started in the mid-1890s and altogether employed just over one hundred men, women, and teenagers.[3]

In Kenosha, the Badger Brass Manufacturing Company had a much larger operation and specialized in bicycle lamps. The company's first product was designed by Edward J. Williams and was awarded a patent on February 7, 1899. The brass lantern had a large glass magnifying lens illuminated by gaslight and sidelights that copied naval traditions with red on the "port" side and blue on the "starboard." Branded a "solar lamp,"

its glow came not from solar power but rather from acetylene gas formed by water dripping on carbide, which was then ignited with a match.[4] As one of the larger sundry companies, Badger Brass employed 150 men and 50 women (including twelve employees under sixteen) when the plant began production in 1898.[5] Poor employee relations soon hurt the factory's working conditions.

Badger Brass Manufacturing Company of Kenosha manufactured acetylene-powered "solar lamps."

Racine Heritage Museum, photo by John Urban

Bicycle Sundries

Its workers successfully unionized in 1898, but when the company underwent a difficult strike from 1907 to 1908, corporate leaders broke the unions and negotiated an open shop.[6] Although they adapted their lamps for automobiles and airplanes, expanding into nascent markets, the company never fully recovered, and the business was sold to Detroit's C. M. Hall Company in 1917.[7]

Bicycle shops were the primary sellers of sundries, but larger manufacturing companies also offered them in their annual catalogs. LAW-approved bicycle shops, such as William Groth in Appleton, D. H. Pollock Company in Beloit, and C. A. Krebaum in La Crosse all advertised sundries in the *Pneumatic*.[8] The Julius Andrae and Sons catalog for 1900 exhibited the wide variety of items available to bicyclists. Catalog subscribers could select from a variety of gas lamps ($2.00 to $3.50), bicycle bells ($.25 to $1.00), air pumps for pneumatic tires ($.25 to $5.00), toe clips ($.15 to $.50), cyclometers to track mileage ($.75 to $1.00), and bicycle locks ($.10 to $.50). The company also offered leather panniers ($1.25 to $1.50), handlebar or rear tire–mounted luggage carriers ($.25 to $2.00), and a frighteningly dangerous handlebar basket designed to carry picnics, luggage, or a small child ($.60). Cole's Baby Seat did not include a seat belt, but it did have a bottom door for the child's legs to hang free above the front wheel.[9]

The disparities and festering problems of the bicycle boom came to the forefront in the late 1890s when members of IUBW and affiliated unions worked to reverse unfair practices by manufacturers. Problems first arose in 1898 at the Charles H. Steig Company in Kenosha when Steig fired two polishers without consulting the union. Steig refused to reinstate the men, causing members of Local 45 to strike to support their brethren. The State Board of Arbitration intervened and, with the two parties, found that wage troubles were the root cause. Steig, IUBW Local 15, and Local 45 agreed to raise the pay scales and reinstate the men.[47] In a similar case in Kenosha, the Board of Arbitration intervened in a labor dispute between the Badger Brass Manufacturing Company and members of the International Polishers and Brass Workers Union, who averaged $2.28 per day for piecework. Union members noted that in some instances the price paid for piecework was too low, while managers argued the wages were fair and had been agreed to by the union and management. The company tried to break the union and threatened to hire nonunion workers to replace the striking union men, and both parties quit the arbitration meeting without an agreement.[48]

With new labor representation, skilled workers at unionized plants now had the opportunity to collectively negotiate working conditions and provide a voice for grievances. One such negotiation, centered around a wage dispute, took place between the IUBW and Beebe Manufacturing Company. On March 28, 1899, representatives from the IUBW and Beebe agreed to a new wage scale for filing and grinding bicycle wheel frames, including a promise by Beebe to relieve replacement workers and bring back all striking men. Negotiated by union president Mulholland and Charles G. Beebe, the new wage agreement was signed and witnessed by the Board of Arbitration.[49] The agreement didn't stick. One month later, claiming conditions had worsened, 125 union men walked off the job. Most of the unionized workers were allowed to return to work, but Beebe kept a few nonunion men on the workforce, to the great frustration of the union. The IUBW demanded that the remaining nonunion men be let go, but Beebe continued to refuse. Police were soon called in to separate the picket line from the replacement workers.[50] In May, according to the *Racine Daily Journal*, the situation intensified when a nonunion man who refused to leave his position was followed home and beaten by a group of union men, led by union employee John Seidel.[51] Although settlement seemed possible after Beebe sold the company, an agreement was never reached under the new ownership by the Wisconsin Wheelworks, and the factory was destroyed in a fire on June 8, 1900. Its demise foreshadowed the dark times ahead for Wisconsin's bicycle manufacturing.[52]

Beebe Manufacturing Company specialized in bicycles with frames made entirely of wood. Unlike many bicycle plants, the factory had a workforce of carpenters to help manufacture the machines, including this model, ca. 1898.

Racine Heritage Museum, photo by John Urban

Bicycle workers at A. D.
Meiselbach posed with
partially assembled safety
bicycles outside their plant in
North Milwaukee, ca. 1896.

*Milwaukee County
Historical Society*

An oversaturated market, poor management, and volatile labor conditions were too much to overcome for Wisconsin's bicycle-manufacturing industry. From 1898 to 1899, the state industry lost over 526 jobs and production declined by $404,896.[53] Starter companies and established companies folded, including Badger Bicycle Company, Bamboo Bicycle Company, Bolte Cycle Manufacturing, Chief Cycle Company, Cream City Cycle Company, and Milwaukee Bicycle Company. The 1890s proved a volatile time for the industry: over its span hundreds of enterprises gained a foothold and generated incredible profits, until the industry virtually collapsed.[54] Only a few companies, like Badger Brass Manufacturing Company and Julius Andrae and Sons, continued production in the twentieth century, in large thanks to their diverse business interests. Both companies relied on manufacturing new technologies to outlast the short bicycle boom, manufacturing automobile lamps and telephones, respectively; both were able to keep a foothold in the industry into the new century.[55]

One strike in 1896 raised discord within the bicycling community and helps illustrate how the state's economy was enmeshed with the bicycling boom during the decade. Hoping to capitalize on the greater mobility bicycles offered employees, Milwaukee's Postal Telegraph Company (like the *Milwaukee Sentinel* and other area businesses) outfitted its messengers with bicycles in the summer of 1895 in order to guarantee faster and more reliable delivery. A year later, in December 1896, with wintry conditions

Employees at Curtis and Yale, makers of window and door sashes, blinds, and molding, used bicycles for transportation to work at their Wausau plant, ca. 1895.

WHi Image ID 77957

settling in over the city's downtown, one of the employees refused to ride his bicycle through the ice and slush. This employee, the *Pneumatic* noted, was "summarily dismissed," but in solidarity, twelve of the twenty employees at the firm "walked out." For two hours, the employees waged a strike and demonstrated their grievances at the corner of East Water and Michigan Streets, just outside the company's headquarters. With news of the strike spreading quickly, other employees of the firm joined the picket line. According to the *Pneumatic*, the company then called the police to restore order. After several hours, management agreed not to force employees to ride their bikes in dangerous wintry conditions.[56]

DESPITE these examples of labor unrest, it was clear that wheel fever was at hand throughout Wisconsin. The late-century pattern of boom and bust hit every corner of the state, opening means of access to new riders who responded with enthusiasm. In

Oshkosh, where the bike boom hit most dramatically in 1895, a reporter from the *Daily Northwestern* estimated that the local bicycling population would grow to two thousand riders by year's end. New technological improvements in bicycles and sharp competition between manufacturers forced prices down, making the bike widely available in Wisconsin's rural and small-town communities. Chicago's big bicycle manufacturers, including Monarch, Sterling, and Ames and Frost, who all sold in Oshkosh, fell behind by several months on their orders and were unable to meet the growing demand. The *Daily Northwestern* noted, "Seldom has any department of human industry taken on such proportions in so short a time as has the bicycle industry of this country." In every area of the state, the boom was keenly felt.[57]

As a microcosm of the broader change sweeping the country, Oshkosh shows how the boom played out locally. During the 1890s, the city had over thirty bicycle dealers, including "curbstone dealers" and "vest pocket" agents who handled a single model by one company. Bicycle sales reached three to four hundred per dealer during the spring of 1895, with high-end models from the prior year priced at discount, around $70 to $75 each. New bicycles could cost riders $85 to $100, but the most popular model was a basic roadster for just $50. "Lady riders," according to the *Daily Northwestern*, "buy [lower priced models] in large numbers and workingmen and the ordinary citizens find them within reach of their means when they feel able to buy at all." The less expensive models were heavier and available with a 26- or 28-inch tire. Bicycles were often sold on installment plans to make them more affordable, but the real savings were from curbstone dealers, who "hustled" for their sales. Slowly but surely, the bike transitioned from a "rich man's carriage" to something very much like a "poor man's horse."[58]

As the bicycle became more widely available with the boom, a conservative backlash developed in the late 1890s that ultimately helped bring the boom to an end. It again took the shape of earlier sexist, class-based, and racist appeals. Over the years of the boom, expanded access to cycling had continued to disturb many of the state's residents. In particular, the popularity of cycling among educated and middle- to upper-class women, with its ties to reformers like Willard, did not sit well with white male conservatives. In a long article decrying the presence of the "reckless" bicycle girl, whom editors suspected hailed from Chicago and "invaded" Milwaukee purely for the pleasure of showing off to men, columnists at the *Milwaukee Sentinel* lashed out. "There is the Chicago bicycle girl," the article complained, "who comes here in whole droves and betakes herself to the avenues and boulevards for a two hours' spin." Playing up the illicit sexuality these young women apparently showcased, *Milwaukee Sentinel* editors wrote, "It isn't that her skirt is always short . . . or her handlebars too low—one occasionally sees all these things in the morning, when the Chicago excursionists are not supposed to be here"—but it was her "rakish air" and level of "assurance" that set her apart from the rest of the riders in the city. In fact, the article said, "It isn't that

Women of all ages began using the bicycle for daily riding. As this woman may have discovered, ca. 1900, learning to ride a bicycle is a timeless activity filled with many bruises.

WHi Image ID 56090

their costumes are so striking. As a rule the Chicago bicycle togs that come up . . . are more noticeable for shabbiness and symptoms of hard usage than anything else." Yet "usually in those cases her cheeks are excessively pink, and her eyebrows suspiciously dark, and she doesn't mind the stares of the men on the sidewalk in the least."[59] From these and other accounts, it is clear that women bicyclists introduced a number of uncomfortable tensions for late 1890s riders, and unfortunately many of these tensions encouraged sexist characterizations that made any woman who wanted to ride a bicycle open to male suspicion, derision, and temptation. In this way, the gains of the bicycle boom were slowly undermined as men in the late 1890s closed the doors on the sport.

It is difficult to say what black men thought of all these new women riders in Wisconsin's streets, but Wisconsin's black newspapers were often more receptive and encouraging of the female and working-class presence in cycling. Still, black enthusiasm alone could not stop the backlash. Milwaukee's *Wisconsin Weekly Advocate* noted that "most housemaids ride the bicycle nowadays, and it is the bicycle skirt that these wear during working hours. . . . Skirts, however, would never have been shortened had not the smart women first set the pace."[60] Another article offered women advice on what to wear while cycling in ways that actually welcomed female innovation in cycling clothing. "Quite the prettiest wheeling costume is the divided skirt, which falls so close together that no one knows whether it is an all-around skirt or the bifurcated one."[61] Women "must relieve the monotony of her duties," another black newspaper article asserted, "by taking outdoor exercises—a walk every day, or a spin on a bicycle."[62] Other black commentators, however, were not always as sure. "When a man's wife and daughter have wheels in their heads," the *Illinois Record* speculated, "it is a bicycle, a pair of blooms, and short skirts that they want. What, oh what, will become of the new woman?"[63]

Where Wisconsin's blacks shared some of the enthusiasm and anxiety expressed by the state's whites, other elements of the cycling culture were certainly not shared. As coverage in Milwaukee's black *Wisconsin Weekly Advocate* made clear, white enthusiasm for the war with Spain in the summer of 1898 reached a crescendo. Black observers met the displays with a characteristic ambivalence, using the patriotic displays of white

Young male cyclists gathered in Madison for a tour in 1897. One member of the 13 Club can be seen wearing his skull-and-crossbones jersey.

WHi Image ID 98615

men as chance to mock white performances of excessive masculinity and patriotism. Fond of taking to the streets with manly chest thumping and flag waving, whites of all classes, black observers noted, sometimes literally fell on their faces. "Those noisy and loud-shouting men," the *Advocate* noted, "talking about wiping Spain out and somebody's bicycle tire happened to explode in their midst." Sounding a bit too much like actual gunfire, the explosion threw the frightened riders to the ground. It exposed white vulnerability in a way that undermined the militaristic displays.[64]

America's war with Spain in 1898 marked the beginning of the end for bicycling's first great national boom. Black newspapers were some of the first locally to comment on how radically the culture had transitioned. One of the first signs was how quickly bicycle clothing fell out of fashion, yielding to more masculine and western-themed designs. "The sombrero of the Western plains is all the fashion in New York," the *Advocate* noted. "It is the favorite outing hat of the Fifth avenue girl, and also of her brother, whether he has gone off to the war with Colonel Theodore Roosevelt's band of rough

riders or whether he plans to be among the chosen few at the summer resorts." The "bicycle hat" was said to be losing its popularity to the "cowboy" spirit.[65] American manhood looked for something more rugged, more patently competitive as it eyed the new American century. At such a time, wheel fever—now marked by a tangible female presence—could not endure.

CHAPTER 8

Walter Sanger, Major Taylor, and Professional Racing at the End of the Boom

Call: "Who wears the wooden shoes?"
Response: "Wallie-e-e"

—Race day chant by Walter Sanger's fans[1]

As historian Gail Bederman has observed, the late 1880s and 1890s saw a transition in men's sporting culture away from notions of "refined" and "civilized" manhood and toward more competitive and aggressive sports such as prize fighting, baseball, and professional bicycle racing.[2] Though not considered mass entertainment today, racing was one of the most popular and influential sports at the turn of the twentieth century. Thousands filled the grandstands at major events across the country, and newspapers carried race results alongside box scores. In some ways, the accessibility of cycling meant the sport was more popular than other early professional sports. Yet racing itself was a sport for individual competition. Much of its appeal, in fact, came from individual racers. Bike racing offered the aggressive, head-to-head sporting and bravado Americans were beginning to like. Racers abandoned the long frock coats and tweed jackets common in the early boom. In their place came tight uniforms, long bare legs, and exposed arms that showcased the raw masculinity of the racers. They were fast, their competitions were fierce, and their fans were ravenous.

In an era of intense nationalism, rampant white supremacy, and profound economic and labor inequalities, bicycle racers helped fashion a new kind of mass culture where professional sports and the men who participated in them became a crucial outlet. This turn helped entrench sporting culture as a preeminent feature of Wisconsin's cultural landscape, even as most early bicyclers have since been long forgotten. The lightning speed and power of these racers seized the popular imagination, and Wisconsin men were often at the forefront. One racer in particular, Milwaukee's Walter C. Sanger, became one of the era's most important sports personalities. His life and times reflect enduring lessons about the role of bicycling in Wisconsin. Long forgotten, few have situated the story of this once-legendary Wisconsin racer within his broader social context. His story, along with the stories of other key racers of the time, especially Marshall "Major" Taylor, illuminates the complexity and meaning of the racing culture in Wisconsin during the last years of the boom.

Walter Sanger grew up in a world where bicycles were both ubiquitous and prized. Born on March 13, 1873, in Milwaukee, he was influenced early on by his father, Casper Sanger, who trained and broke racing horses on his farm in Waukesha. Early in his amateur career, the younger Sanger was often seen riding his bicycle on dirt tracks, pacing his father's animals. Sanger became interested in bicycling as a sport around 1890, just as it was beginning to take hold in Wisconsin. Bicycling was the perfect sport for Sanger.

Printed by the Detroit Lithograph Company in 1895, this scene captures the colors, physical effort, and excitement of a race during the bicycle boom.

Library of Congress, Prints & Photographs Division, LC-DIG-ppmsca-08935

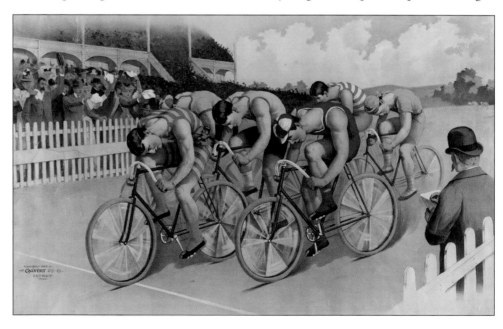

WALTER SANGER.   820 491/1

Known for his "Herculean" figure, Milwaukee's Walter Sanger emerged as one of the greatest cyclists of the bicycle boom in the 1890s.

Milwaukee County Historical Society

Sanger's famous pedal-less finish in the Pullman Race in 1892 earned him notoriety as a fierce competitor and respect from his opponents. The cartoonist predicted a similar finish later in Sanger's career at London's Herne Hill.

Pneumatic, vol. 5, no. 2, 1894

He needed just a small amount of disposable income to purchase a bike, and southeastern Wisconsin's streets offered plenty of chances for him to hone his abilities. Described as having "the build of Hercules," Sanger's physical style of racing and muscular physique put him above other racers. In 1890, he became acquainted with Julius, Henry, and Terry Andrae, who recruited him to become a member of the Milwaukee Wheelmen.[3]

A series of stunning performances in 1891 boosted Sanger onto the cycling scene, and his reputation grew quickly. At the Wisconsin State Fair, in Sanger's first major amateur competition, he swept all four races and set a respectable time of 2:34:30 in the one mile. Sanger further established a reputation as an elite contender during Chicago's Pullman Race in 1892, where his dramatic finish made him a household name. The Pullman Race featured over three hundred of the best riders in the United States, and Sanger was poised to finish strong when his left pedal fell off. Only ten riders were ahead of him at the time, and many of them had been given generous handicaps at the start. Sanger was ready to overtake them and sail to victory had his machine stayed together. After pounding the pedal back on with a brick, he resumed the race only to have it fall off again. Despite the setback, Sanger finished with just one pedal, a feat that helped spread his name through the cycling community.[4] Sportswriters were soon hailing him as one of the preeminent racing prospects in the world.[5]

Sanger's rise occurred so quickly that even foreign reporters were taking notice of the young phenom by 1892. "A rider of whom great things are expected during the cycling year is the young western phenomenon, Walter C. Sanger," the Canadian *Victoria Daily Colonist* wrote in May. "Sanger . . . is a powerfully built young fellow, standing 5 ft. 11 and a half inches, and weighing in the neighborhood of 185 pounds."

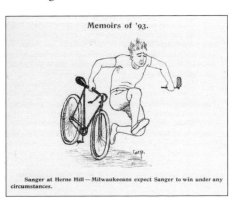

Memoirs of '93.

Sanger at Herne Hill — Milwaukeeans expect Sanger to win under any circumstances.

The report also mentioned that Sanger had finished a close second to his early mentor, Terry Andrae, in races throughout 1891.[6] Sanger's successes effectively supplanted Andrae, icon of the famous Milwaukee-based Julius Andrae and Sons manufacturing company and known to fans as "the Flying Badger." Born on December 5, 1868, in Milwaukee, Andrae stood as tall as Sanger but weighed only 160 pounds.[7] Sanger was

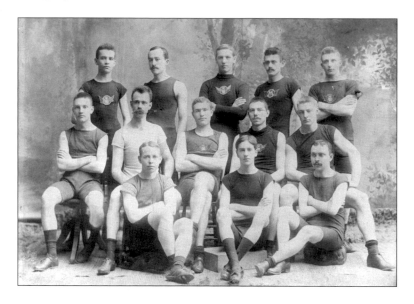

The Milwaukee Push was the most decorated amateur cycling team in the state, featuring such great athletes as Walter Sanger (middle row, far right) and Terry Andrae (seated next to Sanger).

Milwaukee County Historical Society

younger, bigger, and stronger when he arrived on the scene in 1891.

As an amateur, Sanger competed against a wide range of racing's elite professionals. Many of his early victories came close to home, where he knocked off a number of the top names of his day. The year 1892 was particularly momentous. In addition to his legendary performance in the Pullman Race, Sanger appeared at the Exposition Bicycle Tournament in Milwaukee. Organized by the Milwaukee Wheelmen, the tournament gathered amateur and professional racers from Wisconsin and Illinois for three days of competition at the Exposition Building. A large wooden track with banked corners was built in the main hall and surrounded by spectator seating.[8] Although many talented racers were scheduled to compete, including New Jersey's Arthur Zimmerman, the main rivalry centered on the Milwaukee Wheelmen's elite racing team, known as the Milwaukee Push, and the Chicago Cycling Club. The rivalry filled the pages of area bicycling magazines. In their hometown bicycling paper, the *Pneumatic*, the Milwaukee Wheelmen blamed Chicago's team for poor sportsmanship and having falsely disqualified Milwaukee riders in meets during the preceding year.[9]

The Milwaukee tournament suffered a major setback in the early stages of its planning, however. After organizers printed programs featuring photographs and names of the registered elite racers, all of the eastern competitors backed out, citing fears that the event would not be able to pay the award monies it had promised. As a result, the event centered on Sanger and Chicago's Herbert A. Githens, helping to further boost Sanger's young reputation. The event got off to a slow start. On the first day, Sanger and Githens traded wins as each crashed at crucial moments, enabling the other to cruise to easy victory. By the second night, the rivalry finally produced some great races. In the ten-mile event, Githens trailed Sanger for eight laps. But in the final two laps, he passed Sanger and sprinted to the finish, where he was raised up on his teammates' shoulders. On the final day, however, an undaunted Sanger regained his composure and defeated Githens in all three races. In the handicap events, the other members of the Milwaukee Push—including Walter's brother William F. Sanger—all performed well. Despite the intense rivalry that had flared before the tournament, cooler heads ultimately prevailed, and by all accounts the friendship between the Milwaukee and Chicago riders was reestablished, largely because of the fair treatment the Chicago Cycling Club re-

Even amateur cyclists competed for lavish prizes. This medal was awarded to University of Wisconsin student Byron Dixon Paine for a road race victory on May 16, 1891.

WHS Museum 1972.43.2,a, photo by Joel Heiman

Spectators packed the grandstands at the state meet in Oshkosh in 1892. Decked out in their club uniforms, the wheelmen cheered for their local heroes in the amateur competitions.

Courtesy of Oshkosh Public Museum

ceived.[10] Still, both clubs were stung by the decision of the eastern riders to back out of the event.

By the time Sanger appeared on the professional and amateur circuits in Wisconsin, the LAW had become primarily an activist and fraternal organization, but its efforts still included organizing a professional racing circuit. The league helped boost Sanger's celebrity: the racer made a name for himself by competing in league-sponsored races like the rematch event at the state meet in Oshkosh in early July 1892. Hungry for a chance to redeem itself against the Milwaukee Push, the Chicago Cycling Club came north to seek revenge just weeks after their Exposition defeat. Both teams also deepened their rosters in the lead-up to the race, sending their full delegations to the event, including "cracks" (a slang term for racers) and "cranks" (their boisterous fans) from around the region. The Milwaukee Push even chartered its own private train to the event, complete with two baggage cars. One carried the personal items of the racers, including bicycles, while the other carried the racers themselves, along with selected friends and family. Hoping to play host in the grandest style, Oshkosh built the state's first major racing facility on the grounds of the existing ballpark, creating a quarter-mile track without banks. It became the first track in Wisconsin state history built exclusively to suit bicycling events.[11]

Whipped into a frenzy by the coming contest, a great throng descended upon Oshkosh, turning the city into a veritable bicycling haven. Hundreds of riders from all over the state poured into town, alighting at the train depot, where they unloaded their bikes and rode to the event grounds. Milwaukee's contingent was the largest of

WM. F. SANGOR   820 491/1

Walter Sanger's brother William was also a successful racer and amassed his own sponsorships and prizes in the 1890s.

Milwaukee County Historical Society

all. Men, marking a shift from years before when women and children cyclists were also common attendees at events, filled virtually every inbound train. Streetcars and hotels were decorated with banners and flags of the LAW, lending the downtown an air of festivity. The wheelmen, in characteristic gentlemanly style, held a parade, riding four abreast as they toured the city, which the *Oshkosh Weekly Northwestern* called, rather demurely, a "pretty and interesting sight." The enthusiasm for the races made it clear what the real attraction would be in the coming days.[12] Walter entered the quarter-mile dash, one-half mile, one-mile handicap, three mile, and five mile handicap while his brother William also signed up for several events. Winning prizes of a new bicycle suit, opera glasses, and medals from the L.A.W., Sanger won every race except for the one-mile handicap, finishing second to Ripon's Lou Reed.[13]

Wheelmen events often showcased the growing chasm between old-guard bicyclists who saw the machine as a tool of refined leisure and touring and the new generation of "scorchers" who idolized the brute force of racing. The pleasant weather that blessed the Oshkosh event made these growing tensions more pronounced. On the event's last day, the *Oshkosh Daily Northwestern* reported, "Dame nature was again kind to the bicyclists," with riders circling around the town during the cool mornings and the sound of bicycle bells echoing off downtown storefronts. When the sun rose high and warm over the city by afternoon, however, the more measured wheelmen abandoned their bikes and went instead for a ride on Lake Winnebago aboard the steamer *O. B. Reed*. After touring the lake in their formal uniforms and badges and taking in the warm summer sun, the wheelmen left the boat and again hopped on their bikes, this time taking themselves to the track to watch the racers. Sanger won or was competitive in every race he entered. When the sun went down, riders, their friends, family, and assembled onlookers gathered back at the Athearn Hotel, where bands played long into the night as men in jaunty wheelmen uniforms strutted about.[14] The celebrity of the racers would eventually make wheelmen parades and tours a kind of sideshow to the racetrack, but at this event at the height of the boom, good weather and a celebratory atmosphere enabled the kind of showy pomp the wheelmen cherished.

Wisconsin's Racetracks

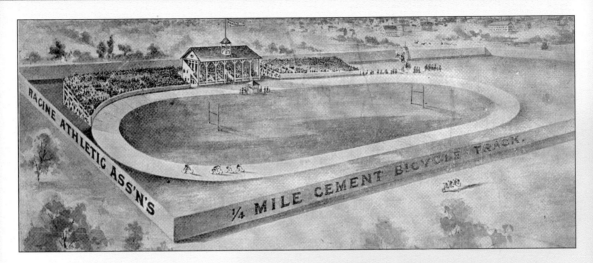

Racine's new velodrome was constructed in preparation for a national circuit and state meet in 1897. The new track offered the finest luxuries for race participants and spectators, as well as a modern cement-banked track.

WHi Image ID 98613

THE RAPID GROWTH and popularity of bicycle racing required an infrastructure of racing venues that would promote competitions and provide a good experience for spectators. Although Wisconsin's racetracks hardly compared to hallowed places like England's Herne Hill Velodrome, the tracks still helped set world records, drew thousands of spectators, and hosted the world-class athletes.

Wisconsin's first bicycle races took place indoors during the spring of 1869. In Milwaukee, spectators watched races inside the Milwaukee Skating Rink, which had been converted to a velocipedrome. Historical evidence suggests the rink remained mostly unaltered, and the amateur riders simply raced for a half mile along the outer edge of the rink while fans stood alongside barriers or on bleachers.[1] Many of the smaller velocipede rinks held similar competitions throughout Wisconsin, but untrained riders and makeshift designs made the venues dangerous.

Indoor races continued to be popular, but few cities had large enough buildings to host spectators and contain a banked track with pitched corners that allowed faster speeds. In Milwaukee, the ideal venue was the enormous Milwaukee Industrial Exposition Building. Twenty-five-year-old A. Martin Patitz, who was employed as a draughts-

Wisconsin's Racetracks

man and designer for the Chicago, Milwaukee, and Saint Paul Railway, designed the track and superintended its construction for a major meet in 1892.[2] Made entirely of wooden boards, the banked track had seating for several thousands. A large fountain completed the center oval.[3] Patitz's design proved successful, and he was later hired to build a similar track for the Minneapolis Track Association.[4]

By 1890, Wisconsin had only a few dedicated racetracks for bicycles; most early meets were held at city or county fairgrounds. State Racing Chairman Irvin F. Strauss described the ideal racetrack for meets as having a half-mile length (or slightly shorter), as long as the surface and turns were safe.[5] Unfortunately, few tracks complied with his standards. Photographic evidence shows that many brought considerable challenges to amateurs and professionals alike. Most of the tracks were primarily used for horse racing and thus made of bare dirt, cinder, or gravel. In some cases, dirt tracks were not even groomed before a meet, as was the case for an amateur women's race in Langlade County.[6] Heavy rainfall the week of a race could damage a track and even cancel the event.

After 1890, Wisconsin underwent a brief surge in the construction of racetracks as the sport's popularity burgeoned. In Oshkosh, local LAW members raised funds and improved a bicycle track at the city's baseball grounds with the intent of holding regular meets.[7] Madison residents looking for a home for area track races purchased the old state fairgrounds at Camp Randall and, under the auspices of the Madison Cycling Club, converted the half-mile horse track into one for bicycles.[8] For Ripon's state meet in 1893, local cycling clubs built a new racetrack described as "the finest regulation half-mile track in the state." With "excellent stretches" and "perfect turns," the large track allowed for twelve riders and a ninety-six-foot-tall grandstand.[9] Tracks became larger and more elaborate, with a track in Neenah even adding luxuries like dressing rooms for riders.[10] By the summer of 1894, tracks went up in Mount Horeb, Weyauwega, and Wausau.[11]

Creating the ideal track required constant upgrades, and cycling clubs annually improved their facilities or built new ones. For the 1896 state meet in Appleton, local wheelmen added banked corners to their dual-use cinder track at the City Fair and Driving Park. An estimated ten thousand people attended the meet, overwhelming the track's large grandstands.[12] In Milwaukee, the primary racing venue was at National Park, where Walter Sanger earned early accolades, but the track failed to meet the expectations of spectators and racers. Despite its place at the center of Wisconsin's bicycling activities,

Wisconsin's Racetracks

the city lacked an adequate race site until 1898, when local wheelmen built a new athletic field with a dedicated bicycle racetrack in preparation for the LAW's national meet two years later.[13]

Wisconsin lacked a modern outdoor velodrome for cycling until a competition to host the 1897 state meet between Green Bay and Racine forced its construction. To secure the nomination, Racine's prominent businessmen and wheelmen promised the construction of a new athletic park with a fully modern banked track made of cement.[14] Racine hired C. E. Hawley of New York, who had recently designed the elite Manhattan Beach Track, to create a new sports complex for bicycling, baseball, tennis, and football.[15] A recent development in the sport, velodromes set a new standard in bicycle racing as they produced faster races and made for a more exciting experience.

Finished in time for the meet, the new Racine Athletic Grounds had a cement "four-lap" quarter-mile track, with each circle banked at 136 degrees. A grandstand of 144 feet by 43 feet held 1,200 spectators, and two additional bleachers provided seating for 2,200 people. Dressing and bathing rooms, as well as lighting for evening races, completed the facility.[16] The modern track brought additional accolades when the meet was designated part of the LAW National Circuit. Held on July 1–3, races on the velodrome tied one world record when Detroit's Thomas Cooper won the half-mile professional in 1:00 4-5 (one minute, 4/5 of a second).[17] After racing's popularity declined, few of the racetracks continued to be solely dedicated to the sport and instead survived into the twentieth century as multiuse tracks or part of a fairground.

Racine's velodrome became the top racing facility in Wisconsin and attracted professional cyclists on the national circuit. Built in 1897, the facility had electric lighted grandstands and a banked cement track.

WHi Image ID 98614

After several days of thrilling races at the state meet in Oshkosh in 1892, wheelmen boarded the *O. B. Reed* for music, dancing, and a moonlit cruise on Lake Winnebago.

Courtesy of Oshkosh Public Museum

Sanger also earned the nickname "Wooden Shoes" during his breakout season in 1892. At the North Side Cycling Club meets in Milwaukee, Gerhard Aussem often worked as the race starter. Aussem had a strong German accent. In an interview long after his retirement from racing, Sanger noted that "[Aussem] has always had trouble getting the sauerkraut out of his language," and visiting riders would often laugh at his English mispronunciations. Soon after the meet, Sanger's ancestry, along with Gerhard's thick accent, Milwaukee's strong German identity, and the European practice of wearing wooden clogs for farming, seemed to provide sportswriters and rivals with a nickname to mock Sanger's old world connections.[15] A *New York Times* article about nicknames of crack riders confirmed that Sanger "could never deny his ancestry" and as a "big, husky German," the nickname fitted him well. Ethnicities were often used to define the nicknames of riders. Sanger's contemporaries included John "the Terrible Swede" Lawson and later Marshall "Major" Taylor, a black racer who was also known as "the Colored Wonder."[16] Outside Milwaukee, "Wooden Shoes" often appeared in race summaries and updates about the LAW race circuit. Eventually, after numerous victories on the track, Walter and his supporters embraced the name.

Sanger's name also attracted the attention of local bicycling manufacturers and the professional racing circuit. To celebrate Sanger's numerous victories in 1892 and the

Walter Sanger's new sponsorship from Sercombe-Bolte Manufacturing Company in September 1892 put his name on advertisements and even a new model called the "Sanger Racer."

Pneumatic, vol. 5, no. 9, 1894

prominence he brought the Milwaukee Push, the club held a banquet in his honor in late October.[17] Unknown to the Milwaukee Wheelmen, Sanger was already in private conversations to join a new local team sponsored by the Sercombe-Bolte Manufacturing Company, the maker of the Telegram brand of bicycles. The relationship began when the company lured Casper Sanger to purchase stock and soon after elected him president of the company.[18] The mid-December announcement of Sanger's resignation caught his Milwaukee Push teammates by complete surprise.[19] By joining the Telegram Bicycle Club and receiving an official sponsorship from Sercombe-Bolte, Sanger joined the ranks of professional racers. He would soon travel the United States and Europe competing against the world's best. In return, Telegram provided Sanger with a personal trainer, Richard Fails, who advised Sanger to withhold training during the winter. An entertaining personality, Fails was described as a man who "can rub his man down to the pink of condition, speak in tongue refined at a banquet, dance a jig and hold his own in a scrap."[20]

Sanger's celebrity status grew as the company used his likeness in advertisements and unveiled a special Telegram Sanger Racer that, for a time, became Sanger's bike of choice at meets. Sensing the appeal that Sanger's name would bring to their products, the company also made a commercial variety that everyday Wisconsinites could buy. At twenty-four to twenty-six pounds and made special to order, the Sanger Racer was the "King of Telegram Bicycles." It was also around this time that Sanger earned the nickname "The Pride of Milwaukee."[21] Sanger stood poised to become an international champion. But little did he know his young career was about to enter a period of dramatic highs and lows.

Arthur "the Jersey Skeeter" Zimmerman was considered the greatest cyclist among Sanger's contemporaries. They competed against each other in Europe in 1893. Zimmerman often raced in Wisconsin—he even swept races at an 1893 meet in Milwaukee, where he was notably heckled by the Milwaukee cranks.

Milwaukee County Historical Society

EARLY in 1893, Sanger left Wisconsin to train in Massachusetts. He would enjoy higher visibility, larger crowds, increased sponsorship dollars, and greater access to world-class cycling venues from the East Coast. With Fails by his side, Sanger started a new training regimen, "where for three weeks strict training will be the order of the day," even as many of the top racers and Wheelmen clubs in the country headed instead for Chicago to take part in the World's Fair.[22] His strict discipline paid off, however, as he won a number of races and set records that summer in Europe, including "two great victories at Brussels" in May against the world's top competitors.[23] A month later, still in Europe, Sanger won more races, including the "much coveted honor" of the blue ribbon at the English championship races on June 10 at Herne Hill in London.[24] Following these stunning victories, he returned to the United States, where his team needed him for more events. He left Europe with Arthur Zimmerman, arguably the most famous and successful US racer who had also taken part in several international cycling events held that summer.[25] Sanger's departure in June forced him to cancel an appearance before the Glasgow Celtic Club, a decision that "was a great disappointment to the club wheelmen."[26] Sanger's star power was soaring.

Fresh from his victories in Europe, Sanger received a hearty welcome home to Milwaukee on July 28, 1893. "A big parade of wheelmen" was followed by a reception at the Telegram clubhouse. There Sanger greeted the immense crowd of fans who had turned out to show their support and voice their admiration. Political dignitaries, including Wisconsin governor George Wilbur Peck and a representative of Milwaukee mayor John C. Koch, also made speeches. In a telling departure from the refinement characteristic of clubhouses in the late 1880s, a large and garish portrait of Sanger atop a high-wheel bicycle was hung in one of the building's large formal parlors.[27]

The world of professional racing could be a volatile place, however. Not long after this celebrated return to Wisconsin, Sanger's fortunes took a turn for the worse. In August, just one month after being welcomed with open arms as a state hero, Sanger was expelled from the Telegram Bicycling Club. On August 22, club leaders advanced a resolution banning the racer because he had refused to compete in an event that the club had supported with advertising dollars. Sanger complained that he was not in the proper condition to race and that the track had four turns—a different configuration than what he was used to. According to the *Oshkosh Daily Northwestern*, Sanger probably did not help his cause when he called the track "fit for only school boys to ride

Each year, a large group of professional racers toured the United States on the national circuit, shown here in Detroit in 1893. Walter Sanger is shown seated crossed legged in the front row (sixth from the left).

Bearings, vol. 8, no. 2, 1893

upon." Real men rode on real tracks, he pleaded. Nevertheless, several of Sanger's rivals did compete. When Sanger's father went to the club to defend the honor of his son, he saw that Walter's picture had been turned upside down and faced toward the wall of the meetinghouse.[28]

Troubles continued in the fall of 1893. After a poor showing at a Chicago race, Sanger returned home to Milwaukee and told reporters that "a trainer should be in perfect harmony with the man he handles," and Sanger apparently concluded he and his new trainer, C.R. Culver, were no longer a good team. Then, in November, Sanger was working on a windmill at his father's farm in Waukesha when he fell and was punctured through the groin by a nail. He assured reporters that he would be fine, and that in the coming season he would return stronger than ever. Rumors persisted nonetheless, and some wondered if he would gain weight with the injury keeping him from training. "All this talk about my gaining flesh rapidly is all bosh," he said. He seemed confident about his abilities to get back into shape as the year 1894 opened.[29]

With the warming weather of spring and early summer, Sanger left Wisconsin to escape his distractions and pursue stiffer competition on the East Coast. In July, he joined the Springfield Cycling Club of Massachusetts, where he dominated the racing scene just as he had predicted. On July 17, at the Waltham Bicycle Park, Sanger tried for a mile record without pacemakers (riders who would pedal alongside the competitors to help them measure their pace) and with a flying start. The existing record was set in France at 2:16. Poor winds forced the trial to be delayed until the afternoon, but at 5:00 p.m. Sanger decided to go ahead. Facing a stiff wind, he burst onto the track, setting records in every fraction of the mile. The *New York Times* trumpeted his new records: at the quarter mile, 0:29; at a third of a mile, 0:40; at a half-mile, 1:01; at two-thirds, 1:24; at three-fourths, 1:35; and at the mile, 2:11.[30] This accomplishment, along with others, was picked up and covered in Wisconsin newspapers and by Sanger's friends at

Tandem racing became a popular event as riders working together could reach extreme speeds. One of Milwaukee's best tandem teams was the Telegram Tandem of Edward Crocker and Edward Roth, ca. 1896.

Milwaukee County Historical Society

FAMOUS MILWAUKEE TANDEM TEAM—"TELEGRAM TANDEM."
ED. H.W. CROCKER   EDW. ROTH.

the *Pneumatic*, who continued to cover Sanger's feats. Slowly, the scorn from the Milwaukee Wheelmen faded, and the city again embraced its hero.

On August 6, 1894, Sanger again returned to Milwaukee to great fanfare. Almost six thousand of the city's residents turned out to see him race. Though his return was triumphant, woes continued to plague the Milwaukee bicycling scene more generally. The Milwaukee Wheelmen had organized a boycott of the event in protest of the Association of Cycling Clubs, who organized the meet. The association seems to have done a lackluster job with its planning, as reports indicated that the track was in terrible shape, the prizes were less than lucrative, and Sanger wasn't going to ride at all were it not for the hometown crowd. Sanger, nonetheless, easily won several of the races held that day. Charges of corruption, scandal, and general trickery would plague the sport throughout the coming years, ultimately tarnishing the reputations of many athletes.[31]

The ups and downs of Milwaukee's most famous bicyclist continued in 1895. In March, Sanger fell ill with typhoid and was confined to his bed for several days with a temperature around 105 degrees. This unfortunate news was paired with reports that he had received a new bike that was almost two and a half times lighter than anything he had ridden before. As soon as he recovered from typhoid, Sanger said, he would resume his dominance of the sport.[32] "It would not be surprising if nearly every bicycle record . . . was lowered in this season," commentators noted in April. With Sanger competing at the highest levels, his name became synonymous with the upper echelons of the sport. "In Walter Sanger the cycle world has one of the greatest all-around bicycle riders that has ever been developed," noted the *New York World*. "He will do great things on the wheel this season."[33] His increasing celebrity caused further tensions, however, when in June 1895 the L.A.W. suspended Sanger for thirty days from all races on charges that he had sold one of his racing prizes for cash and also had taken a check instead of the prize itself.[34] It was around this time that Sanger made his decision to go "pro" full time. Mired in persisting allegations of scandal, the Milwaukee racer prepared to enter the world's most elite group of riders.[35]

Yet before this could happen, family tragedy struck when Walter's brother Emil was killed in a domestic dispute in the summer of 1895. According to the defendant, testifying during the trial, Emil attacked his wife Nellie during an argument. Reports indicated that Emil may have kicked her in the stomach, as she suffered a deep puncture wound just above her navel. When Emil's wife called her brother, Robert Luscombe, for help, Luscombe rushed over and found that Emil had left the scene. When Emil returned, Luscombe thought he saw a weapon and shot Emil in what was claimed as self-defense. Walter Sanger seemed willing to believe Luscombe's claim, even if he could not corroborate the story entirely. Emil had made repeated threats against his wife's family. Out of respect for his reputation and stature, Walter Sanger's appearance before the court was scheduled so as not to conflict with an upcoming race in Saginaw, Michigan.[36] Later in the month, there were also massive races at Lynn, Massachusetts. More than five thousand people watched Sanger and other riders on July 27. "It was a very knowing and enthusiastic gathering," the *Boston Sunday Globe* reported. Sanger finished strong but did not win.[37]

Sanger was back in the winner's circle two months later. One of the great triumphs of his career came on September 11, 1895, when he won several races at the American Cycling Derby in Springfield, Massachusetts. In front of a crowd of ten thousand, the meet featured some of the finest athletes in the world, with Eddie "the Cannon" Bald, Arthur "the Jersey Skeeter" Zimmerman, Thomas Cooper of Detroit, and Arthur Gardiner of Chicago. In a meet that saw numerous records broken, Sanger stole the spotlight with an incredible record-setting victory in the one-mile international professional race. During the race, Sanger held to the middle of the pack until the final back turn, when he saw a brief gap as a competitor slipped to the outside. Nearing the finish line, Sanger and Henry Tyler took to the front for thirty desperate feet, and in the final moments Sanger found another burst to win by ten feet.[38] "It has been generally conceded that Sanger rode the greatest races of the year on this track, and that he stands far above the common run of cycle racers," *Scientific American* reported. Playing the role of a bona-fide international professional racer, and in some ways angling to break free from his ties to Wisconsin, Sanger thanked the manufacturers and designers of his pneumatic tires for the victory. Made by the Boston Wove Hose and Rubber Company,

SPRINGFIELD BICYCLE CLUB TOURNAMENT

SPRINGFIELD MASS SEPT. 11 AND 12, 1895

Spectators who attended the Springfield Cycling Club Tournament on September 11–12, 1895, witnessed Walter Sanger's greatest race as he defeated Zimmerman and set a new world record in the one-mile international professional.

Library of Congress, Prints & Photographs Division, LC-USZC4-1951

they used a rough surface to guarantee better traction coming out of the corners, precisely the moment when most riders tended to slide high on the track. Sanger managed to keep a steady line through the turns and came out on top at one of the premier races of the season.[39] With the win, he established himself as a household name in sports, as his exploits graced every major newspaper in the United States, including the *New York Times.*

As their celebrity status grew, racers on the circuit found ample opportunity to taunt and jeer at one another. With his career on the rebound, Sanger shared details with reporters regarding his growing dislike of fellow rider John "the Minneapolis Wonder" Johnson in November 1895. Sanger accused his rival of cheating. "I am not looking for a race with Johnson at the present time," Sanger said. "I know a little too much about the methods of Johnson and his manager to be after a race with them." Johnson had allegedly used a slow watch in recording his time trials, giving him more competitive times. "All I ask is for a fair show, and, if I am beaten fairly, I am willing to accord the other man all credit for his victory," Sanger said. Increasingly an advocate and spokesman for his sport, Sanger helped lead efforts to reform racing in a time of increasing skepticism because of its well-publicized corruption.[40]

With his career in high gear and somewhat settled for the first time in many years, Sanger started courting a young woman named Katherine Kotzenburg. Father McGill of Holy Rosary Church married them in a quiet ceremony at the Oakland Avenue church on December 27, 1895. For hours afterward, newspapers noted, Katherine and Walter ice-skated with friends and family on the frozen Milwaukee River. Just two days after the Christmas holiday, it is easy to imagine the wedding party rushing home through Milwaukee's freezing streets to warm homes filled with family and friends. Ultimately, however, Sanger's time for celebration was short. The racetrack beckoned.[41]

A key event in 1896 was the state meet in Appleton, which offered a chance for Sanger to race in his home state once again. He raced in front of three massive grandstands filled with almost eight thousand spectators. The scene was a dazzling one, as "the fair ones, and there were hundreds of them, were attired in dainty light gowns of rich materials," newspapers observed. Adding to the scene, the Milwaukee Wheelmen and Green Bay's Pastime Cycling Club rode around town in "Indian fashion," making "real war whoop accompaniments." The crowd relished the opportunity to see Sanger and others. "The best in America were on hand and the crowd was satisfied," reports said.[42]

While the celebrity power of the racers was real, the continued success of these events reflected the enduring institutional power of the wheelmen. Despite having the second largest membership of wheelmen in the state, Appleton was viewed by profes-

THIS IS THE TREAD OF THE PEBBLED VIM

This is a picture of . . . . .

WALTER SANGER,

as he looked when he won those three races at Springfield on

VIM TIRES,

made by the Boston Woven Hose and Rubber Company. He won because the VIM TIRE is fast. Enough said, it has the pebble tread, and it does not slip. By the way, don't fail to send 10 cents in stamps for our "Art Book" on tires.

Sanger's record-setting performance in Springfield made him a household name and brought continued attention from sponsors, including Boston Wove Hose and Rubber Company's Vim Tires.

Courtesy of Nicholas J. Hoffman

sional cyclists as having a lackluster bike scene, mostly due to its not having a successful brand-name racer like Sanger. Hoping to rebrand its image, the Appleton Cycling Club petitioned to host the Wisconsin state meet. It also sought official circuit sponsorship from the national chapter of the LAW. When the *New York Times* announced the host cities for the league's national race circuit, it listed both Milwaukee and Appleton for Wisconsin. The increased coverage resulted in the largest and most successful meet in the state to date, setting new standards for early professional racing.[43]

Designated as a national meet, with lavish prizes of new safety bicycles and diamond medallions, the event at Appleton attracted some of the biggest names in late nineteenth-century racing. Among the most anticipated contests was the one between Sanger and Eddie "the Cannon" Bald. Sanger was, of course, the state darling of bicycle racing. Following his marriage and his success in the east, Massachusetts's elite Waltham Manufacturing Company, makers of the Orient bicycle, became his new sponsor.[44] Unknown to the meet organizers, however, Sanger was suffering from a lame leg due to a crash at a meet in Galesburg, Illinois. He was late for the first competition and delayed the scheduled professional races.[45] The injury no doubt limited the explosive power his fans relished. Sanger liked to stay behind the pack for most of the race and then burst forward to claim victory. His rival, Eddie "the Cannon" Ball of Buffalo, had sponsorship from Alexander Pope's Columbia Bicycle Company and was the reigning national champion. Perhaps most thrilling for fans, the event featured many of the superstars of bicycle racing, including Thomas Cooper, Arthur Gardiner, and Otto Ziegler of San Jose.[46]

An early entry by a racer was often seen as a challenge to others. Bald was the first star to commit to the meet. Sanger and Cooper quickly followed to "not allow Bald or anyone else to carry off the big cash prizes without a contest on their part." The *Appleton Crescent* predicted the race would be the hottest of the year and perhaps the fiercest of all time. By July 4, more than sixty-two amateur riders and seven professionals had registered to participate. Some of the amateur races would include over fifty bicyclists divided into multiple heats. Entire LAW chapters registered at local hotels and rented special trains from all corners of Wisconsin. Just a few days prior to the meet, the *Crescent* declared, "Club members started out with the intention of making the Appleton meet one of the greatest. . . . Today it seems that success will surely crown their efforts." For a town barely on the nation's bicycling map before the event, the big-name racers ensured that Appleton, Wisconsin, would join the list of top cycling destinations.[47]

The star power at the races meant the entire city mobilized to accommodate fans

Walter Sanger raced under the Orient brand, made by the Waltham Manufacturing Company of Waltham, Massachusetts, at the Appleton meet in 1896.

Library of Congress, Prints & Photographs Division, LC-USZC4-3026

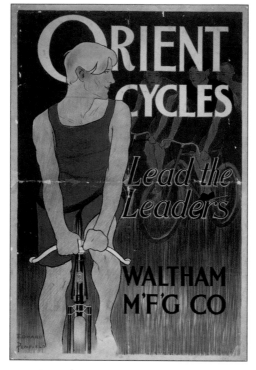

Professional cyclists from around the United States, including Otto Ziegler of San Jose, gathered in Appleton in 1876 to participate in a national circuit race.

History San Jose

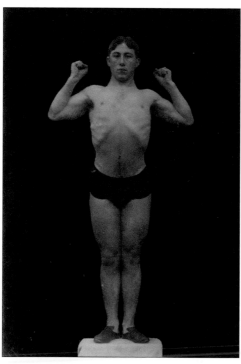

and participants. Local businesses decorated their storefronts with red and white bunting, matching the colors of the Appleton Cycle Club. City officials used special dollar-sized red and green stickers to mark outgoing mail. At the same time, even as storefronts and streetscapes were decorated to the hilt, downtown businesses actually closed during the meet so everyone had a chance to go. The crowds were so thick that disputes erupted over where pedestrians should be allowed to go and where bicyclists could ride. On the eve of the meet, the issue came to a boil, as residents feared that bicyclists would flood sidewalks and overwhelm local streets. Hoping to signal its goodwill to the city and its residents, the clubs issued a formal proclamation against "scorchers," bicyclists who sped quickly past pedestrians, and asked the "road hogs" of "truck, farm wagon, or speed cart" to share the road in turn. It is difficult to know, however, what effect these requests had on the traffic that must have followed the influx of riders. The city's bicycle path from the downtown neighborhood to the fairgrounds was "doctored up" for the expected large traffic volume.[48]

When the meet opened on July 8, members of the Winnebago Wheelmen of Fond du Lac described the city as decorated in "gay attire and crowded with enthusiastic Wheelmen."[49] Perfect, warm, sunny weather brought an estimated five to seven thousand people to the half-mile racetrack. Spectators jammed the grandstands, clung to the

Eddie "the Cannon" Bald cruised to a world record in the half-mile open race at the Appleton meet in 1896.

Milwawkee Public Museum Photography Collection

sides of buildings, and sat on fences. Festivities also occurred around the track and throughout the downtown district. There were concerts by the Standard Band at City Park, and spontaneous parades of wheelmen cruised down College Avenue, including a boisterous single-file parade of the Green Bay Wheelmen behind a bass drum. Each evening the meet organizers held a dance at Armory Hall to the music of Maeder's Orchestra. It was the premiere event of the summer.[50]

Despite the widespread fanfare, the races remained the main attraction. Bald and Sanger were the featured competitors, with Sanger defending his home state against the national champion. In the finals for the one-mile open professional event on July 10, the first day of the meet, Sanger reportedly hoped to thoroughly defeat Bald. The entire nation awaited the results. Race officials placed Bald at the second line and Sanger at fourth. At the crack of the starter's pistol, the men chased after the pacer and held their positions until the final lap. Sanger, in his customary style, floated behind the pack and waited for the final straightaway to make his move. Knowing and anticipating Sanger's plan, Bald held his sprint until the final leg where he increased his lead. His ferocious sprint energized the crowd. With thousands of spectators on their feet, screaming at the top of their lungs, the racers neared the finished line. Down the stretch, the entire crowd stood and started changing, "Bald! Bald! Bald!" as he cruised through the tape. Winning by four wheel-lengths, Bald finished ahead of Gardiner, who was followed by Ziegler. In what must have been a crushing disappointment for the "Pride of Milwaukee," Sanger did not even place.[51]

Sanger's opportunity to redeem himself occurred in the one-half mile open professional event, which took place at the conclusion of the first day. At the start, Ziegler jumped to a narrow lead, but Sanger and Bald quickly passed him. At the finish line, Bald narrowly defeated Sanger with an astounding time of one minute flat to set an unconfirmed new world record. Sanger's Wisconsin supporters quickly assured themselves that their hero had lost because of his lingering leg injury. Bald then cruised to a third victory in the two-mile open and thus swept all three professional races. Despite Sanger's poor showing, the spectators could reconcile themselves in having witnessed a legendary and potentially world-record breaking performance by international sensation Eddie Bald.[52]

As the meet concluded, reporters throughout the state agreed that Appleton's meet was the best to date. The *Neenah News* thought the event was "perfect in every way and merited the commendation of all." Reporters from the *Milwaukee Sentinel* added, "The Wheelmen are well pleased with the treatment accorded them by the people of Appleton." Yet in a meet complete with a world record and the allure of international sporting celebrity, the stuffy stereotype of the cycling clubs still lingered as a point of contention. The Green Bay Wheelmen jeered their Appleton rivals, saying their own presence "added more enthusiasm to the meet than the Appleton boys." Green Bay's posturing was due to their continued interest in hosting the state meet and probably some jealousy over the success of the two-day event. Although the city later enjoyed small meets between local clubs, Appleton never again hosted a major meet with so many celebrity athletes.[53]

Sanger's poor showing at Appleton opened another round of bad luck. On July 30, 1896, he was briefly embroiled in a controversy involving the death of Joe Griebler, a professional rider from Saint Paul, Minnesota, who died during a race in Lima, Ohio. Sanger was at the race, and some early reports accused him of having caused Griebler's fatal crash. The rumors were quickly put to rest when it became clear that Griebler

Marshall "Major" Taylor, ca. 1898, was quickly becoming a celebrity on the national circuit. Routinely mocked by white racers, he was not allowed to race below the Mason-Dixon Line.

Indiana State Museum and Historic Sites

had simply lost control and flown off course. According to the *Milwaukee Journal*, onlookers carried Griebler to a nearby copse of trees, where witnesses saw him bleeding from the mouth and nose. His caretakers then removed him to a nearby house, where he died within the hour. Sanger and the other riders must have been reminded of the incredible dangers they faced each time they entered the racing track.[54]

Eager to move on, Sanger entered new races in July and August at Springfield, Massachusetts, and Indianapolis. His entrance into these races ultimately put him on a collision course with one of the most famous athletes of the late nineteenth century, Marshall "Major" Taylor, a remarkable figure that most Americans today have never even heard of. The stage for their dramatic showdown was set when Sanger recorded a new track record in the one-and-a-half-mile race on the Capital City track in Indianapolis. Two days after Sanger's triumph, Taylor shattered Sanger's time and set a new track record by over eight seconds, dealing the legendary Milwaukee rider a defeat he never fully recovered from.

Within a few years, Major Taylor would become one of the greatest professional riders of his time—a champion of international renown and arguably one of the most dominating athletes in all of bicycling history. On the occasion of his race with Sanger, however, he was just getting his start in the sport. An African American born in Indianapolis on November 8, 1878, Taylor was roughly five years younger than Walter Sanger. As Taylor later explained in his 1928 autobiography, he was working in a bike shop in Indiana when Sanger announced his intention to set a new track record at the Capital City track, then one of the premier venues in the Midwest. Taylor clearly respected Sanger's talents, but he also saw an opportunity to capitalize on the defeat of a high-profile racer. Taylor later called his rival "one of the greatest bicycle riders of the day," but this respect seemed only to fuel Taylor's drive to better him.[55] Because of the racist attitudes of the time, however, it was sometimes the case that white and black riders weren't allowed to race head-to-head. Additionally, it was often true that amateur racers were not allowed to race professional racers head-to-head. In this instance, Taylor appears to have raced alone, but he still managed a clear victory by far outpacing Sanger's time. Sanger entered a period of long decline as his dominance of the sport neared an end.

As Gregory Bond writes, Major Taylor and other professional black athletes of the late nineteenth century helped forge a new manly ideal that welcomed exceptional "colored gentlemen" like Taylor, but rarely others. Taylor won over skeptical whites with his sobriety, hard work, conduct, dress, and financial independence. Taylor's entry as a professional would lend new opportunities for head-to-head competition with whites.[56] Taylor's first professional race occurred at Madison Square Garden in the fall of 1896. His appearance in professional racing generated fierce racist antagonism in a sport that had long worked to preserve itself as a white man's domain. As black riders challenged claims of white superiority, many of the old legends in the sport started to fall by the wayside. Taylor endured intense hatred throughout his career, something his followers constantly watched out for at events, as white riders would try to trick, elbow, or otherwise injure him during races to avoid being beaten. As Boston's *Colored American Magazine* put it in 1902, "It makes a white man blush to know that a colored rider is to-day . . . the banner man for clean sport and gentlemanly conduct." "When he first started to ride," the paper continued, "a colored man was not allowed on the circuit tracks, but by degrees he has won the esteem of not only the race promoters, but the

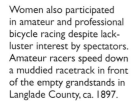

public generally."[57] In fact, Major Taylor's image was repeatedly used in bicycle advertisements, including ads for the E.C. Stearns Company and the Iver Johnson Arms and Cycle Works. As his power grew, he forged alliances with white racers who vowed to protect him against the more racist competitors in the field.[58]

By the end of 1897, a year or so after his defeat by the rising star Taylor, Sanger readied his retirement announcement. That year, Sanger had competed well in National Circuit Meets and occasionally raced unsuccessfully with other white cyclists against Major Taylor.[59] Both athletes also committed early to a meet in Racine in 1897, but they each scratched and did not participate.[60] The truth is that though Sanger was still training at a high level and had perfected his workouts, he simply could not compete at the level he once had. Having come full circle in his career, Sanger participated in early July in a publicity stunt to race against the famous pacing horse Albatross just as he had as a young boy, training horses on the family farm. Sanger won two of the three races, again earning recognition in newspapers across the country.[61] He tried to repeat the performance at the Wisconsin State Fair, but a long speech by ex-Congressman Robert M. La Follette caused its cancellation.[62] Still a regular spokesman for the importance of good eating and exercise, Sanger explained some of his training regimen to reporters that year, emphasizing how he had cut coffee and alcohol out of his diet.[63] By September, a few months after the birth of the Sangers' first child, *Milwaukee Journal* reporters speculated that "the expert bicycle rider is likely to leave the track soon and settle down to a home life."[64] Sanger's departure from the sport occurred at the precise moment when bicycle racing entered a period of turbulence and decline in Wisconsin.

Women also participated in amateur and professional bicycle racing despite lackluster interest by spectators. Amateur racers speed down a muddied racetrack in front of the empty grandstands in Langlade County, ca. 1897.

WHi Image ID 98611

The story of this decline is still not well understood, but it is likely that bicycling's increasing association with women and nonwhites like Taylor contributed to a redirection of white male attention elsewhere—particularly toward the military, with the onset of the Spanish-American War, but also to prize fighting and other popular male sports. Bicycling's downfall may also be understood in other terms. While racing often promoted fierce antagonisms, both Sanger and Taylor enjoyed the benefits of a sport that still ensured male control through the large prizes and high salaries for male racers.

These inequalities were made clear during the summer of 1898, when racers from all over the country descended on Green Bay for two major cycling events. The first of these was a women's meet during the last week of June and early July. The second was the LAW's Thirteenth Annual Wisconsin Division Meet, scheduled for August 16–18, 1898. Planning for both events was already well underway in June, and it was clear from the start which of the events would attract the most attention. Green Bay's main cycling club, the Pastime Cycle Club, had already received letters from leading high-profile male racers from around the country. Sanger, who was beginning to pull out of racing, was a notable exception and did not attend, but Taylor did register.[65]

The women's event, by contrast, drew almost no attention, except for scant advertisements in the local paper in the week or so before the race. Admission was set at 25 cents for adults, 15 cents for kids. Promoters did what they could to place ads, promising the "fastest female flyers" on a "brilliantly illuminated" new track attended by live music.[66] Little is known about the racers or how the event transpired, however—the events by and large went unrecorded. What did get recorded was the story that the promoters of the race, having failed to draw large ticket sales, could not pay their board at local hotels and had their luggage held until they were able to scrounge up the cash. Acknowledging that the women's races had been a "complete failure," the promoters were ridiculed in local papers. Barely able to pay for their lodging, the women and their male managers left town in shame shortly after the Fourth of July.[67]

Paying for hotel rooms would not be a problem for the men who invaded the city the next month. Where the women's races had struggled to get people in the door at 25 cents or less, nearly all of Green Bay's business establishment, including area hotel owners, came down to support the men's event. On June 28, the city's Pastime Cycle Club met to strategize how best to use this support.[68] By July 7, a few days after the close of the failed women's meet, Green Bay's Business Men's Association announced that it would forward cash to help sponsor the men's event.[69] In meetings held over the coming days, Green Bay's business leaders hashed out how this money would be allocated and announced their formal support, along with a full range of committees and subcommittees to further organize the event.[70] Throughout, the question was never whether the city's business elite would help plan the events but at what scale. Men's professional cycling had become big business.

Dressed in the epitome of cycling fashion, these riders from Montello cut a handsome figure, ca. 1898. Leisure riding and touring remained popular in the late 1890s.

WHi Image ID 47195

Green Bay's wheelmen and business leaders had the added benefit, of course, of history. For years, men like Sanger had slowly assembled a fraternal machine around bicycling, and in planning for major cycling events the power of that machine was made clear. The star power of racers like Sanger and Taylor further emboldened these efforts. In 1898, Green Bay's business leaders had the luxury of using the wheelmen's existing infrastructure to help plan the event. In the middle of July, Pastime Cycle Club used clubhouse space to conduct its meetings.[71] Between August 1 and 3, the first entries to the event started appearing as planning by the Pastime Cycle Club continued—these entries were then passed on to local newspapers and edited and printed by male-dominated newsrooms.[72] Newspapers also printed enthusiastic stories documenting the entry papers for racers like Eddie Bald. "Bald is noted for his fast work all over the country and will be another great drawing card for the LAW races in this city," the *Green Bay Daily Gazette* noted. The celebrity of the racers found a ready-made market in eager fans and readers throughout the city.[73]

With the cooperation of major hotel and restaurant owners, the organizers, all white business men, freely moved throughout the planning process to secure whatever they asked for. Wheelmen met on the night of August 8 and chose the Beaumont Hotel as their headquarters for the upcoming meet. Arriving members were instructed to pick up an envelope containing a badge and a ticket to the event when they registered. At the same time, workers and volunteers organized last-minute improvements of the racetrack and grandstands while league organizers finalized plans for a fireworks show and band performance to accompany what newspapers assured readers would be a night "in which every citizen in Green Bay can take part."[74] Entries were still being received as late as August 12. As the opening day drew near, planners even put out a call to Green Bay residents hoping that some families would be willing to host overflow racers and guests. "Private homes who can accommodate the outside riders in large or small parties are requested to leave their names," a notice in the *Green Bay Daily Gazette* read.[75]

Wherever they went on the professional circuit, racers like Taylor and Sanger partook in a grand commercial spectacle. The *Green Bay Daily Gazette* greeted "L.A.W. Week" with large ads that read, "We are ready for it with the biggest bargains you ever saw."[76] Area companies such as Otto Merkel & Co., a maker of bike lamps, ran ads in the local paper hoping to draw the influx of out-of-towners into their shops.[77] The A. Spuhler Company offered "royal purple bunting" for those decorating their homes "for the meet."[78] Bicycles were sold at "less than cost" at Mueller and Man.[79] Meanwhile, the night before races began, area newspaper writers noted the arrival of the racers and their managers. "The whole push of the fast racing men arrived this morning over the Chicago & Northwestern road."[80] Supporting the cyclists was the duty not only of good bicycling fans but also of Green Bay's businesses, newspapers, and everyday residents.

The presence of Major Taylor elicited a telling array of feelings in the community, including curiosity, fear, and suspicion. It seemed impossible for journalists not to mention Taylor's race wherever he appeared, and from the accounts it becomes clear that curious fans and observers followed him wherever he went. As the only black rider at the meet, Taylor competed in a state with roughly 2,500 blacks in 1900, most of them in Milwaukee. It was entirely possible that many in Green Bay would be seeing a black person for the first time. "Mr. Taylor, the little colored wonder," reporters said, "will be one of the favorites here without a doubt." Taylor's potent claim to manhood as a professional racer, along with what was probably a sincere desire to play a good host and thus appear benevolent on the race issue, led Green Bay's whites to find other venues for reasserting male authority and control. Further down the page from where Taylor's arrival in the city was announced, editors relayed a story about "four damsels" and "some of their gentleman friends" who were standing downtown on one of the nights of the event, admiring a storefront window where the LAW had filled the display with a small shrine to cycling. The story offered a chance to ridicule the supposedly unintelligent minds of women. When one of the girls turned to her "escort" and asked what LAW meant, the newspaper reported that the men laughed at her, turning her away from the window and walking her further down the street so that she would not further publicly embarrass herself.[81]

Despite Major Taylor's success on the track, he was still treated as a curiosity by whites and followed by reporters who documented the "Colored Wonder's" doings off the track.

Indiana State Museum and Historic Sites

Throughout the following morning and afternoon, people from all over the country attended races in filled grandstands. They were met with exceptional weather, and "excitement ran high." Major Taylor "showed wonderful speed qualities and was not in the least crowded at any time during the race."[82] Taylor continued to attract voyeuristic attention in the *Green Bay Daily Gazette*. In addition to referencing his skin color every time he was mentioned in reports, local writers also made note of his appearance in other ways. "Major Taylor . . . is a very neat dresser," reporters noted, offering commentary they rarely offered in reference to whites. "The little major after eating a hearty supper last night dressed in a swell suit of black and took a stroll through the streets of the city. It is needless to say that he created much enthusiasm wherever he went."[83]

There was a tangible amount of local pride at stake in Green Bay's treatment of Major Taylor. When the "colored whirlwind" won the races that afternoon, the *Green Bay Daily Gazette* noted that the "southern race problem" had not affected the day's events, an indication that Taylor's treatment by area whites would be taken as a reflection of Wisconsin's attitudes toward blacks—if not the North's generally.[84] It did not matter, apparently, that Wisconsin's small population of blacks faced profound inequality and racist resentments. Taylor was an exception, worthy of respect because he was a bicycle racer, just as black men who had fought for the Union deserved the respect of white veterans. Wisconsin's whites at the time were usually not willing to extend such courtesies to other, "unmanly" black men. Taylor's identity as a racer tapped into a complicated mix of white assumptions about power, authority, and respectability in the late 1890s.

These complicated tensions help shed light on bicycling's increasingly beleaguered place, both within Wisconsin and throughout the nation at the end of the nineteenth century. The second day of the event, August 17, saw the biggest races. While the *Green Bay Daily Gazette* estimated almost two thousand out-of-state guests among the thousands gathered at the grandstands, behind closed doors that evening, LAW meetings revealed that attendance at racing events was actually down across the state. League leaders had no real explanation for the cause and blamed the Spanish-American War, asking that the national organization renew the memberships of those men who had left to fight in order to keep the ranks of the wheelmen strong, at least on paper. After two days of great success in Green Bay, rain moved in. "A drizzling rain set in making the track very bad and impossible to ride upon."[85] Organizers had no choice but to cancel the remaining events.

Despite the bad weather, the Green Bay meet had been a success, with all involved expressing appreciation for the hard work that went into making it happen. In fact, Major Taylor was quoted in the *Green Bay Daily Gazette* as saying, "The boys who have promoted the races are all right. They are a good lot of race promoters. I am perfectly satisfied with the treatment I received and wish the boys success." Meanwhile, the racers exited town to make their way to Saint Louis, where additional races were to be held in the coming days. Business went back to usual in Green Bay.[86] Nobody complained about unpaid hotel rooms.

SANGER'S exit from the sport and nonappearance in Green Bay signaled ominous changes for the future. In late December 1898 and early 1899, the state's racing fans yearned for the rise of another amateur racer to take his place. Frank Mulkern of Milwaukee seemed likely to fill the void, but it quickly became clear that nobody could fill Sanger's shoes. Mulkern had no previous training and only limited success in his first season of racing, winning amateur races in Green Bay and earning first-place finishes in Watertown and Seymour. Some suggested he might take the sport by storm, but these hopes never panned out, even as many noted that his build was perfect for racing. The *Pneumatic* warned, "Mulkern will probably enter the field for blood next season, and, if he does, beware, ye heroes of the wheel." Though the warning echoed the masculine thirst for competition characteristic of the time, it vastly overrated Mulkern. The end of the great bicycling boom in Wisconsin was coming.[87]

Other names came forward and fell flat. As new racers attracted the attention of sports writers and enthusiasts, expectations were quick to cool. Along with Mulkern, Wisconsin's Edward Aldridge became the state's newest darling. At the Milwaukee Exposition Tournament on January 1, 1898, Aldridge set two new unpaced world records in front of his home audience. His effort to ride 24.5 miles in an hour and 25 miles in 1:01:32 placed him among the elite racers near the end of the 1890s. Unfortunately, because of a bizarre LAW rule under which no records were accepted between January 1 and March 1, his record was not made official. As the *Pneumatic* stated, "Aldrich is one of the new generation of Wisconsin's racing men" to occupy the spotlight as former champions Sanger, Cooper, Bald, and Zimmerman began to fade. But the Milwaukee event was Aldrich's last hurrah as a statewide bicycling icon.[88]

The North Side Cycling Club Team won many amateur races throughout the state.

Milwaukee County Historical Society

Eager for more action during the 1899 racing season, Wisconsin's wheelmen debated whose performances merited championship honors. Reporter O. F. Cody stated his support for Major Taylor, but acknowledged his opinion was an unpopular one in Wisconsin, which largely remained loyal to Sanger.[89] Taylor made periodic returns to Wisconsin but appears never to have shared a racetrack with Sanger, or have ever raced against him head-to-head. Janesville hosted Taylor and the state LAW meet in 1899. Early hopes for the event were high. On July 10, the *Janesville Daily Gazette* reported that Tom Eck, one of the world's most famous managers and trainers of bicycle riders, had arrived from Saint Louis and personally inspected the mile-long track at the fairgrounds. "The track is a great surprise to me," he said. "It is simply great and I consider it today one of the fastest tracks for bicycle racing in America."[90]

But the event became a major debacle and embarrassment for Wisconsin. Major Taylor had signed up to participate in several of the races when reports surfaced that they might be cancelled because promoters wanted higher entry fees for the professional riders. The problem was soon resolved, however, and the races were back on track. State newspapers continued the tradition of highlighting Taylor's color. "All of the professional races were good, and some fast time was made. When Taylor, the colored rider, appeared he was applauded," one report read.[91] The *Janesville Daily Gazette* referred to him as the "ebony streak."[92] Despite the success of racers like Taylor, however, poor management led to professional and amateur racers being short-changed on their prize winnings. Major Taylor took home only $40 of the $125 he won, while many other amateur racers received nothing at all. Behind the scenes, more trouble was brewing.[92]

Event planners had ambitious expectations for how the meet would go, no doubt remembering the enormous successes of the Appleton races in 1896 and the Green Bay races in 1898. The opening day was successful, with good weather, almost two thousand spectators in the stands, and good souvenir sales. Trouble started when the mayor of Chicago, Carter H. Harrison, failed to show despite the promises of event planners that he would make an appearance. When rains canceled the races on following days and news of the lack of cash reached the racers, the remaining events were called off.[93] "The fourteenth annual meet of the Wisconsin Division L.A.W. has ended miserably after one day's racing," the Janesville *Daily Gazette* reported. The city, it went on, now occupied the dubious distinction of "being the first in fourteen years to throw up the sponge before the end of the meeting."[94] Because many professional racers made the journey to Janesville at their own expense, the lack of pay reflected poorly on the organizers and called into question the likelihood of professional riders returning to the state.

"The Janesville Affair," as it came to be known, failed to deliver on many promises. The band that was scheduled to play at the courthouse, for example, did not show up. Riders complained that the entry fees were higher than normal. The rain prompted event organizers to call the whole thing off. "The annual state bicycle meet," one report

Amateur race at the Neenah Driving Park, ca. 1897

Neenah Historical Society

read, "proved to be a great fizzle. . . . [It] has been the most miserably conducted bicycle meet ever pulled off in this section of the country." Stanley Tallman, one of the Janesville organizers and a local bicycle aficionado, as well as several other event planners from the city, were surrounded with clouds of suspicion in the days after the event. The failure also diminished the reputations of the Wisconsin business leaders who had long helped keep cycling afloat.[95]

Wisconsin found one last opportunity to redeem the failures of the "Janesville Affair." After a long and frustrating effort to bring the event back to the Badger State, Milwaukee finally earned the right to host the LAW National Meet on July 10–15, 1900.[96] Major Taylor expressed his excitement for the event, particularly his matchup with cycling great Thomas Cooper. In June, citing "a letter received from Taylor here this morning," the *Weekly Wisconsin Advocate* proclaimed that Taylor "never was able to follow the pace better than he is now" and "should the two men meet on the indoor track at the Industrial Exposition Building, those interested in cycling will undoubtedly not only witness one of the fast match records for indoor track, but also one in which skill will go a great distance."[97] The promised matchup took place on July 11 in a head-to-head mile-long race for a $1,000 prize.[98] As the racers arrived in Milwaukee and began practicing on the banked track, several noted its dangerous speeds and steeply banked turns. After Cooper fell on a practice ride, both he and Taylor refused to race, and quit the meet altogether along with the other professionals.[99] Describing the racers as a labor union on strike, Connecticut's *Naugatuck Daily News* wrote, "[The] meet will go down as one of the biggest fizzles in the history of the League of American Wheelmen."[100] Yet another major cycling race in Wisconsin had ended in failure as news of the debacle filtered throughout the country.

Despite the dismal affair of the national meet, the *Weekly Wisconsin Advocate* continued to follow Taylor's career closely. In September 1900, it reported that the "fastest sprinter in the world" was about to enter his name in several new racing competitions and that "unprejudiced experts" would be wise to see that "he will easily realize his ambition." The report ran alongside an image of the rider atop his bike, head lowered, with hands on his handlebars. Overhead, the paper ran the headline, "Black Wonder of the Wheel."[101] Taylor's enduring presence in the sport challenged not only longstanding white assumptions but also paved the way for new opportunities for black men in professional sports more generally.[102]

Yet his successes also illuminated the difficulties facing African Americans at the turn of the century. After an illustrious racing career, Major Taylor found few opportunities for advancement. Where many of his white competitors found work in the upstart automobile industry, Major Taylor struggled to earn a living through a variety of odd jobs. Though he tried to generate support from the sale of his 1928 autobiography, he found few buyers. He died tragically, alone and in poverty in the charity ward of the

Cook County Hospital in Chicago on June 21, 1932, whereupon he was placed in an unmarked grave. He was just fifty-three years old.[103]

In a culture that seemed to value white manly competition above all else, the fate of bicycling became increasingly tied to the fate of its individual racers. Thus, as racing greats like Sanger left the cycling scene, racing slowly fell out of favor—and the whole bicycle industry was about to undergo a similarly dramatic change. The "Janesville Affair" and Milwaukee's failed national meet cannot be isolated as a cause of the boom's decline, but it certainly contributed. The end of boom seemed clear by the summer of 1898, as the late-night meetings at the Green Bay meet show. Membership in the LAW went into a dramatic tailspin that summer. The *New York Times* reported on the irony that while the league's membership had actually peaked at an all-time high in January 1898, by the first of April its ranks had shrunk by almost ten percent, with greater falloff through May and June. This tailspin occurred directly after the United States declared war on Spain. The nation's biggest LAW state divisions—New York and Pennsylvania—lost significant numbers as the war progressed. In interviews with the *New York Times*, the New York LAW secretary said the decline was not constrained to any particular section and was being witnessed all across the country. By the time of the 1900 national LAW meet at Milwaukee, despite Taylor's enthusiastic participation, the fate of racing was all but sealed. The causes of its downfall were a common topic of debate around the nation.[104]

There is probably much to be said for the argument that America's white men simply found a bigger and bolder venue for competition. Isaac B. Potter, then the league's president, said explicitly that he thought the war was to blame. "Every one was thinking war, talking war, and going to war," he said. "War has knocked everything into a cocked hat," a Delaware league representative said. Sterling Elliott, the publisher of the league's *Bulletin*, said the cycling trade was "suffering acutely from the war fever. . . . Interest in everything but war is temporarily slack."[105]

His bicycle days nearing an end, Sanger continued to race sporadically until 1900, when he transitioned to focus on a handlebar manufacturing company he opened in 1899 in Milwaukee. His company's patent for adjustable handlebars had been approved in December 1898. The following year, his factory began production on a new automated system capable of producing one thousand bars in twenty-four hours. Sanger and his co-owners traveled throughout the United States to advertise their product. Sales manager J. Cordes traveled east on a promotional tour and was joined by Sanger in New York

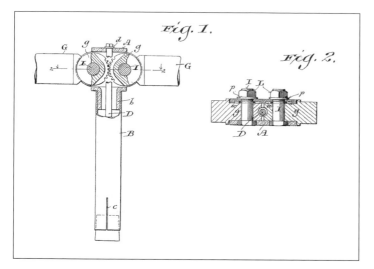

Sanger briefly operated
a handlebar company in
Milwaukee after his cycling
career ended. The unique
adjustable design earned
a patent in 1899.

US Patent #634,505,
October 10, 1899,
courtesy of Google Patents

City.[106] Sanger's design was for track riding, with drop-front handlebars that lowered the rider into an aggressive, forward, aerodynamic position.[107] Although the Sanger bar was popular among racers, its limitation to track riding offered a small market. In 1901, the Sanger Handle-Bar and Plating Company went bankrupt. "Mr. Sanger said the firm would probably make a settlement and continue the business," the *Janesville Gazette* reported. Sanger regrouped and tried to turn his attention elsewhere.[108]

The champion bicycle rider from Milwaukee was left to ponder his options. Perhaps hoping to rejuvenate some of the star power he had once enjoyed, Sanger announced on June 26, 1902, that he intended to begin participating in local motorcycle races, a new fad then sweeping the state. His move is telling. As new technologies allowed even greater thrills, the bicycle slowly became a relic of an older and slower age. "Motor racing has never been witnessed in Milwaukee and the chances are that people will take to it from the start," one report said.[109] Often held at the same venues where bicycle races had occurred just a couple years before, motorcycle and automobile races helped bring an end to the bicycle boom. Some of Sanger's fiercest competitors, such as Eddie Bald, retired from bicycling and became heroes in automobile racing. By 1929, Sanger too had joined the automobile fever with his brother as the owners of the Sanger Automobile Company located on the upper east side of Milwaukee.[110]

Sanger's brief grip on the national imagination faded into obscurity. Sanger's obituary in the *Milwaukee Journal* on December 6, 1941, the day before the Japanese bombed Pearl Harbor, indicated that Sanger had participated in 404 races, of which 293 were amateur and 111 were professional events. He had amassed over $35,000 in prize money, medals, and trophies throughout his career. When he died December 5, 1941, the *Milwaukee Journal* called him "the idol of bicycling racing enthusiasts."[111] Nonetheless, Walter Sanger's name has almost entirely faded from local memory. Only a small monument in Wisconsin's Sports Hall of Fame remains to remind Wisconsinites of his story.

CONCLUSION

Walter Sanger's brief foray into motorcycle racing following the bankruptcy of his handlebar company was a telling sign of what was to come for the nation's professional and amateur cyclists. As Americans faced a new century, bicycling slowly faded in the United States as a recreational and professional pastime, and new professional motorsports like automobile and motorcycle racing rose to take its place. Between 1869 and 1900, Americans had developed a deep love for speed, power, and the freedoms offered by the bicycle, but this appreciation was about to take a new shape. Slowly but surely, as the purr of automobile engines replaced the sound of ringing bicycle bells on America's streets, the transportation landscape shifted. Where steam engines, railroads, and bicycles had defined transportation in the nineteenth century, the twentieth century would hold out the promise of a gas-powered, combustible revolution built directly upon the culture and infrastructure established by those nineteenth-century Americans gripped by wheel fever.[1]

The automobile trade, in fact, built its early successes upon the innovations first unleashed during the bicycle boom. In cities such as Detroit, Chicago, Saint Louis, and Milwaukee, and many towns in between, bike shops and factories converted to gas stations, garages, and assemblies, providing products and services to a new kind of wheel. Many bicycle factories simply switched their production from bikes to cars after 1900. The automobile boom even followed the same basic narrative arc as the bicycle: as with the velocipede, the first key technological innovations took place overseas, with French and German engineers leading the way. Nikolaus Otto, Gottlieb Daimler, and Carl Benz helped develop the new industry from 1901, when Daimler's Mercedes was marketed as the world's first motorcar, to 1909, when it became clear that a domestic industry in the United States had gained a foothold.

Hoping to capitalize on the car in much the same way that they had capitalized on

An early horseless carriage parked at the Ballard Bicycle Company in Oshkosh, ca. 1900, heralded the end of the bicycle boom.

Milwaukee Public Library Historic Photo Collection

bikes a few decades before, manufacturers in the Badger State and throughout the United States worked hard to get the most cars into the most hands. Car designers in the United States, such as Ransom E. Olds in Lansing, Michigan, made cars that were smaller and less powerful than their European counterparts. In this way, the first domestic automobiles were better suited for the country's still unimproved dirt and rural roads, yet they also appealed to expanding consumer desires. The Oldsmobile, for example, was essentially a motorized horse buggy with spoked bike wheels that initially sold for $650. Like many early bikes, this fairly hefty price tag ensured that the first cars would only be accessible to the white middle and upper-middle classes. Yet in time, as had happened with the safety model bicycle in the 1880s, American producers would lower the cost of their cars, and their expanded affordability would fuel a rapid sales boom.

The automobile industry also co-opted the bicycling lobby, using the accumulated gains of the LAW, the good roads movement, and thousands of cycling enthusiasts to generate support among the white middle class. As Jeff Mapes has written, the good roads movement was essentially taken over by car lobbyists between 1900 and 1920, leading to a bond between the white middle class and the car that remains strong to this day. Calling the bicycle the "consciousness raiser that led to the car," Mapes highlights the sheer number of people who abandoned the bicycle industry for the automobile industry in this period. J. Frank and Charles E. Duryea of Springfield, Massachusetts, for example, were early bike mechanics who designed the first successful gas-powered automobile in the United States in 1893. Although their historic debut went almost entirely unnoticed at the time—in part because it happened near the height of the bicycle boom—their entry into the car business signaled the beginning of a massive transfer of wealth, status, and property established during the bike boom over to the leaders of the automobile industry. What began as a trickle away from bike manufacturing in the United States and throughout Wisconsin slowly became a flood. By 1920, many of the men who had stood at the helm of the bike industry had re-established their dominance in automobiles. This transition helped ensure that they would oversee key changes in transportation in the twentieth century.[2]

Not every former cyclist embraced the growing automobile culture. After Sercombe-Bolte Manufacturing Company failed in 1894, Parker H. Sercombe quit the LAW and relocated to Mexico to recover his finances. He then returned to the Midwest, and took up residence in Chicago where he became an advocate for socialism and free love. Sercombe operated a free-thinking organization called the Spencer-Whitman Center on Chicago's Calumet Avenue and was the publisher and owner of a magazine called *To-Morrow: For People Who Think*. Sercombe described his magazine's focus as "rationalism and human liberty," while critics viewed it as an organ advocating socialism, anarchism, sex reform, and eugenics. Carl Sandburg briefly lived with Sercombe, working as an editor and contributor for the magazine, and mingled with Sercombe's friends, such as Jack London and H.G. Wells.[3]

For the most part, however, everyday bicyclists were rarely hostile to the new emerging status quo. In fact, they welcomed and celebrated it. By 1910, it seemed as if the transition from bikes to cars had been both inevitable and natural. While grassroots cycling advocates recognized that old bike factories were increasingly producing automobiles, they welcomed the change as an example of technological progress and the forward march of civilization. They rejoiced that their victories in securing better traffic laws and cycling regulations in the 1880s and 1890s proved so adaptable for the new industry. In truth, the car's eventual dominance of transportation would lead many Americans to forget that cyclists deserve credit not only for infrastructure developments such as highway and road systems but for road laws, car-friendly hotels and

Thomas B. Jeffery in an automobile he designed in Chicago, ca. 1900

WHi Image ID 40834

Workers strength-testing a Rambler automobile, ca. 1901, near their new plant in Kenosha

WHi Image ID 40840

restaurants, and highly detailed road maps. This oversight took root in the rapid and almost seamless ascension of the car industry in the first decade of the twentieth century. During this period, some five hundred new automobile businesses entered the trade. Many had gotten their start in the bicycle industry. Henry Ford, once a bike mechanic in Detroit, introduced his Model T in that city in 1908. That same year, William C. Durant founded General Motors in Flint, Michigan. Durant would later partner with Louis-Joseph Chevrolet, also a former bike racer, to help form Chevrolet Motors.[4]

For blacks the story went quite differently in the early twentieth century. Black athletes like Major Taylor were formally excluded from a number of professional sports around the time of World War I, and would become more marginalized interwar period. For Taylor, who was effectively pushed into foreign exile after he won the bicycling US championship in 1900, sympathetic newspapers noted that "in France there is not the same prejudice against Afro-Americans that Taylor found [in the United States]." By 1902, Taylor was effectively done with racing in the United States. He tried mounting a comeback later in the decade, but found that many hotels and restaurants were no longer willing to serve him. In 1928, broke and struggling to make ends meet, Major Taylor hoped that sales of his autobiography would provide him with some much-need financial support. That support, sadly, never came.[5]

Whites found paths to success far easier. Thomas B. Jeffrey, a former bicycle manufacturer, illuminates how this was often the case. Trained in England as a maker of scientific instruments, Jeffrey came to the United States in 1863 to build bicycles, hoping to make his mark on the growing industry. His first stop was Chicago, where he helped create a brand of bicycles called Ramblers, experimenting with newfound automobile technologies on the side. In 1900, he moved out of the bicycle industry and relocated to Kenosha, Wisconsin, where he refocused his efforts on automobiles. In 1902, he produced 1,500 new Ramblers, simply swapping the old name of his bikes for the new name of his cars. The Jeffrey family sold the business in 1916 to Charles W. Nash, who quickly made the Kenosha plant the largest producer of automobiles outside of Detroit. Nash Motor Company would go on to become one of the largest automobile makers in the country.[6] A number of early twentieth-century Wisconsin-based automotive companies, such as Mitchell-Lewis in Racine, Kissel Kars in Hartford, and the Four Wheel Drive Company in Clintonville, also helped establish Wisconsin as a regional center for the automobile industry. But few of the opportunities lent to these men were extended to blacks like Taylor.[7]

The legacy of wheel fever was palpable in other ways throughout this period. In Appleton, for example, which had boasted one of the state's strongest LAW organizations throughout the 1890s, the first car arrived around 1898. A local physician named James Reeve purchased a Duryea Physicians Runabout for transportation to and from his appointments. Like many early cars, this "boneshaker" of a vehicle was extremely unreliable. Reeve actually tied a bicycle to the back of it just in case it broke down. By 1900, Reeve had replaced the Duryea with the more innovative (though no less trouble ridden) steam-powered Locomobile, which combined characteristics of a locomotive, horse carriage, and bicycle. Using pneumatic bicycle wheels and a central chain drive, the vehicle adopted many of the same basic technologies that had driven the safety's rise during the bicycle boom.[8] Recognizing a growing market, small businesses took the lead in providing for the needs of automobile owners. Appleton-area shops such as the Schlafer Hardware Company, whose bicycle sales had helped the business thrive during the earlier boom, serviced and monitored the nine hundred automobiles owned by Outagamie County residents in 1915.[9]

Dr. James Reeve used his Locomobile for medical visits in Appleton, ca. 1900. The horseless carriage's design was influenced by technologies developed through the bicycle.

History Museum at the Castle, Appleton, WI

By World War I, automobile producers across Europe and the United States employed thousands of people, turning out hundreds of new cars each year. Many of these companies could point to workers, designers, and engineers who had been employed in bicycle industries just ten or twenty years before. Early converts included a num-

Mr. and Mrs. Albert G. Zimmerman taking their Locomobile down Lake Mendota Drive outside Madison, 1902. The route was popular with touring cyclists, but automobiles began appearing by 1901.

WHi Image ID 40837

ber of recognizable faces. Walter Sanger joined his brothers Casper and William in 1911 as an employee at their automobile garage at 2578 North Farwell Avenue.[10] Meanwhile, under the slogan, "Andrae Never Disappoints"—used for more than a decade to sell Milwaukee residents their bicycles—Julius Andrae and Sons converted their works to make automobile parts and electronic accessories for cars.[11]

The bicycle boom influenced American transportation in other ways after 1900. As Walter Sanger's story helps show, bikes played an important role in the development of Wisconsin's early motorcycle industry, particularly for Harley-Davidson in Milwaukee. Although they were not the first to engineer a motorized bicycle, William Harley and the Davidson brothers (William, Walter, and Arthur) were able to perfect and effectively market their design in the years before World War I. During the fighting that ensued, Harley-Davidson produced eighteen thousand motorcycles for the military, effectively launching of one of Milwaukee's proudest and most enduring companies.[12] The aviation industry also expanded thanks to early bike mechanics and shopkeepers. Perhaps the most famous example is that of Orville and Wilbur Wright, who started out as bike mechanics. In 1892, almost a decade before their first flight at Kitty Hawk, North Carolina, the Wright brothers opened a bike shop in Dayton, Ohio. The Wright brothers credited their experiences as mechanics in helping them hone the fine-tuned machining in metal and wood that later enabled them to develop the first airplane.[13]

Wisconsin's early cyclists helped transform cultural expectations and attitudes regarding road infrastructure and transportation networks in the early twentieth century. In fact, the automobile's rise helped rejuvenate efforts at road reform that had begun during the good roads movement of the 1890s. With the help of many who had first worked for reform under the umbrella of this earlier lobby, Wisconsin passed its State Aid Road Law in 1911. After World War I, the state's dirt roads were slowly converted to gravel, macadam (layered crushed rock), and finally pavement. By 1916, the State Highway Commission started integrating these improved roads into a unified state highway system. As a result, Wisconsin saw a boom in regional tourism. A 1922 highway census revealed that more than three thousand automobiles had passed through once-remote northern Wisconsin towns like Rhinelander, effectively laying the groundwork for the North Woods tourism industry. Early wheelmen surely would have been thrilled to see their state covered in new roads, with so many new communities opened up for cycling adventures. But the enthusiasm for automobiles in this period made it clear that Wisconsinites much preferred visiting such places in their cars—at least for the time being.[14]

FOR much of the early twentieth century, the story of Wisconsin's investment in cycling takes a backseat to the automobile. Yet from 1900 to 1920, Europe's love affair with the bicycle only continued to grow. There, cycling remained broadly popular for a number of reasons. David Herlihy has credited cycling's enduring European popularity on tighter street patterns, a cultural appreciation for cycling that made it less prone to cycles of "boom and bust," and the tendency to see bicycles as a utilitarian transportation choice, particularly after World War I. In the United States and throughout Wisconsin, by contrast, only competitive venues like bicycle racing managed to keep cycling relevant as the automobile gained traction. The 1920s became something of a golden era for bicycle track racing in the country, but the massive crowds characteristic of cycling events during the earlier boom were a thing of the past. Europe also saw a rejuvenation of bicycle racing, but unlike the sprinters and speedsters common in the United States,

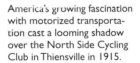

America's growing fascination with motorized transportation cast a looming shadow over the North Side Cycling Club in Thiensville in 1915.

Milwaukee County Historical Society

most European races were road races spread over several days. The Tour de France, for example, was first held in 1903. Over a hundred years later it remains the event most synonymous in the public mind with competitive cycling.[15]

In the United States, those who remembered the boom of the 1890s turned to commemorating and celebrating it. In 1928, for example, Elsbeth Andrae, the wife of the former Milwaukee bicycling great Terry Andrae, donated lands along the Lake Michigan shoreline near Sheboygan as a state park. To this day, thousands of Wisconsinites relax in Terry Andrae State Park, even as most remain unaware of its link to early cycling history.[16] As the decades passed, LAW members and members of other amateur clubs gathered for reunions. In 1936, the North Side Cycling Club celebrated forty-seven years of continuous bicycle advocacy for Wisconsin's communities. Pioneer wheelmen such as Louis Pierron and J. W. Warnken helped host the anniversary festivities with a program titled "Fight-Fight-Fight." It implored the aging wheelmen in attendance to "ride bikes and enjoy their health and sport as well as we do."[17]

In contrast, scarcity and hopelessness helped drive another spike in bicycle sales in the United States as people sought cheaper and more utilitarian transportation options. In 1936, sales actually broke one million bikes per year for the first time since the 1890s. Yet American manufacturers lagged well behind their European competitors as World War II opened. Bicycling remained so popular in the years just before the war in Europe that people joked Dutch children would be born on bicycles in the twenty-first century.[18] The Depression may have been a boon for the industry, but it was keenly felt by those who had lived through bicycling's earlier heyday. In October 1931, Otto Dorner, the apostle of the good roads movement, was traveling along the Port Washington Road when his car collided with another vehicle. Although everyone else survived the crash with just a few minor cuts and bruises, Dorner's left leg was crushed. Never quite able to recover his health, Dorner sank into a deep depression. On July 7, 1938, he walked to a park bench on the lakefront in Milwaukee along Lincoln Memorial Drive. He sat down, read an edition of the day's news, and then put a gun to his head. When he was found, he was holding the gun as a copy of his newspaper fluttered in the nearby grass.[19]

Another Wisconsin native, George F. Kennan, offered perspective on Wisconsin's place in biking as the Depression came to a close. In June 1938, Kennan, who would become one of the most influential architects of twentieth century foreign policy, returned from his diplomatic work in the Soviet Union to take a bike tour of his home state. Kennan described a landscape transformed by the rise of the automobile, but one that differed substantially from the descriptions of the LAW published just thirty years before. "All of the roads," he said, "were beautifully graded and surfaced. They led through prosperous and thickly populated farming country." Such roads presented a lonely and haunting place for Kennan, however. "It seemed to me that these beautiful highways were the most deserted places I had ever encountered. In the course of a one-hundred mile journey, I was destined to encounter on the open road no single fellow-cyclist." Compared to the motorists who "had no more real association with the highway than their fellow-travelers in the cabins of the transport planes that occasionally droned overhead," Kennan found the new car culture dangerous, a "natural menace." Kennan worried that cars, and the feelings of solitude they seemed to breed, represented the "sad climax of individualism, the blind-alley of a generation which had forgotten to think or live collectively." It symbolized, he believed, a "people who felt neither curiosity nor responsibility for the mass of those who shared their community life and their community problems." Kennan's poignant critique could not contrast more with the descriptions of busy rural roads and highways jam-packed with cyclists throughout the state in the 1890s, or of early cyclist's descriptions of the roadside conversations and picnics of the first bike boom. Kennan and Dorner did not know each other, most likely, but in the summer of 1938 both came to terribly bleak conclusions about what the future might hold.[20]

The experience of World War II seemed to confirm the dark suspicions both men held. With the course of human history in question as the world staggered into a new and frightening atomic age, institutions looked for comforting reminders of the past. Long-honored Wheelmen traditions, such as the annual forty-eight-mile Milwaukee Road Race, continued in 1945. In that same year the Milwaukee Public Museum used wheelmen reunions to gather a large collection of early historic bicycles. The collection, initiated by Milwaukee alderman and bicycle enthusiast Carl P. Deitz, had nearly forty-five models in its holdings by the war's end. On February 11, 1945, Deitz pre-

Wheelmen kept a fraternal bond even after the glory days of cycling were over. Old members routinely met for reunions, including this one of the Milwaukee Wheelmen in 1950.

Milwaukee County Historical Society

You are invited to the
Gathering of Old Time Bicycle Riders
in the Conference Room of the
MILWAUKEE PUBLIC MUSEUM
West Wisconsin Avenue and North Eighth Street
Take Library Elevator to Second Floor
SUNDAY, FEBRUARY 11, 1945, at 3:45 P. M.

We suggest that you **COME EARLIER** (after 1:30 P. M.) and view the col-
lection of Rare Old Bikes gathered by Ald. Carl P. Dietz and presented to the
Museum, **BEFORE** going to the Conference Room.
Bring along any old photographs, catalogs or clippings. Movies of old timers
will be shown. We are expecting you. Bring the ladies.
THE COMMITTEE

Wheelmen gathered in 1945 to celebrate a collection of rare bicycles donated by Carl Deitz to the Milwaukee Public Museum. The Dietz collection remains the most extensive set of early bicycles in Wisconsin.

Milwaukee Public Museum Photography Collection

By 1945, many Americans viewed cycling as a children's activity. Groups of young boy and girl cyclists, like Carolyn Hall, Bruce Mohs, and David Culver, were common sights around Madison.

WHi Image ID 39488

sented the museum's bicycle collection to a "Gathering of Old Time Bicycle Riders." Organizers also asked the veteran riders to bring their photographs, catalogs, and clippings from the first boom.[21]

One of the more heartwarming stories of the postwar period involved the re-interment of Major Taylor from his unmarked grave into a new plot at Chicago's Glenwood Cemetery on May 23, 1948. While it is difficult to say what, precisely, motivated a group of ex-professional bike racers in Chicago to locate and move Taylor to a more respectable location, they managed to hold a small ceremony for Taylor that helped restore his name and place to the historical record. The re-burial represented something of a generational changing-of-the-guard. With Jackie Robinson, the first black Major League Baseball player of the modern era then playing in his second season for the Brooklyn Dodgers, it was increasingly clear for many Americans that profound shifts were about to take place in American life. Those changes would also be seen in the cycling community. Between 1945 and 1960, with many of the sport's old-timers fading into obscurity, cycling became increasingly aligned with a new demographic.[22]

In the United States, bicycling in the postwar era was dominated by youth. American children and adolescents were increasingly the only ones seen on bicycles, parading around their neighborhoods with packs of friends born to suburban baby boomers and war veterans. Once they became teenagers, however, white suburban Americans tended to abandon their bikes for cars, which allowed them greater mobility, increased privacy, and greater access to new consumption options including fast food and drive-in movie theatres.[23] In the same period, bikes became more popular with the adult population worldwide. After 1945, bicycling exploded as a global phenomenon in ways that were simply not so in the United States. In nations such as India and Pakistan, and throughout the continents of Southeast Asia and parts of Africa, cycling became a truly ubiquitous transportation option. China

Women remain an important presence in Wisconsin's cycling community today. Milwaukeeans Kate and Claire Riordan completed a tour from the Pacific Ocean to Milwaukee in 2010.

Kate Riordan

built multilane bicycle highways to accommodate the flood of bicycle traffic that appeared after 1945. Driven by the abundance of cheap labor and parts produced overseas, cycling today is very much a globalized industry. Millions worldwide commute to work, to food, and to enjoy leisure on their bikes.

In the United States, however, the story of the post-World War II decades was quite different, with bicycling seen primarily as a recreational option and not a utilitarian one. The postwar dominance of the automobile simply repeated patterns of exclusivity first learned in the years of early cycling. After 1945, road projects gave middle-class whites unprecedented access to jobs and recreation while effectively cutting nonwhites off from those same opportunities. The automobile lobby, centered in Detroit, used its considerable power to convince federal and state governments to invest in suburban neighborhoods, further marginalizing urban communities while fueling white middle-class economic expansion. Urban whites relied on the improved road networks to flee to new and often all-white suburban housing and shopping developments, leaving behind urban centers populated with black and immigrant laborers who came during the Great Migration. Between 1945 and 1975, suburban Milwaukee became one of the largest white population centers in the state while inner-city Milwaukee became solidly black. New interstates, meanwhile, limited the mobility of poorer inner-city communities by dividing neighborhoods and deepening racial segregation. The growth of the modern suburb also cut off black and increasingly Latino and Asian communities from marketplaces and services, including grocery stores, markets, parks, and access to public transportation. At the same time, the United States became more and more dependent on cheap oil and gasoline.

Slowly but perceptibly, these larger demographic and economic changes led to increased concerns about the availability of fossil fuels, the sustainability of the new suburbanized landscape, and the declining health conditions of suburban residents. In the 1960s, as bicycle sales reached four million for the first time in the United States, white Americans reawakened to the need for change. A segment of that reawakening looked to Europe. New European-made ten-speeds were faster, lighter, and easier to use than the heavy cruiser-style bikes that were common in 1950s suburban neighborhoods. As more European bikes filled the marketplace, demand rose for better access to bicycling infrastructure. After several decades of car dominance, Wisconsin made its first significant move back toward an embrace of bicycling with its creation of the Elroy-Sparta State Trail, the storied former home of the Chicago and North Western Railway, in 1967. The use of abandoned nineteenth-century railroad beds to create a 32-mile bike path demonstrated the adaptability of older infrastructure for new ends.[24]

In the early 1970s, many American bicycle companies were taken by surprise when they noticed a spike in sales across the nation's dealerships. Everyone had theories as to why it was happening, but as sales went from 6.9 million bikes in 1970 to 15.2 million in 1973, speculation grew more urgent. Some pointed to a rising environmental consciousness led, in part, by Senator Gaylord Nelson of Wisconsin, who helped create Earth Day on April 22, 1970. Others, as Jeff Mapes has helped highlight, pointed to an emerging physical fitness craze. Calls for more radical reform were also in the air, as the great social movements of the late 1960s and early 1970s, including women's liberation, civil rights, the antiwar movement, and gay rights moved to center stage, offering a powerful critique of the status quo in the country. Not surprisingly, given the sport's long tradition of advocacy, several new bicycling companies formed during this period. In Wisconsin, bicycling's long ties to southeastern Wisconsin and Milwaukee would again shine through as an enduring legacy of the bike boom.[25]

Following in the footsteps of bicycle pioneers like Terry Andrae and A. D. Meiselbach, Richard Burke and Bevel Hogg formed Trek Bicycle Corporation in December 1975 (established 1976) as a subsidiary of the Milwaukee-based Roth Corporation, an appliance distributor. Trek's origins help illuminate the variety of ways the first boom helped shape what has become one of the world's largest and premier bicycle manufacturers. In a direct reflection of the state's rural and small-shop roots, Trek initially employed just five workers, who got their start making bikes in a rented barn located in rural Waterloo, Wisconsin. Its founders chose the location for simple and practical reasons, hoping to divide the space between Milwaukee and Madison, the two cities where they each lived. On another level, however, it made for a perfect choice, as it stood directly between the two great cycling cities in the state. For the first few years, Trek built its reputation as a purveyor of traditional steel-frame bicycles. By the early 1980s, however, it would change direction to meet the demand of what was by then clearly becoming America's second great bicycle boom.[26]

Long-dormant advocacy organizations also re-established themselves in the state during this period. After a long period of inactivity in the early and middle part of the twentieth century, the League of American Wheelmen was rejuvenated as a new organization, the League of American Bicyclists. The changing demands of these and other groups again led manufacturers, as they had during the first boom, to initiate sweeping design changes to meet the new tastes of the bicycling community. One of the key inno-

Quarterbacks Jerry Tagge and Scott Hunter celebrated the Green Bay Packers' unique bicycle tradition with young fans during training camp in 1973.

WHi Image ID 59758

vations of the mid-1970s was the creation of the mountain bike, which is now one of the biggest parts of the domestic bicycling industry.[27]

In Wisconsin, kids in Green Bay helped the Green Bay Packers foster a much-beloved Wisconsin bicycling tradition. A photograph in the collections of the Wisconsin Historical Society from 1973, the year of the oil crisis, documents Packers quarterbacks Jerry Tagge and Scott Hunter riding bicycles loaned to them by young fans assembled outside of Lambeau field. The players borrowed the bikes to "commute" to a nearby practice facility. For several decades now, the Packers have continued this tradition by inviting youngsters from the community to lend their bikes to Packer players who still follow the same routine during training camp. Former Packers CEO and chairman of the board Bob Harlan celebrated the kid's ongoing participation in 2011: "You see them rain or shine waiting for the players to come out."[28]

Like the first bicycle boom, however, the second boom did not appear without various fits and starts. As Jeff Mapes has concluded, sales were actually slackening nationwide by the time of Trek's appearance, and bike shops were closing in alarming numbers around the country by the middle of the decade. Scholars continue to debate whether it was high-minded environmentalism or changing demographic patterns that drove the first wave of booms and busts in this period. After all, by the early 1970s, many of the baby-boomers who had enjoyed cycling as kids had grown up to embrace ten-speeds as adults. Hoping to meet their new demand, American manufacturers reacted in precisely the same way as their forebears during the panic of 1893, when they oversaturated the market with cheap bicycles and drove down demand.[29]

By the early 1980s, however, there were signs that the bicycle market was set to stabilize. Trek helped foster this new domestic manufacturing environment. Sensing an opportunity to answer the growing demand among high-end consumers hoping to have an American-made product, Trek started recalibrating its approach, echoing the pattern of early manufacturers in the time of the first boom. Driven again by the ongoing demands of the white middle and upper class, Trek helped put thousands of new bikes into the hands of consumers willing to pay a little extra for their machines. With more and more cyclists back on the roads, state governments and local advocacy groups responded by creating new trail infrastructure around the state.[30]

Bikes continued to be a popular, though not ubiquitous, transportation option through the 1980s and 1990s in Wisconsin and beyond. As they had during the first boom, advocacy organizations again helped increase ease of access to the sport for Wisconsinites. In 1986, for example, the Rails-to-Trails Conservancy was formed, giving new momentum to bike trail projects throughout the country. Competitive racing again re-emerged, increasing the sport's popularity. In 1986, Greg LeMond became the first American cyclist to win the Tour de France. Bikes, as increasing numbers of converts pointed out, were more widely accessible, easier to use, and cheaper than perhaps any other transportation option on earth. Yet the second boom was again characterized by sexism. Women bicyclists, for example, did not have representation at the Olympics until the 1988 games in Seoul.[31]

Led by Greg LeMond, bicycle racing re-emerged as a popular spectator sport in the 1980s. Road races and venues like Kenosha's Washington Park Velodrome provide a local outlet for racing enthusiasts.

Wisconsin Department of Tourism, RJ & Linda Miller

Since the early 1990s, however, it is clear there has been yet another cultural return to many of early cycling's promises. Driven by a resurgence of modern-day environmentalism and a flood of Asian-produced bicycles and bicycling components, it remains difficult to say where this recent, still unfolding boom might go. Certainly, big legislative gains for cyclists in the early 1990s helped rejuvenate and embolden the current cycling climate in Wisconsin and elsewhere. Strong bipartisan support of cycling legislation, first forged as an explicit goal of the LAW's activism in the 1880s and 1890s, remained key to the sport through its resurgence in the 1990s and early 2000s. Wisconsin Republican Tom Petri, for example, played a crucial role in the 1990s in broadening access to cycling at both the state and federal level. Such bipartisanship is fading, however, as the Republican Party has become less and less interested in advocating for the environmental benefits of the sport. Nothing has better symbolized the sport's radicalizing partisan make-up, perhaps, than the 1992 emergence of Critical Mass, a militant activist ride where bicyclists used their numbers to block traffic, calling attention not only to cyclist's presence, but also to the dependencies fostered by automobile use and fossil fuel consumption.[32]

Since the 1990s, then, a distinct countercultural influence has made inroads into today's cycling culture, where it remains in a sometimes-uneasy relation to the sport's more conservative elements. As activists hammer home the point that riding a bike produces far less pollution and demands far fewer resources than driving a car, their message is finding a home among increasing numbers who see the bicycle as a practical solution to many of the world's ills. Bikes, they point out, are far cheaper than other modes of transportation. Working families can save hundreds, if not thousands, of dollars per year by replacing

basic trips they take by car everyday with trips they might take by bike. Groups such as Revolution Cycles in Madison have advocated for not only a greener world through bicycle recycling programs, but also bicycle awareness and owner self-sufficiency. They teach people how to repair and build their own bikes, and they work to get bikes into the hands of anyone who has a desire to ride, no matter their economic position. They embody the newest generation of bicycling's continuing egalitarian tradition.[33] But many questions persist. A look at the enduring lessons in *Wheel Fever*, we hope, can help shed light on these concerns and inform their ongoing debate.

HISTORICALLY speaking, bicycling is one of the rare sports that requires a tremendous amount of space in order to be truly enjoyed. Since at least the late 1860s, bicycle advocates across the country, including Wisconsin, have worked to secure access to space for their sport in a variety of ways. During the velocipede mania, cities and local governments reacted with hostility to these demands and effectively used local ordinances to curtail velocipede use. Advocates, however, kept pushing, and by the 1880s it was clear that bicyclists constituted a powerful enough lobby that no city government could afford to stand in the cyclist's way. From the early 1880s through the early 1900s, cyclists and local governments worked together to determine what the culture of the roads would look like. This work involved answering basic questions: Who should ride? Where should they ride? When? And how? The ways early cyclists worked out these questions, often in tandem with elements of both the private and public spheres, has largely been the story of this book. We hope we have shown that the answers often lie in challenging systems of exclusion that inform popular understandings of the sport's history and legacies.

One clear lesson that *Wheel Fever* illuminates, we believe, is that while private industry often assumes credit for generating access to the sport through sponsorships, innovative product designs, and the quality of manufacture, its historical role in fostering cycling is easy to overstate. Since the 1860s, business leaders and manufacturers in Wisconsin and throughout the United States have lagged behind their overseas peers in providing cutting-edge technologies and products to American consumers. Only after demand has risen have domestic manufacturers typically reacted, yet their products are often subpar in comparison to those produced overseas. Still, American manufacturers and workers can be credited with providing thousands of American riders with quality and even high-end bikes, especially since the 1980s. This isn't the entire story, however. The reality is that outside of a few American cities, the real reason for the private

Rural towns like New Glarus, located along the Sugar River State Trail, have benefited from partnerships between the government and bicycle advocates.

Wisconsin Department of Tourism, RJ & Linda Miller

sector's triumph in the United States during the late nineteenth and twentieth centuries belongs to car companies. Bikes, despite a growing presence in total market share, take a backseat in contemporary transportation sector discussions. Today's multinational car companies spend more on Super Bowl ads than the entire domestic bicycle industry generates in a single year. Yet the $1.5 billion generated annually by cyclists in the state of Wisconsin is no small number.

Egalitarians working from outside the industry deserve far more attention. Indeed, one of the great legacies of the first bicycle boom is the continuing partnership forged between everyday bicycle advocates and their representatives in local government. Since the late 1960s and early 1970s, for example, Wisconsin has developed hundreds of miles of bike trails through a combination of state, federal, and private initiatives. Today, Wisconsin is a national leader not only in terms of its total bike path mileage, but also for being one of the first states to adopt the popular rails-to-trails program which converts abandoned railroad lines into bike paths. The success of trail systems like the Elroy-Sparta State Trail, now in the Rails-to-Trails Conservancy "Hall of Fame," highlights the strong support local advocates have had from the state in the form of grants and other incentives for bike infrastructure developments. According to a 2010 study, the state of Wisconsin invested $40 million in the state's bike infrastructure between 1993 and 2008, with federal support reaching $156 million during the same period.[34]

In fact, in recent years the government has proven far more reliable in supporting bike infrastructure projects in poorer Wisconsin communities than has the private sector. In Janesville, for example, area bike advocates gained twenty-eight miles of paved trails from 1998 to 2008, linking the city's north and south sides. Further plans are in the works to link these paths to nearby Beloit, a city with a historically strong African American and Latino presence. Planners in Rock County are investigating the possibility of extending the Janesville/Beloit trail corridor to northern Illinois and then Chicago, which would provide a link not only to one of the country's largest urban cycling communities but to the largest city in the Midwest. As the *Janesville Gazette* reported in June 2012, such plans often depend on the availability of state grants. Once again, however, those grants would not be possible without the strong support cycling has had at the grassroots level in the state.[35] Indeed, through the combined help of local governments and independent advocacy groups including the Bicycle Federation of Wisconsin, state residents can now access the Great River State Trail (linking Onalaska, Holmen, and Trempealeau), the La Crosse River State Trail (which links the Great River Trail to the Elroy-Sparta State Trail), the Sugar River State Trail (between New Glarus and Brodhead), and the Hank Aaron State Trail (in Milwaukee, with access to Miller Park, home of the Milwaukee Brewers). Together, these efforts and many others help highlight the victories Wisconsin has had in giving its riders strong infrastructure options and show what private and public efforts can achieve when they work together.[36]

Wisconsin has remained an innovative leader by offering bicyclists the opportunity to ride across rolling farmland, through repurposed railroad tunnels, and over old rail bridges, like this one on the Great River State Trail.

Wisconsin Department of Tourism, RJ & Linda Miller

Americans can point to a long list of great bicycling cities in the country, but very few truly great states and even fewer great bicycling regions. In Europe, cities such as Copenhagen and Amsterdam have far greater bicycle participation rates than any US city. An estimated fifty percent of the population rides a bike on any given day, a substantial figure compared to Madison's still-small tally of roughly ten to twelve percent during the peak bicycling season of late spring, summer, and early fall. The reason, as we hope to have made clear in this book, is that bicycling in the United States emerged out of a profoundly inegalitarian culture fueled by elitism and exclusion. This, along with the dominance of car culture, explains why the benefits of bicycling have not been extended to or embraced by a broader public.[37] Still, there are examples that indicate this story is not quite over. Looking abroad, many cities in the United States have again taken inspiration from overseas and are re-energizing efforts to improve access to cycling in ways that recall some of the more progressive initiatives currently underway in Europe. The City of Milwaukee offers a good example. In 2011, after making a study of European biking infrastructure, the city installed what the Bicycle Federation of Wisconsin has described as the first "raised bike lane[s] east of Eugene, Oregon." These lanes, situated directly next to the route of car traffic, have helped segregate bikes from cars, providing a buffer between the road surface and the bike path surface that improves safety and encourages bike traffic.[38]

Advocates do not need to look so far from home for inspiration, however. One of the great legacies of the wheel fever that gripped Wisconsin in the last part of the nineteenth century is the uncontested truth that cycling presents a broad range of health and environmental benefits. This is all the more important in a state where public health experts warn that more than half the residents are obese or will soon reach obesity levels, and where cheese curds, brats, ice cream, and beer provide an experience bordering on the sacred. In 2010, the journal *Environmental Health Perspectives* helped quantify the benefits of cycling nationwide. It estimated that $3.8 billion in health care costs could be saved annually if Americans simply replaced their daily (less than five-mile) car trips with bicycle rides. Further, they estimated that 1,100 lives would be saved each year through the contributions of bicycling to cutting obesity and curbing diabetes, heart disease, and other ailments common to a population notorious for its unhealthy diet and woeful lack of exercise. Maggie Grabow, a PhD candidate at the University of Wisconsin–Madison's Nelson Institute, which studies a broad number of environmental and public health issues, has put it bluntly: "The majority of Americans do not get the recommended minimum level of exercise." Grabow adds, "In a busy daily schedule, if that exercise can automatically occur while commuting to work, we anticipate a major benefit in stemming the obesity epidemic." The challenge, of course, is that many people, particularly the state's poor, disabled, and working people, simply lack the money, time, and easy access to trails that make bicycling an easy choice that fits comfortably into their daily routine.[39]

Bipartisan support for bicycling legislation remains strong in Wisconsin, but like national policy, it often fails to address broader issues to democratize transportation.

Wisconsin Department of Tourism, RJ & Linda Miller

The environmental movement has also been tremendously influential in shaping the continuing work of bicycle advocates in Wisconsin, and it remains a key part of contemporary bicycling politics in the state. Few are willing to refute the idea that bikes promote a range of sensible transportation options for anyone concerned about the health of the planet. Bicycling reduces the amount of carbon released into the atmosphere. "If we can swap bikes for cars, we gain in fitness, local air quality, a reduction in greenhouse gases, and the personal economic benefits of biking rather than driving. It's a four-way win," Jonathan Patz of the University of Wisconsin's Global Health Institute has said. Indeed, the improvements in bicycle infrastructure are already making cities like Portland, Oregon, and Madison, Wisconsin, increasingly popular places to live and ride. Many US cities are also seeing an explosion of interest and participation in cycling. From New York City to Detroit, and from Phoenix to San Francisco and beyond, exciting new developments in bicycle advocacy are making US cities more bike friendly and more sustainable as a result.[40] More importantly, these benefits extend beyond the cycling community. Everyone breathes cleaner air as more people choose biking as a primary mode of transportation.

Bringing all of these issues together, it seems necessary to reiterate the importance of bipartisan support that combines not only public and private initiatives but also the work of independent advocacy organizations like nonprofits, activist groups, and, of course, concerned individuals and families. Though late nineteenth-century LAW members in Wisconsin often had clear partisan preferences, they also knew that the sport's future could not be built without support from across the aisle or from across more important divides, such as those drawn between whites and blacks, men and women, and farmers and city folk. The future of bipartisanship in cycling, however, appears to be at risk. As recently as 2004, President George W. Bush, a Republican, and presidential nominee John Kerry, a Democrat, both spoke openly and routinely about their love of cycling, but only Democrat Barack Obama continued this stance in 2008. But in the 2012 electoral cycle, the GOP effectively distanced itself only from the cycling community. In the wake of this shift, an unlikely array of independents including Michael Bloomberg and Janette Sadik-Kahn (*New York Magazine* wrote in 2009 that her opponents often dismiss her as "hipster bureaucrat") have moved recent reforms along in places such as New York City. Countless others, representing positions far less privileged, have also carried on cycling's egalitarian vision.[41]

Of course, not all of the blame for partisan collapse can be pinned on bipartisan failures. Both parties remain primarily invested, it seems, in keeping the automobile industry paramount as the transportation option of choice in the United States through subsidies, bailouts, and other government supports. In addition to receiving drastically lower federal expenditures, moreover, bicyclists have recently served as scapegoats for problems in the car culture, as when the United States Transportation Secretary under George W. Bush, Mary Peters, partially blamed spending on bike paths for the deadly collapse of a Minneapolis freeway bridge in August 2007.[42] Still, bicyclists across the country are working on a variety of urban planning, public health, children's education, and energy policy fronts to increase the visibility and viability of biking.

While it remains limited in scope, work across the aisle is still possible, even as politics at the county and state level remain deeply divided. A good example of this is how, in 2011, during the controversial recall of Governor Scott Walker, the Bicycle Federation of Wisconsin managed to get the bipartisan support of Wisconsin's Republicans and Democrats for its bicycle "tune-up" bill, which updated a number of the state's bicycling laws and improved a few basic safety standards. "Given the current political climate," the federation's website read, "it is good to see that members of both parties can agree on making bicycling safer in Wisconsin." The federation was obscuring more than it revealed, however, when it said that it had brought the two warring parties into line. In reality, the parties agreed that bicyclists should have basic safety equipment like helmets and lights, and that government had a role in enforcing penalties against those who did not have them. What the seeming victory reveals is that Wisconsin had basically returned to the battles it had already fought more than a hundred years previously. While bipartisan support of a bill is helpful, support in this case simply indicated that basic safety measures are a good idea. Legislators are much less willing to touch broader issues that might have bigger implications for society.[43]

In the end, informed bicycle advocacy is still the key to ensuring bicycling's continuing successes. Nevertheless, many challenges and questions linger. Chief among them is the simple reality that bicycling still benefits wealthier and white communities more than it benefits poor and nonwhite communities.[44] Because government has often been the most reliable source of bicycle advocacy, the current emphasis on rolling back government means that disadvantaged communities suffer while wealthier communities—acting through separate, often private revenue streams—can continue to install new bike infrastructure. Yet many nonprofit groups are at work to expand access across common divides. The Bicycle Federation of Wisconsin, for example, takes as its mission the task of securing the sport's benefits for the widest range of people possible, all while making bicycling a more common and seamless part of everyday life. It has played a key role in sponsoring a range of popular cycling events throughout the state, and it routinely works with area government and industry leaders to promote cycling to new riders, including programs that create incentives for biking to work. The federation's "Ride Guide," an annual compilation of area rides and events, boasted more than 250 bicycle rides in the state of Wisconsin alone in 2012. The federation also updates its membership on the various legislative gains bicyclists have made each year, both in state and out of state.[45]

Wisconsin continues to be an innovative center for state-made bicycles and components. Here a Milwaukee Bicycle Company head badge is installed on a new bicycle at Ben's Cycle in Milwaukee.

Photo by Drew Triplett

A long tradition of bicycle advocacy has lured bicycle manufacturers to the state, but their continued presence still rests, ultimately, on the passion cyclists bring to their sport. Trek Bicycle Corporation, Waterford Precision Cycles, Ellis Cycles, Saris Cycling Group, MadRax, Rudy Rack, Hayes Disc Brake, Pacific Cycle, and Mt. Borah, Inc. all call the state home, and all stand as a tribute to the legacies of the first bicycle boom. Some of these companies have huge national and international market shares, like Trek, while others are small-scale or "artisanal" shops, much in the vein of some of Wisconsin's early producers. Ellis, for example, is a small producer that crafts handmade frames in Waterford. Wisconsin's bike riders also support several key industry distributors, including Planet Bike and Olympic Supply. Bike messenger companies like Breakaway Bicycle in Milwaukee and Scram! in Madison compliment the 270-or-so bicycle stores and shops that employ hundreds of workers in retail and mechanic positions throughout the state. All depend on the seemingly simple yet potentially revolutionary act of going for a bike ride.

Wisconsin's advocates know that the most effective politics are often local politics. Cycling's local presence has helped Madison become a national and even international cycling destination, a standard bearer among America's top cycling destinations. John Burke, the son of Richard Burke and the current chairman of Trek, has emerged as one of the nation's most powerful bicycle proponents. City leaders remain key to leading the way in local affairs. Former Madison mayor Dave Cieslewicz, for example, was one of the first of more than seven hundred US mayors to sign a pledge to limit the city's greenhouse gas production in 2007. The year before, Cieslewicz announced a new initiative to make Madison the best city in America for cycling. Even a brief glance gives plenty of evidence that Madison is well on its way to becoming just that.[46]

Wisconsin's stamp on the nation's bicycling industry remains clear. The best recent estimates suggest Wisconsin's cyclists have helped build what today accounts for a substantial chunk, perhaps one-fifth, of the nation's bicycling industry.[47] Estimates of the yearly contributions to the state's economy have added to the total manufacturing, service, and sales numbers, estimated at $556 million in 2006, to a more recent 2010 figure that includes recreation and tourism dollars, concluding that bicycling pumps more than $1.5 billion annually into the local economy. Add to this an estimated

Few monuments recognize Wisconsin's early bicycle history. Sparta's Ben Bikin' statue is a tribute to the high-wheel and stands thirty-two feet tall near the Elroy-Sparta State Trail.

Wisconsin Department of Tourism, RJ & Linda Miller

jobs impact of an approximate 3,500 positions statewide, and you begin to get a sense of bicycling's significance to the Badger State.[48] Taken together, the combined strengths of government, industry, and advocacy organizations have also led to a dramatic proliferation of cycling-related events, races, and rides that have only deepened the cultural significance of the sport to Wisconsin. Though area companies take tremendous pride in sponsoring them, it is the riders who ultimately lend these events their power. Bike MS's Best Dam Bike Ride, for example, will celebrate its thirtieth anniversary in 2013 with the help of the Bicycle Federation of Wisconsin and the National Multiple Sclerosis Society. The ride took its name from Beaver Dam, Wisconsin, which was the overnight stop in what started as a two-day ride from Milwaukee to Beaver Dam and back in the early 1980s. Today, the ride goes from Pewaukee to Whitewater to Madison and typically draws around 1,700 cyclists. It has helped raise millions of dollars to find a cure for the disease.[49]

Participating in the state's culture sometimes means involving yourself in the state's great cycling events, large and small. In the recently organized Riverwest 24-Hour Bike Race, riders tour the Riverwest neighborhood in Milwaukee, assembling as many laps as possible over the course of twenty-four hours. Riders can race solo, or they can sign up as a team and split the time however they please between team members. While the race does not support a particular charity, organizers do not dissuade riders from raising money for a cause. Pedal Across Wisconsin (PAW) offers an event that, since 1989, has taken riders across Wisconsin's North Woods in a loop that includes the Nicolet National Forest, Eagle River, and dozens of miles along Wisconsin's beautiful inland lakes. Planners also include off-bike scenic opportunities for riders. Like many organized group rides in the state, it caters to riders of all ability levels. Wisconsinites also delight in events that have a decidedly independent streak. The World Naked Bike Ride, for example, is a yearly event that draws participants together from dozens of cities around the world. Over the past several years, a dedicated following in Madison has turned out to make the event one of the highlights in the city's yearly bicycling calendar. Asking its riders to "bear as they dare,"

Cyclists at the Chequamegon Fat Tire Festival continue to redefine bicycle culture by racing along the grounds of the American Birkebeiner cross-country ski trail.

Wisconsin Department of Tourism, RJ & Linda Miller

the ride is just what its title implies: a clothing-optional jaunt through town meant to foster positive body images for a cleaner, safer, and more energy independent world.[50]

Through their own experiences with riding, through ongoing efforts by organizations like the Bicycle Federation, and through other state and local educational programs, Wisconsin's residents have increasingly awoken to the many improvements bicycles make to quality of life. Bicycles reduce traffic congestion by taking cars off the roads. They decrease the need and spaces required for parking. They calm automobile traffic, making it safer not only for motorists and cyclists but also for pedestrians walking on the sidewalks. Bicycles get riders to nearby destinations faster than cars, as anyone who has travelled State Street in downtown Madison can readily attest. And while many of bicycling's benefits can be hard to quantify and measure, a number of studies have shown that people who live in areas where bikers and walkers are common generally enjoy a much happier existence. Residents find that they can easily fold bicycling into life's daily routines, such as going to the grocery store, visiting the bank, or getting to work. Running errands on your bicycle is often less stressful, less expensive, and always more healthy than riding in a car. It can save you hundreds of dollars per year in fuel costs. These are all markers of a great cycling state, but it would be a mistake to assume all great things last forever.[51]

Perhaps the most exciting legacy of Wisconsin's wheel fever is recognizing the substantial gap that has opened between the world experienced on bicycles throughout the last part of the nineteenth century and the one that might yet be created with the lessons of history in mind. Many state advocates, for example, were disappointed when Madison narrowly missed becoming a host to a portion of the 2016 Olympic Games. Chicago made a concerted and aggressive bid to host the 2016 event and ultimately advanced as a finalist city to the selection committee. Madison, cited by the Chicago organizers for its outstanding bicycling opportunities, would have hosted the bicycling events. Some took the loss as a stinging defeat for local businesses, but what is ultimately more important? Building for a future that might benefit a few world-class athletes? Or building a future in which all of us, star athletes or not, might find ways to make cycling more central to our lives?[52]

THE stories told in *Wheel Fever* underscore the tremendous challenges faced by cyclists in Wisconsin and throughout the country today. In this book, we have tried to highlight the ways bicycles, bicyclists, and the cultures they have produced are in fact part of broader cultural trends. Indeed, the state's bicycling history illustrates just how powerfully cycling has worked as a force of both political inclusion and exclusion, often benefitting the white middle and upper class in ways that have not been shared by others who also call the United States home.

It is clear that we still have a long way to go. In Wisconsin, the poor and working classes continue to live in zones that remain environmentally at risk. Working-class communities are often cut off from public recreational spaces such as parks and bike paths. Wisconsin's enduring racial segregation also makes it hard for members of one community to bike to another community comfortably. The bicycling community stands to lose many of its historic gains if its advocates do not stand up for the value and equity of America's public spaces, like the highways and biking trails once championed by the good roads movement. More than this, cycling advocates need to fight for spaces that are truly shared and open to all. Cycling works best, after all, as a solution for society when it is paired with and integrated into other modes of transportation that take the ideas of sustainability and public access seriously, like high-speed rail, electric and hybrid vehicles, and innovative public transportation networks that connect the state's cities and towns.

Increasingly positioned at the forefront of America's many ongoing struggles, bicycling's history goes back far beyond what most people might assume. In the last part of the nineteenth century, cycling revolutionized America's transportation culture, offering a working alternative to today's high-consumption, oil-dependent automobile

Milwaukee's annual Santa Cycle Rampage fuses wintertime riding with a holiday celebration.

Kate Riordan

Today, Wisconsin is known as a great bicycling destination, but many challenges to its reputation persist.

Wisconsin Department of Tourism, Brian Malloy

industry. Although the first boom failed to secure the bicycle as the preferred vehicle for navigating America's cities and towns, it is impossible to know how far it might have gone had cycling's early advocates worked to better integrate their sport with a more sustainable democratic vision. For all the stories of cycling's early successes shared here, then, the early history of cycling is also a story of limitations and false starts. A widespread cultural assumption of white authority and control kept the bicycle from achieving its true potential, even as it worked to expand bicycling's benefits to growing numbers of white middle-class men. In this way, visions of a poor man's and poor woman's horse ultimately lost out to a more conservative mindset that simply used the bicycle, more often than not, to re-assert the lines of white male control. This triumph of inequality was never predetermined, and it was never totalizing. Challenges to its reign persist.

At each turn, women and other challengers have routinely shifted the lines of power. As Mapes has written, "Bicycling, once largely seen as a simple pleasure from childhood, has become a political act."[51] This, of course, has always been true, but to differing degrees. It depends on your time and place, and upon your idea of what is political. In their day, women such as Frances Willard and Edith Shuler were formally barred from the political stage. People of color such as Major Taylor were also kept outside the formal realm of policy making when they took up cycling. Yet these men and women helped remap not only the meaning of cycling but also the broader meaning of equality in the United States. Their challenges, importantly, have never ceased. In recent decades, the bicycle has found itself at the heart of key policy discussions. As the nation's second great bicycling boom unfolds, with ramifications shaping society both here in Wisconsin and abroad, the dream of a cleaner, freer, more efficient, and more democratic world is still within our reach. You might not think it, but your next bike ride is very much a political act.

Notes

INTRODUCTION: How Wisconsin Became a Great Bicycling State

1. The website for the Fox Cities Cycling Association can be found at http://foxcitiescycling.org/about-fcca/.

2. The most comprehensive history of early cycling, and a key model for the discussions that follow, is David V. Herlihy's *Bicycle: The History* (New Haven: Yale University Press, 2004). The term "bicycle boom" is used throughout his book and throughout much of the historical writing on cycling's history.

3. The numbers cited in this paragraph come from a key study for understanding bicycling's impact in Wisconsin by the University of Wisconsin–Madison's Nelson Institute for Environmental Studies, conducted in 2010. See Maggie Grabow, Micah Hahn, and Melissa Whited, *Valuing Bicycling's Economic and Health Impacts in Wisconsin* (Madison: The Nelson Institute for Environmental Studies, Center for Sustainability and the Global Environment, January 2010). For bicycling's numbers in comparison to deer hunting, see Tom Held, "Report Finds Cycling Tops Deer Hunting in Economic Impact," *Journal Interactive: A Blog of the Milwaukee Journal Sentinel*, 2 February 2010.

4. For the best general history of cycling written in recent years, see Herlihy, *Bicycle*. Also helpful for an introduction to cycling's history in the United States are Robert A. Smith, *A Social History of the Bicycle: Its Early Life and Times in America* (New York: American Heritage Press, 1972), and Norman L. Dunham, "The Bicycle Era in American History" (PhD diss., Harvard University, 1956). The only comparable state study we have seen is Michael C. Gabriele's *The Golden Age of Bicycle Racing in New Jersey* (New York: The History Press, 2011). As its title suggests, Gabriele's book is primarily concerned with early bicycle racing, not the full scope of the sport's impact.

5. Frances Willard, who lived in Janesville for a time, wrote about her love of cycling in *A Wheel Within a Wheel: How I Learned to Bicycle with Some Reflections Along the Way* (London: Hutchinson & Company, 1895).

6.   Susan B. Anthony, "Interview by Nelly Bly," *New York World*, 2 February 1896. Anthony remained an outspoken advocate for women's cycling throughout her life. She even took lessons at bicycling rinks, as Herlihy recounted in *Bicycle*, 110.

7.   Herlihy's *Bicycle* serves as a great introduction to the sport's early politics, including its egalitarian impulse. For more nuanced work, see, for example, Ellen Gruber Garvey, "Re-Framing the Bicycle: Advertising Supported Magazines and Scorching Women," *American Quarterly* 47, no. 1 (March 1995). For a good representation of the more emancipatory narratives often seen in popular or trade presses, see Sue Macy, *Wheels of Change*: *How Women Rode the Bicycle to Freedom (With a Few Flat Tires Along the Way)* (Washington, DC: National Geographic, 2010). A good example of a recent work that has more fully historicized the recent dynamics of the sport is Jeff Mapes, *Pedaling Revolution: How Cyclists Are Changing American Cities* (Corvallis, OR: Oregon State University Press, 2009).

8.   There is still much to be said about the sport's historic conservative advocacy. Herlihy's section on "Racial Restrictions" provided the authors with early inspiration for exploring these issues as they related to Wisconsin and to the League of American Wheelmen in particular (see *Bicycle*, 263 and following). A good example of how conservative advocacy continues to play a role in the sport is Robert Penn's *It's All About the Bike: The Pursuit of Happiness on Two Wheels* (New York: Bloomsbury, 2010). A book-length tribute to his $5,500 dollar bicycle, a sum he admits is high but well worth the price, Penn writes about the individual benefits his bike provides, citing a range of mental health and physical health concerns it helped him alleviate during his quixotic "pursuit of happiness." Yet the book seems only minimally concerned with the sport's larger implications outside the realm of his personal individual performance and enjoyment. When he insists that "[i]t's *all* about the bike," he underlines the conservative line of thinking that any consideration of the bicycle beyond self-improvement is unimportant. (186)

9.   Many books have provided inspiration for the racial and gender analysis developed for this project. Two particularly significant influences include Gail Bederman, *Manliness and Civilization: A Cultural History of Race and Gender in the United States, 1880–1917* (Chicago: University of Chicago Press, 1996), and Kristin L. Hoganson, *Fighting for American Manhood: How Gender Politics Provoked the Spanish-American and Philippine-American Wars* (New Haven: Yale University Press, 2008), particularly its introduction and first chapter.

10.   We are not the first to notice a link between cycling and increasing American demand for private transportation options. See Gary Allan Tobin, "The Bi-

cycle Boom of the 1890's: The Development of Private Transportation and the Birth of the Modern Tourist," *Journal of Popular Culture* 7, no. 4 (Spring 1974): 838–849.

11. One of the best introductions to the good roads movement in Wisconsin is Ballard Campbell, "The Good Roads Movement in Wisconsin, 1890–1911" *Wisconsin Magazine of History* 49, no. 4 (Summer 1966): 273–293. For a discussion of the bicycle's role in 1890s electoral politics, see Michael Taylor, "The Bicycle Boom and the Bicycle Bloc: Cycling and Politics in the 1890s," *Indiana Magazine of History* 104 (Spring 2008): 213–240.

12. David Herlihy credits either Karl von Drais or his French agent, Louis Dineur, for the first usage of "velocipede" (from the Latin *velox pedis*, meaning "swift of foot") in 1818 to describe the new machines. The term quickly became the generic word for a human-powered, wheeled vehicle, and it remained in use until the 1870s, when it yielded to "bicycle." For more on this history, see Herlihy, *Bicycle*, 23.

13. For more information on velocipede mania, see Herlihy, *Bicycle*, 75–101.

14. For more on Towne's historic ride, see "The Velocipede," *Milwaukee Sentinel*, 7 January 1869, and chapter 1 of this book.

15. For more on this important early set of rides in Racine, see "Neighborhood Notes: Racine," *Milwaukee Sentinel*, 2 July 1879, 2; "Wisconsin Waifs: Racine," *Milwaukee Sentinel*, 3 July 1879, 2.

16. Herlihy describes the formation of the League of American Wheelmen in *Bicycle*, 204–205. For an early article detailing the formation of the Milwaukee Cycling Club, see "The Bicycle Boys," *Milwaukee Daily Sentinel*, 28 January 1881, 4.

17. See *Wright's Directory for Milwaukee*, Volumes 27–31 (Milwaukee: Alfred G. Wright, 1894–1897).

18. For a description of an early Milwaukee bicycling party for women, see "Untitled," *Yenowine's News*, 26 May 1889, 4. For Ward's book, see *Bicycling for Ladies: With Hints at the Art of Wheeling* (New York: Brentano's, 1896). See also Kate Parke, "Bicycle-Lock," US Patent 436,800, filed 28 April 1890 and issued 23 September 1890.

19. The LAW had opened their ranks to all races in 1892, but in 1894 barred blacks. For more information, see Herlihy, *Bicycle*, 263.

20. For details on a drunken spectacle white riders from Wisconsin created on their visit to Chicago, see "Racing in the Cold: Cracks Were Full," *Daily Inter Ocean* (Chicago), 4 January 1893.

21. See factory inspection reports in J. Dobbs, Commissioner, *6th Biennial Report of the Commissioner of Labor, Census, and Industrial Statistics of Wis-*

consin, 1893–1894 (Madison: Democrat Printing Company, State Printer, 1894); and Halford Erickson, Commissioner, *9th Biennial Report of the Bureau of Labor and Industrial Statistics: State of Wisconsin, 1898–1899* (Madison, WI: Democrat Printing Company, State Printer, 1901).

22. In addition to the sources listed in note 11 on good roads activism, see David P. Thelen, *The New Citizenship: Origins of Progressivism in Wisconsin, 1885–1900* (Columbia: University of Missouri Press, 1972), 78–79; and Philip Parker Mason, "The League of American Wheelmen and the Good-Roads Movement, 1880–1905" (PhD diss., University of Michigan, 1957).

23. For more on Londonberry, see Sue Macy, *Wheels of Change*, 68–69. Macy details the stories of several marathon riders in her book.

24. For a description of the ridicule of "Sam Wing," see "Chinamen as Cyclists," *Pneumatic* 7, no. 1 (April 1896); for a summary of how riding a bike threatens marriage, see "Bicycles Harm Marrying Business," *Pneumatic* 7, no. 4 (July 1896).

25. Our book presents the first sustained look at Sanger's story. In fact, there are minimal published secondary sources and few helpful primary sources to point readers to, beyond what we include in chapter 8. For a helpful introduction to the racing culture of the late nineteenth century that includes some references to Sanger, see Peter Nye, *Hearts of Lions: The History of American Bicycle Racing* (New York: Norton, 1988). Milwaukee's *Pneumatic*, the city's top source for cycling news and entertainment during the boom, is one reliable source of Sanger coverage. One of the articles to provide a rare biographical glimpse is "Walter C. Sanger," *Pneumatic* 1, no. 3 (June 1892): 7. Major Taylor, on the other hand, has generated some attention from scholars and other writers. He also wrote an autobiography, *The Fastest Bicycle Rider in the World: The Story of a Colored Boy's Indomitable Courage and Success Against Great Odds* (Worcester, MA: Wormsley Publishing Company, 1928). For secondary literature, see, for example, Todd Balf, *Major: A Black Athlete, a White Era, and the Fight to Be the World's Fastest Human Being* (New York: Three Rivers Press, 2008); and Andrew Ritchie, *Major Taylor: The Fastest Bicycle Rider in the World* (San Francisco: Van der Plas/Cycle Publishing, 2009).

26. Randy Gant has earned a local reputation for his bike riding. The *Janesville Gazette* interviewed him in 2009 to learn more about his dedication to the sport. See Anna Marie Lux, "Cyclist Discovers Health in Daily Commute: Janesville Township Man Rides 24-Mile Route Five Days a Week," *Janesville Gazette*, 11 June 2009, 1A.

27. See "We Are Now in the Lead," *Pneumatic* 6, no. 3 (June 1895).

28. The League of American Bicyclists, along with its 2012 Bicycle Friendly State Rankings, can be found online at http://www.bikeleague.org.

CHAPTER 1: Velocipede Mania

1. "The Velocipede," *Milwaukee Daily Sentinel*, 7 January 1869.

2. It is difficult to confirm exactly when the first velocipede ride in Wisconsin took place. In the 1890s, Milwaukee's main cycling magazine, the *Pneumatic*, remembered (incorrectly, perhaps) that the first bicycle ever built in the state belonged to Louis West, who apparently made the first ride down the streets of Appleton in 1868. If true, this means West, not Towne, deserves the credit for the first velocipede ride. West claimed that a blacksmith in Milwaukee named H. J. Brecht assembled the first Wisconsin velocipede in 1866. This story, while plausible, did not reach the newspapers and was not corroborated by any other sources in our research. Without any further evidence, we credit Towne with the first ride because his ride drew the first newspaper coverage and because these contemporary newspaper accounts seemed certain that Towne's ride was the first of its kind. To see the *Pneumatic*'s recollection of the West ride, published almost three decades after the alleged first ride took place, see "Wisconsin's First Wheel," *Pneumatic* 7, no. 2 (May 1896). For the *Sentinel*'s firsthand account of Towne's ride, published only a day or two after it occurred, see "The Velocipede," *Milwaukee Sentinel*, 7 January 1869.

   There are also instances of local newspapers claiming the appearance of velocipedes in Wisconsin towns as early as 1868. In February 1869, for example, the *Citizen* (Beaver Dam) claimed it had seen its first velocipedes back in September 1868, but no reports we saw corroborated the story. For the *Citizen*'s claims, see "Velocipedes," *Citizen*, 4 February 1869.

3. France's significance to the early history of the bicycle is a key theme of David Herlihy's *Bicycle: The History* (New Haven: Yale University Press, 2004), especially 75–101.

4. For more on the contested origins of the velocipede, see Herlihy, *Bicycle*, 19–21. Herlihy shows that the velocipede has a complex and contested origin. While Herlihy grants substantial attention to Pierre Michaux, another French mechanic named Pierre Lallement also deserves credit. Lallement brought a prototype of the velocipede to the United States on a steamship that travelled from Paris to Brooklyn, New York, in 1867. He eventually secured the first patent for a velocipede, but his bid to popularize the technology in the United States failed. Only after its appearance at the Paris Universal Exhibition did the velocipede become popular in the United States. Lallement went back to France in 1868 because he failed to secure a manufacturer for his patent. Ironically, the technology he had tried to popularize became fashionable al-

most immediately after he left. See Herlihy, *Bicycle*, 102–103, for more information.

5. Herlihy, *Bicycle*, 19–21.
6. *Scientific American*, 30 January 1869, quoted in Herlihy, *Bicycle*, 75; *Journal Universel*, 12 June 1869, quoted in Herlihy, *Bicycle*, 78.
7. *Le Sport* quoted in Herlihy, *Bicycle*, 78; see also Herlihy, *Bicycle*, 81.
8. "Velocipedestrian" was a term commonly used in early newspaper accounts describing the velocipede and its riders. See, for example, "Mania Velocipedestrian," *Milwaukee Daily News*, 5 March 1869. The *New York Times* coverage can be found in "Affairs in France," *New York Times*, 22 August 1867. Both articles are quoted in Herlihy, *Bicycle*, 78.
9. Herlihy, *Bicycle*, 78, 81.
10. "A Woman Velocipedestrian," *Appleton Crescent*, reprinted from the *Dispatch* (Reading, PA), 27 March 1869.
11. A. Favre was a French velocipede maker and commentator. For more information, see A. Favre, *Le Vélocipède: Sa Structure, Ses Accessoires Indispensables*, 2nd ed. (Marseille: Barlatier-Feissat et Demonchy, 1868).
12. Herlihy, *Bicycle*, 96–99.
13. Ibid., 102–103, 105.
14. "The Velocipede Exhibition," *Milwaukee Daily Sentinel*, 5 February 1869.
15. "Frightful Velocipede Accident," *Daily Milwaukee News*, 21 February 1869. The article mentions that it is quoting an account from the *Cincinnati Commercial* of 18 February 1869.
16. "Mania Velocipedestrian," *Daily Milwaukee News*, 5 March 1869.
17. "Velocipedes—Their Destiny," *Daily Milwaukee News*, 14 March 1869.
18. "Rink Velocipede School," *Milwaukee Daily Sentinel*, 26 March 1869.
19. "The Rink," *Daily Milwaukee News*, 2 April 1869.
20. Bates chronicled his journey in Gilbert H. Bates, *Triumphal March of Sergeant Bates from Vicksburg to Washington* (Washington: Intelligencer Print House, 1868).
21. "Velocipede Riding School," *Daily Milwaukee News*, 3 April 1869.
22. "Velocipede Rink," *Milwaukee Daily Sentinel*, 10 April 1869.
23. "Velocipedestrianism," *Daily Milwaukee News*, 16 April 1869.
24. "The Velocipede Rink," *Daily Milwaukee News*, 21 April 1869.
25. "Velocipedlar," *Milwaukee Daily Sentinel*, 14 April 1869.
26. "The Greatest Velocipede Exploit on Record," *Daily Milwaukee News*, 22 April 1869. The editors credited the *Jacksonville Journal* for the story.
27. "The Rink," *Daily Milwaukee News*, 22 April 1869.
28. "Great Attraction at the Rink Tonight," *Milwaukee Daily Sentinel*, 20 April 1869.
29. "Velocipedrome," *Milwaukee Daily Sentinel*, 22 April 1869.

30. "The Rink," *Daily Milwaukee News*, 23 April 1869.

31. "The Rink," *Daily Milwaukee News*, 24 April 1869.

32. "The Rink," *Daily Milwaukee News*, 25 April 1869. See also, "The Rink," *Milwaukee Daily Sentinel*, 26 April 1869, 1.

33. "Western Patents," *Milwaukee Sentinel*, 11 January 1869; "State News," *Janesville Gazette*, 7 December 1868.

34. Ralph Gordon Plumb, *A History of Manitowoc County* (Manitowoc, WI: Brandt Printing and Binding Company, 1904), 96.

35. Sylvester A. Wood. "Improvements in Velocipedes." US Patent 85,501, filed 20 November 1868 and issued 29 December 1868.

36. "State Items," *Milwaukee Sentinel*, 16 January 1869.

37. A. T. Glaze, *Incidents and Anecdotes of Early Days and History of Business in the City and County of Fond du Lac from Early Times to the Present: Personal Reminiscences, Remarkable Events, Election Results, Military History, Etc.* (Fond du Lac, WI: P. B. Haber Print Co., 1905), xx.

38. "The Velocipede: Ye Editor Rideth the Animule to Excess, and is Hurted," *Appleton Crescent*, reprinted from the *Ripon Representative*, 3 March 1869.

39. "Velocipede," *Northwestern* (Oshkosh), 28 January 1869.

40. "Velocipede," *Northwestern* (Oshkosh), 4 February 1869.

41. Scott Cross, "The Life of J. Frank Waldo," compiled from information files at the Oshkosh Public Museum. Online photograph exhibit accessed 7 September, 2012, http://oshkosh.pastperfect-online.com.

42. "Velocipede," *Northwestern* (Oshkosh), 4 February 1869.

43. Ibid.

44. "More Velocipedes," *Northwestern* (Oshkosh), 11 February 1869.

45. "Velocipede Rink," *Eau Claire Free Press*, 1 April 1869.

46. "Untitled," *Milwaukee Daily Sentinel*, 15 April 1869, 2, reprinted from *Eau Claire Free Press*.

47. "Velocipede Rink," *Eau Claire Free Press*, 1 April 1869.

48. "The Velocipede," *Appleton Crescent*, 27 February 1869; "Velocipede School," *Appleton Crescent*, 20 March 1869; "Untitled," *The Citizen* (Beaver Dam), 11 February 1869.

49. "Velocipede Race," *Eau Claire Free Press*, 8 April 1869.

50. "Untitled," *Eau Claire Free Press*, 15 April 1869.

51. "State News," *Milwaukee Daily Sentinel*, 31 May 1869, 2.

52. "Velocipede," *Appleton Crescent*, 27 March 1869.

53. "The Velocipede Mania," *Northwestern* (Oshkosh), 18 February 1869.

54. "The Velocipedestrian," *Appleton Crescent*, 27 March 1869. It is possible the

fictional "Augustus L." is a reference to A.L. Smith, who briefly managed a velocipede rink in the city.

55. The gender dynamics of early bicycling remain an important but understudied element of bicycling's early history. For a brief but entertaining introduction to this subject, see Sue Macy, *Wheels of Change: How Women Rode the Bicycle to Freedom (With a Few Flat Tires Along the Way)* (Washington, DC: National Geographic, 2011).

56. "Velocipede," *Appleton Crescent*, 27 March 1869; "Velocipede," *Appleton Crescent*, May 1, 1869.

57. "Velocipede," *Appleton Crescent*, 1 May 1869.

58. "A Word for Velocipedes," *The Daily Milwaukee News*, 12 May 1869.

59. "Commissioner Delano," *Milwaukee Daily Sentinel*, 19 May 1869, 1.

60. "An Ordinance," *Janesville Gazette*, 6 July 1869.

61. "A Word for Velocipedes," *Daily Milwaukee News*, 12 May 1869.

CHAPTER 1: SIDEBAR NOTES

How to Mount a Machine

1. "Velocipedestrianation," *Milwaukee Sentinel*, 23 April 1869.

Fancy Riding

1. "The Rink," *Milwaukee Sentinel*, 23 April 1869; "The Rink," *Daily Milwaukee News*, 23 April 1869.

2. "The Art of Trick Riding," *Scientific American*, 12 May 1899, 299.

3. "The State Bicycle Meet," *Stevens Point Gazette*, 17 June 1896; "Appleton Will Have a Meet," *Pneumatic* 6, no. 5 (August 1895); "State Meet and Circuit Races," *Pneumatic* 7, no. 2 (May 1896); "Appleton's State Meet," *Pneumatic*, 7, no. 4 (July 1896); "Brief State Notes," *Pneumatic* 7, no. 5 (August 1896).

4. "The L.A.W. Races," *Evening Record*, 17 July 1896.

5. "The Art of Trick Riding," *Scientific American*, 12 May 1899, 299.

6. "Brief Bicycle Notes," *Sunday Chronicle* (Paterson, New Jersey), 7 March 1897; "Among the Wheelmen," *New York Times*, 16 April 1897.

7. "State Circuit Races," *Pneumatic* 7, no. 5 (August 1896); "Appleton's State Meet," *Pneumatic* 7, no. 4 (July 1896).

CHAPTER 2: The Dawn of Wisconsin's High-Wheel Era

1. "The Bicycle Men," *Oshkosh Daily Northwestern*, 25 July 1879.

2. "Bicycles," *New York Times*, 1 November 1872, 4.

3. David V. Herlihy, *Bicycle: The History* (New Haven: Yale University Press, 2004), 159.

4. The reference to a "fast age" comes from "Sheboygan," *Milwaukee Sentinel*, 20 October 1876, 2; for information on developments in Waupun, see "Velocipede Riding," *Milwaukee Sentinel*, 5 May 1877, 2.

5. "Watertown," *Milwaukee Sentinel*, 7 April 1877, 2.

6. Herlihy, *Bicycle*, 159. One of the first usages of the term "bicycle" in Wisconsin's newspapers appeared during the velocipede mania. See "Velocipede and Aerobatic Exhibition," *Milwaukee Sentinel*, 5 February 1869. This suggests that as early as 1869, the word was already becoming synonymous with the new technology.

7. Herlihy, *Bicycle*, 160–161.

8. "Bicycle Race," *Milwaukee Daily Sentinel*, 26 August 1874, 3.

9. "Horse and Velocipede," *Milwaukee Daily Sentinel*, 2 May 1876, 3.

10. "English Gossip," *Harper's Bazaar* 8, no. 50 (11 December 1875): 802.

11. Herlihy, *Bicycle*, 163. See also, "Bicycle Riding," *Scientific American* 33, no. 3 (17 July 1875): 39.

12. Julia Hornbostel, *A Good and Caring Woman: The Life and Times of Nellie Tallman* (Lakeville, MN: Galde Press, Inc., 1996), 61–62.

13. Sue Macy, *Wheels of Change: How Women Rode the Bicycle to Freedom (With a Few Flat Tires Along the Way)* (Washington, DC: National Geographic, 2011), 12–13, 18.

14. Herlihy, *Bicycle*, 163.

15. "On Wheels: Growing Popularity of the New Bicycle," *Milwaukee Daily Sentinel*, 10 November 1874, 2.

16. "Bicycling," *Forest and Stream: A Journal of Outdoor Life, Travel, Nature Study, Shooting, Fishing, and Yachting* 3, no. 19 (17 December 1874): 297.

17. Herlihy, *Bicycle*, 163.

18. Ibid., 183–184.

19. Ibid., 185.

20. Ibid., 170.

21. Ibid., 187.

22. Ibid.

23. Ibid. See also Gail Bederman, *Manliness and Civilization: A Cultural History of Race and Gender in the United States, 1880–1917* (Chicago: University of Chicago Press, 1996).

24. Herlihy, *Bicycle*, 179–181.

25. Ibid., 188.

26. Ibid., 189–192.

27. Herlihy, *Bicycle*, 196.

28. Ibid.

29. Ibid., 194.

30. "A Bicycle Journey," *Milwaukee Daily Sentinel*, 10 July 1879, 2.

31. "Racine," *Milwaukee Sentinel*, 2 July 1879, 2; "Wisconsin Waifs: Racine," *Milwaukee Sentinel*, 3 July 1879, 2.

32. "The Bicycle Men," *Oshkosh Daily Northwestern*, 25 July 1879.

33. "Untitled," *Eau Claire Daily Free Press*, 6 December 1878, 1.

34. "A Terrible Storm," *Milwaukee Daily Sentinel*, 3 September 1879, 5.

35. "News," *Milwaukee Daily Sentinel*, 2 July 1880, 7.

36. "Bicycle Trip," *Janesville Gazette*, 11 July 1879, 1.

37. "Untitled," *Oshkosh Daily Northwestern*, 27 December 1879, 3.

38. "A Bycicle Club," *Milwaukee Sentinel*, 14 March 1880, 5.

39. "Bicycling," *Milwaukee Sentinel*, 16 May 1880, 4.

40. "How to Pronounce Bicycle: To the Editor of the Sentinel," *Milwaukee Daily Sentinel*, 7 August 1880, 3.

41. "The Situation," *Janesville Daily Gazette*, 2 November 1880.

42. "Milwaukee Man One of Seventeen Who Christened Republican Party," 1 December 1906, unidentified newspaper clipping accessed at http://www.wisconsinhistory.org/turningpoints/search.asp?id-948.

CHAPTER 3: The Rise of Wisconsin's Amateur Cycling Clubs

1. "The Man on the Bicycle," *Milwaukee Daily Sentinel*, 8 July 1881.

2. Sue Macy, *Wheels of Change: How Women Rode the Bicycle to Freedom (With a Few Flat Tires Along the Way)* (Washington, DC: National Geographic, 2011), 25.

3. Ibid., 18–25.

4. David V. Herlihy, *Bicycle: The History* (New Haven: Yale University Press, 2004), 205.

5. For a helpful discussion of the origins of amateur clubs on a national scale, see Philip Parker Mason, "The League of American Wheelmen and the Good Roads Movement" (PhD diss., University of Michigan, 1957), 35–44.

6. League members envisioned "better infrastructure" as including not only the roads but also the businesses servicing those who traveled them. In this way, they were also concerned with ensuring good hotel rates, cheap meals, plentiful rest areas, and plenty of bicycle shops along the way.

7. Charles E. Pratt, *The American Bicycler: A Manual for the Observer, the Learner, and the Expert* (Boston: Houghton, Osgood, and Company, 1879), 3–5.

8. Ibid., 193.
9. Mason, "The League of American Wheelmen," 44–60.
10. Pratt, *The American Bicycler*, 118.
11. Herlihy, *Bicycle*, 225.
12. "Shorts," *Milwaukee Sentinel*, 1 August 1880, 4.
13. "The Bicycle Boys," *Milwaukee Daily Sentinel*, 28 January 1881, 4.
14. "Untitled," *Milwaukee Sentinel*, 30 January 1881, 8.
15. "Bicycle Spokes," *Milwaukee Sentinel*, 26 May 1881.
16. "The Man on the Bicycle," *Milwaukee Daily Sentinel*, 8 July 1881, 5.
17. "Richardson's Rink," *Milwaukee Daily Sentinel*, 23 November 1881, 4.
18. "Bicycle Gossip," *Milwaukee Sentinel*, 30 April 1882, 8; "Whirling Wheels," *Milwaukee Sentinel*, 21 May 1882, 3.
19. "General City News," *Milwaukee Sentinel*, 14 April 1882, 6; "Milwaukee Bicycle Club," *Milwaukee Sentinel*, 25 May 1882, 2.
20. "Untitled," *Milwaukee Sentinel*, 16 April 1882, 8.
21. "Sporting," *Milwaukee Sentinel*, 30 April 1882, 8.
22. "Bicycle Bon Mots," *Milwaukee Sentinel*, 21 May 1882, 3; "Untitled," *Milwaukee Sentinel*, 15 June 1884, 9.
23. "The Wheel," *Milwaukee Sentinel*, 19 November 1882, 5.
24. "Short Notes," *Oshkosh Daily Northwestern*, 11 April 1881. Hooper married Jessie Jack Hooper in 1888. By 1900, she was among the leaders of the state's suffrage movement.
25. "Oshkosh Bicycle Club," *Oshkosh Daily Northwestern*, 29 June 1882; "The Bicycle Race," *Oshkosh Daily Northwestern*, 25 August 1882.
26. "Advertisement, Oshkosh Bicycle Agency," *Oshkosh Daily Northwestern*, 6 April 1883.
27. "Advertisement, Oshkosh Bicycle Agency," *Oshkosh Daily Northwestern*, 28 April 1883.
28. "A Mile a Minute," *Oshkosh Daily Northwestern*, 21 March 1885.
29. Louise Armaindo, who called herself the "Champion Female Bicyclist of the World," challenged men to a race in Chicago, for example, in 1888. See "Mdlle [Mademoiselle] Armaindo's Challenge," *Daily Inter Ocean*, 5 August 1888. It seems likely that Armaindo was the woman described in the *Milwaukee Daily Journal*. Our thanks to David Herlihy for alerting us to Armaindo's story.
30. "Louisa and Her Legs," *Milwaukee Daily Journal*, 21 June 1883.
31. "Connoisseur of Bicycles," *Milwaukee Sentinel*, 21 June 1883, 5.
32. Herlihy, *Bicycle*, 229.
33. Ibid., 229–230; Lyman Hotchkiss Bragg, *Ten Thousand Miles on a Bicycle* (New York: Karl Kron, 1887); Thomas Stevens, *Around the World on a Bicy-*

cle: With a New Introduction by Thomas Pauly (1887; repr., Mechanicsburg, PA: Stackpole Books, 2001).

34. Nellie Tallman's journal entry for June 13, 1883, is quoted in Julia Hornbostel's *A Good and Caring Woman: The Life and Times of Nellie Tallman* (Lakeville, MN: Galde Press, 1996), 89. For coverage of Stanley Tallman's later cycling successes, see "Fair Races and State News," *Pneumatic* 4, no. 1 (16 October 1893).

35. "World of Sports: The Bicycle Club to Wheel Through Waukesha," *Milwaukee Sentinel*, 9 April 1883, 6.

36. Herlihy, *Bicycle*, 232–235.

37. *Club Songs for the Wheelmen: Big 4 Tour Edition*, ed. T. S. Miller (Chicago: T. S. Miller and Company, 1885); in the Junius Beal Papers, Box 12, Folder 2, Bentley Historical Library, University of Michigan.

38. "Brevities," *Milwaukee Sentinel*, 18 April 1885, 8.

39. "By the Light of the Moon," *Milwaukee Sentinel*, 26 June 1885, 3.

CHAPTER 4: The Safety Model and the Beginning of Wisconsin's Bicycling Boom

1.   "Fun on a Wheel: How Cycling Has Grown in Milwaukee," *Milwaukee Sentinel*, 29 June 1890.

2.   Details on the pneumatic tire can be found in David V. Herlihy, *Bicycle: The History* (New Haven: Yale University Press, 2004), 246–247.

3.   Ibid., 236, 244.

4.   Ibid., 241, 243.

5.   Ibid., 244.

6.   "At the Roller Rinks," *Milwaukee Sentinel*, 11 October 1885, 3.

7.   See, for example, "Reduction in Bicycle Prices," *Wisconsin Weekly Advocate*, 2 July 1898, 7; "Advertisement," *Wisconsin Weekly Advocate*, 9 July 1898, 5.

8.   "Inventor of the 'Wheel,'" *Wisconsin Labor Advocate*, 20 August 1886, 3.

9.   "Pulpit Brokerage," *Wisconsin Labor Advocate*, 27 August 1886.

10. "Untitled," *Wisconsin Labor Advocate*, 10 September 1886, 1.

11. Advertisement, *Wisconsin Labor Advocate*, 11 March 1887, 4.

12. For more on the rise of "colored gentleman" in sports during this period, see Gregory Bond, "Jim Crow at Play: Race, Manliness, and the Color Line in American Sports, 1876–1916" (PhD diss., University of Wisconsin–Madison, 2008), x–xi, 15–20.

13. "Amateur Sports," *Milwaukee Sentinel*, 23 February 1887.

14. Philip Parker Mason, "The League of American Wheelmen and the Good Roads Movement" (PhD diss., University of Michigan, 1957), 51–55.

15. "Untitled," *Milwaukee Sentinel*, 17 August 1887. Commonly known as Terry Andrae, Franz Theodor Andrae would later change his legal name to Frank during the intense anti-German hysteria of World War I.

16. "The Lantern Bicycle Parade," *Milwaukee Sentinel*, 25 September 1887, 3.

17. Ibid., 2.

18. "Something About the Bicycle," *Wisconsin State Register* (Portage), 10 September 1887, 1.

19. "A Day in the City: Peculiar Collision Between Horse and Bicycle," *Milwaukee Sentinel*, 27 October 1887, 3.

20. "Injured by Fall from a Bicycle," *Milwaukee Sentinel*, 5 July 1888.

21. "A Bad Place for Bicycle Riders," *Milwaukee Journal*, 6 May 1899, 12.

22. Herlihy, *Bicycle*, 244.

23. "How She Mounts a Bicycle," *Milwaukee Sentinel*, 9 August 1888, 11.

24. "Not a Political Parade," *Milwaukee Sentinel*, 26 October 1888, 3.

25. "On Iron Steeds," *Milwaukee Sentinel*, 29 May 1889, 5.

26. Ibid.

27. "Untitled," *Yenowine's News*, 26 May 1889, 4.

28. "Ladies' Bicycle Club," *Milwaukee Sentinel*, 12 July 1889, 8.

29. "Lady Bicyclists Rebuked," *Sporting Life*, 20 June 1891, 1. "Home," *Congregationalist* (Boston), 9 October 1890, 6.

30. Florence Finch Kelley, "The Fair Cyclers: The Bicycle Conquered at Last By Women," *Milwaukee Sentinel*, 14 July 1889.

31. Ibid.

32. "G.A.R. Visitors," *Milwaukee Sentinel*, 26 August 1889, 8.

33. "They All Like It," *Milwaukee Sentinel*, 3 November 1889, 11.

34. "Illinois' Champion Beaten," *Milwaukee Sentinel*, 27 October 1889, 3.

35. "Cyclers Have a Book Party," *Milwaukee Sentinel*, 8 December 1889, 3.

36. "Winter Bicycle Tournament," *Milwaukee Sentinel*, 15 December 1889, 3.

37. Herlihy, *Bicycle*, 244.

38. "Must Keep Off of Sidewalks," *Milwaukee Sentinel*, 14 June 1890, 3.

39. "The Bicyclers and the Chief of Police," *Milwaukee Sentinel*, 15 June 1890, 7.

40. "Fun on a Wheel: How Cycling Has Grown in Milwaukee," *Milwaukee Sentinel*, 29 June 1890. By 1892, Parker H. Sercombe with F. H. Bolte had formed the Sercombe-Bolte Manufacturing Company. Together they sponsored Walter C. Sanger, who broke a world record on their Telegram Light Roadster.

41. "Julius Andrae Celebrates 85th Birthday Wednesday," *Evening Wisconsin*, 1 December 1914; "Obituary," *Electrical Review* 71, no. 23 (8 December 1917): 997; "Firm that Brought Electricity to Milwaukee Recalls History," *Milwaukee Journal*, 3 March 1957.

42. Terry was referred to as the Flying Badger in the souvenir program for the 1892 Milwaukee "Bicycle Exposition Tournament," Sports Collection, Mss-1518, Box 6, File 41, Milwaukee County Historical Society.

43. "Town Trade Topics," *Pneumatic* 4, no. 6 (March 1894); *Wright's Directory of Milwaukee for 1894*, vol. 27 (Milwaukee: Alfred G. Wright, 1894); "The Andraes Will Move," *Pneumatic* 6, no. 3 (June 1895); advertisement for "Julius Andrae & Sons Company's Repair Department," *Pneumatic* 7, no. 2 (May 1896). The first Andrae manufacturing plant was located at 225 West Water Street. In 1895 the plant relocated to a larger factory building at 162 to 168 West Water Street, while their original shop at 225 West Water Street continued service as a repair shop.

44. *Constitution and By-Laws: Milwaukee Wheelmen* (Milwaukee: Meisenheimer Print Company, 1893), Pamphlet Collection, Wisconsin Historical Society; "The Colonel Talks," *Pneumatic* 3, no. 1 (15 April 1893); "The First Meet a Success," *Pneumatic* 3 no. 4 (15 July 1893); "Milwaukee Notes" *Pneumatic* 1, no. 2 (14 May 1892): 4; "The Stroller," *Pneumatic* 1, no. 4 (15 July 1892); "Pneus of Milwaukee," *Pneumatic* 1, no. 6 (15 September 1892).

45. *The Badger* (Madison: Junior Class of the University of Wisconsin, 1888), 221; *The Badger* (Madison: Junior Class of the University of Wisconsin, 1890).

46. "The Andrae Cycles," *Pneumatic* 4, no. 4 (January 1894).

47. "Third Annual Road Race of the Badger Wheelmen," (Milwaukee: Meyer-Rotier Printing Company, 1896), Sports Collection, Mss-1518, Box 6, File 41, Milwaukee County Historical Society.

48. "Andrae Riding School at Broadway Armory," *Milwaukee Journal*, 1 May 1897.

49. The total valued goods in 1896 was $1,340,014; one year later it was $1,509,852. State of Wisconsin, *Ninth Biennial Report of the Bureau of Labor and Industrial Statistics* (Madison, WI: Democrat Printing Company, State Printing, 1901), 186.

50. "The Fair Cyclers," *Milwaukee Sentinel*, 14 July 1889.

51. Kate Parke, "Bicycle-Lock," US Patent 436,800, filed 28 April, 1890 and issued 23 September, 1890; Alice E. Bennitt, "Bicycle-Canopy," US Patent 574,235, filed 6 March 1896 and issued 29 December 1896.

52. Herlihy, *Bicycle*, 250.

53. Ibid., 251.

54. Bond, "Jim Crow at Play," 113, 134.

CHAPTER 5: The Troubled Beginnings of Wheel Fever

1.   "The Negro and the League: Letter to the Editor," *Bearings* 8, no. 24 (12 January 1894).

2.   "Milwaukee's Cyclers," *Weekly Wisconsin*, 21 March 1891, 9.

3.   Ibid.

4.   "New Use for a Bicycle," *Chicago Herald*, 7 January 1890.

5.   "Winnebago Wheelmen, L.A.W. 400: Bicycling 1891–1941," article numbers 61, 67, 71, 72, 73, 75, Box: "Oshkosh, Sports, Bicycling," Local History Collection, Oshkosh Public Library.

6.   David V. Herlihy, *Bicycle: The History* (New Haven: Yale University Press, 2004), 258, 264.

7.   Ibid., 254.

8.   Gail Bederman, *Manliness and Civilization: A Cultural History of Gender and Race in the United States, 1880–1917* (Chicago: University of Chicago Press, 1995), 31.

9.   We can only speculate as to whether black bike riders sought admission to the World's Fair, or joined in the protests. Chicago did have several black bicycling clubs, including the Chicago Colored Cycling Club, formed in 1891, a Frederick Douglass cycling club, formed sometime after 1893, and others. The Chicago Colored Cycling Club was also later admitted to the Associated Cycling Clubs of Chicago. See Gregory Bond, "Jim Crow at Play: Race, Manliness, and the Color Line in American Sports, 1876–1916" (PhD diss., University of Wisconsin–Madison, 2008), 51.

10. Bederman, *Manliness and Civilization*, 38–39.

11. "The Lantern Parade," *Bearings* 8, no. 3 (August 1893).

12. Ballard Campbell, "The Good Roads Movement in Wisconsin, 1890–1911," *Wisconsin Magazine of History* 49, no. 4 (Summer 1966): 276–277n7.

13. Philip Parker Mason, "The League of American Wheelmen and the Good Roads Movement" (PhD diss., University of Michigan, 1957), 69.

14. Mason, "The League of American Wheelmen," 69. All of Mason's chapter 3 is helpful on this point.

15. Campbell, "Good Roads Movement in Wisconsin," 278n7.

16. Mason, "The League of American Wheelmen," 35–37.

17. Ibid., 61.

18. "Rights and Privileges," *Pneumatic* 1, no. 1 (15 April 1892), 6–7.

19. Mason, "The League of American Wheelmen," 62–63.

20. "Struck by a Pulley," *Daily Northwestern* (Oshkosh), 28 July 1893, 1.

21. "Before the Board: Wheelmen Keeping the Board of Review Very Busy," *Daily Northwestern* (Oshkosh), 24 July 1893.

22. Ibid.

23. "Far and Wide," *Sporting Life* 20, no. 26 (25 March 1893); "Chose the Quaker Team," *New York Times*, 5 June 1895.

24. "The '13' Club's Road Race," *Pneumatic* 3, no. 2 (15 May 1893); "Condensed Local Items," *Pneumatic* 5, no. 7 (November 1894). The *Pneumatic* editors incorrectly dated the November 1894 (volume 5, number 7) issue—it came out in October 1894. The 13 Clubs were mysterious, but not at all secretive. Photos from the period show 13 Club members wearing their club sweaters at public road races, and many 13 Club members were also LAW members. Any male wheelmen could join the club so long as they met the 13 Club's requirements, and while racial restrictions may not have been a formal part of the club's charter, certainly whiteness was an implied and unstated prerequisite.

25. "The Coming Minstrel Show," *Pneumatic* 1, no. 1 (15 April 1892): 5.

26. For details on the minstrel shows, see "Milwaukee Happenings," *Bearings* 8, no. 16–17 (November 1893); "What Milwaukeeans Are Doing," *Bearings* 8, no. 17 (24 November 1893); "Still Fighting in Milwaukee," *Bearings* 8, no. 24 (12 January 1894).

27. Herlihy, *Bicycle*, 263.

28. Ibid.

29. Quoted in Bond, "Jim Crow at Play," 294.

30. "The Negro Question Again," *Bearings* 8, no. 8 (September 1893).

31. "The Negro Question Again," *Bearings* 8, no. 22 (29 December 1893).

32. For more on the debate on exclusion at the Milwaukee–Waukesha Road Race, see "News of the Sports: No Color Line at the Milwaukee–Waukesha Road Race," *Milwaukee Journal*, 9 May 1893.

33. The photo appeared in *Bearings* 8, no. 5 (1 September 1893), 3. The racer with the mascot was Arthur Zimmerman, as documented in Bond, "Jim Crow at Play," 81, with further details on black mascots generally at 74–75. See also "He Ate His Prize," *Bearings* 8, no. 3 (18 August 1883).

34. "Front Matter," *Pneumatic* 4, no. 3 (December 1893); "Cycling in the Sunny South," *Pneumatic* 5, no. 12 (March 1895).

35. "The Doctor and Good Roads," *Wisconsin Afro-American*, 13 August 1892, 3.

36. "The Pioneer Lady-Rider," *Wisconsin Afro-American*, 20 August 1892, 2.

37. "Racing in the Cold: Cracks Were Full," *Daily Inter Ocean* (Chicago), 4 January 1893.

38. "Local Pneus," *Pneumatic* 3, no. 1 (15 April 1893); "A Chinese Newspaper," *Pneumatic* 3, no. 4 (15 July 1893).

39. "Ladies' Department," *Pneumatic* 3, no. 3 (15 June 1893).

40. "Untitled," *Pneumatic* 4, no. 1 (16 October 1893); "Ladies' Department," *Pneumatic* 3, no. 3 (15 June 1893).

41. "Gossip about Lady Cyclers," *Pneumatic* 1, no. 2 (14 May 1892): 1.

42. "Women and Bicycling," *Pneumatic* 1, no. 5 (15 August 1892): 10.

43. "Editorial Information," *Pneumatic* 1, no. 1 (15 April 1892).

44. "Front Matter," *Pneumatic* 3, no. 3 (15 June 1893); "Front Matter," *Pneumatic* 3, no. 6 (15 September 1893).

45. For a brief mention of their triumph in the *Pneumatic*, see "Notes from Everywhere," *Pneumatic* 5, no. 1 (April 1894). See also Herlihy, *Bicycle*, 250, 255.

46. See two pieces of correspondence detailing diplomatic arrangements for Lenz, "George J. Shoeffel to Hon. J.M. Rusk, Secretary of Agriculture," 18 May 1892 and "George J. Shoeffel to Hon. J. M. Rusk," 18 May 1892 (the letters were dated the same day), Box 3, Folder 3, *Jeremiah Rusk Papers, 1862–1898*, Wis Mss ER, Wisconsin Historical Society, Madison, Wisconsin. Our sincere thanks to David Herlihy for alerting us to these documents late in our research.

47. The *Pneumatic* mentioned that Lenz's mother had received a letter from him as he traveled through China in August 1893. Lenz apparently described scenes of famine as he moved through the country. In November 1894, the *Pneumatic* reported that he wrote a man in Chicago to say that he was leaving "Teheran" [*sic*] and was about 1,200 miles from Constantinople. See "Lenz Has Been Heard From," *Pneumatic* 3, no. 5 (15 August 1893); "The Lenz Relief," *Pneumatic* 5, no. 9 (December 1894).

48. Historian David Herlihy reconstructed Lenz's dramatic story in *The Lost Cyclist: The Epic Tale of an American Adventurer and His Mysterious Disappearance* (New York: Houghton Mifflin Harcourt, 2010); see also Herlihy, *Bicycle*, 254–255. For the *Pneumatic*'s mention of the relief effort sent to find Lenz, see "The Lenz Relief," *Pneumatic* 5, no. 9 (December 1894).

49. "Lenz Was Killed by Kurds," *Pneumatic* 6, no. 2 (May 1895); "The Search for Frank Lenz," *Pneumatic* 6, no. 12 (March 1896).

50. "Opinions and Criticisms," *Pneumatic* 3, no. 5 (15 August 1893).

51. "Patriotism," *Pneumatic* 3, no. 1 (15 April 1893); "Grand Parade to the Home," *Pneumatic* 5, no. 1 (April 1894); "City Cycling Notes," *Pneumatic* 5, no. 3 (June 1894).

52. Michael Taylor, "The Bicycle Boom and the Bicycle Bloc: Cycling and Politics in the 1890s," *Indiana Magazine of History* 104 (September 2008), especially 213–214 and 220–221.

53. *Constitution and By-Laws: Milwaukee Wheelmen* (Milwaukee: Meisenheimer Print Company, 1893), Pamphlet Collection, Wisconsin Historical Society.

54. "Our New Home," *Pneumatic* 3, no. 1 (15 April 1893).

55. "'Colonel' Andrae," *Pneumatic* 5, no. 1 (April 1894).

56. Herlihy, *Bicycle*, 259–260.

57. "The Late Mayor Harrison," *Pneumatic* 4, no. 2 (15 November 1893); "Commentator Commentates," *Pneumatic* 4, no. 3 (December 1893).

58. "A Just Tribute," *Pneumatic* 5, no. 12 (March 1895).

59. "Untitled," *Pneumatic* 4, no. 1 (16 October 1893).

60. *Wright's Directory of Milwaukee for 1894, Vol. 27* (Milwaukee: Alfred G. Wright, 1894).

61. Ibid.

62. "Local Trade Shots," *Pneumatic* 3, no. 1 (15 April 1893).

63. "Chicago's Cycle Row," *Pneumatic* 4, no. 3 (December 1893).

64. "Bicycles Will Be Taxed," *Pneumatic* 3, no. 2 (15 May 1893).

65. For more on LAW tactics and McKinley, see Taylor, "The Bicycle Boom and the Bicycle Bloc."

66. For more on the Clarion, see Herlihy, *Bicycle*, 274.

67. Ibid., 275.

68. "Wisconsin Division Notes," *Pneumatic* 5, no. 2 (May 1894); "Wear Coats While Dining," *Pneumatic* 6, no. 6 (September 1895).

69. Mason, "The League of American Wheelmen," 60.

70. "Of a Cycling Nature," *Pneumatic* 3, no. 5 (15 August 1893).

71. "The Gospel of Cycling," *Pneumatic* 4, no. 2 (15 November 1893).

72. "Untitled," *Pneumatic* 3, no. 5 (15 August 1893).

CHAPTER 6: The Leading Division of the West

1. "Influence of Good Roads on Country Life," *Pneumatic* 4, no. 5 (February 1894).

2. Stephen Crane, "The Transformed Boulevard: Bicycling Has Made It the Most Interesting of City Streets," *New York Sun*, 5 July 1895, 5.

3. Gail Bederman, *Manliness and Civilization: A Cultural History of Race and Gender in the United States, 1880–1917* (Chicago: University of Chicago Press, 1996), 31–41.

4. David V. Herlihy, *Bicycle: The History* (New Haven: Yale University Press, 2004), 263, 275.

5. Wrights City Directory for Appleton, 1896, and *Appleton Crescent*, 29 May 1890.

6. "Untitled," *Daily Northwestern*, 24 May 1890; "Wisconsin Small Talk," *Weekly Wisconsin*, 31 May 1890.

7. "Untitled," *Daily Northwestern*, 28 June 1892.

8. "Speeches Made at the Banquet of the League of American Wheelmen, Monday, May 28, 1883, at Metropolitan Hotel, New York City," *Wheelman* 2 (August 1883): 371. Quoted in Michael Taylor, "The Bicycle Boom and the Bicycle Bloc," *Indiana Magazine of History* 104 (2008): 217.

9. "His Record Is Broken," *Chicago Daily Tribune*, 4 October 1896, 5. Quoted in Taylor, "The Bicycle Boom," 215.

10. "Front Matter," *Pneumatic* 5, no. 6 (September 1894).

11. "Momentary Meditations," *Pneumatic* 5, no. 7 (November 1894). The editors incorrectly dated the vol. 5, no. 7, 1894, issue as November—it came out in October 1894.

12. "A Chance for Bargain," *Pneumatic* 4, no. 2 (15 November 1893).

13. "Wheelmen in Politics," *Pneumatic* 7, no. 7 (October 1896).

14. "Campaign Pins and Buttons," *Pneumatic* 7, no. 7 (October 1896).

15. "Front Matter," *Pneumatic* 4, no. 5 (February 1894); "Entering the Third Year," *Pneumatic* 5, no. 1 (April 1894). *Pneumatic* writers often wrote columns parodying black speech and mocking black culture. For example, see "Rev. Moakley McKoon on the Bicycle," *Pneumatic* 5, no. 7 (November 1894). The editors incorrectly dated the vol. 5, no. 7, 1894, issue as November—it came out in October 1894.

16. "Wisconsin Notes," *Pneumatic* 5, no. 11 (February 1895).

17. "Momentary Meditations," *Pneumatic* 5, no. 1 (April 1894).

18. "The Freemasonry of Cycling," *Pneumatic* 4, no. 6 (March 1894).

19. Martin C. Rotier, *Bicycle Road Map of Wisconsin* (Milwaukee: League of American Wheelmen, ca. 1896–1897), Map Collection, Wisconsin Historical Society. Christina E. Dando has also written about the significance of the maps. See Christina E. Dando, "Riding the Wheel: Selling American Women Mobility and Geographic Knowledge," *ACME: An International E-Journal for Critical Geographies* 6, no. 2 (2007): 174–210.

20. Samuel J. Ryan, *Wisconsin Tour and Handbook.* (Appleton, WI: Wisconsin Division, League of American Wheelmen, 1897), Pamphlet Collection, Wisconsin Historical Society Library.

21. "Commentator Commentaries," *Pneumatic* 4, no. 1 (16 October 1893); "The Use of Our Convicts," *Pneumatic* 4, no. 2 (16 October 1893); "Commentator Commentates," *Pneumatic* 4, no. 4 (January 1894); "Ideal Southern Roads," *Pneumatic* 4, no. 4 (January 1894); "What Milwaukeans are Doing," *Bearings* 8, no. 17 (24 November 1893).

22. Milwaukee Wheelmen, "Constitution and By-Laws: Milwaukee Wheelmen" (Milwaukee: Meisenheimer Print Company, 1893), 2.

23. Ballard Campbell, "The Good Roads Movement in Wisconsin, 1890–1911," *Wisconsin Magazine of History* 49, no. 4 (Summer 1966): 278.

24. "An Energetic Secretary," *Pneumatic* 5, no. 11 (February 1895).

25. "Dorner as a Tourist," *Pneumatic* 6, no. 6 (September 1895).

26. The close ties between early highway lobbying, the bicycle industry, and Albert Pope are detailed throughout Philip Parker Mason, "The League of American Wheelmen and the Good Roads Movement" (PhD diss., University of Michigan, 1957). See especially 125, 140, and 182.

27. "Front Matter," *Pneumatic* 4, no. 4 (January 1894).

28. "Influence of Good Roads on Country Life," *Pneumatic* 4, no. 5 (February 1894).

29. Ballard Campbell, "Good Roads Movement in Wisconsin," 280.

30. Ibid, 278–280.

31. "Wisconsin's First Cycle Path," *Pneumatic* 6, no. 5 (August 1895).

32. "Building Cycle Paths," *Pneumatic* 6, no. 12 (March 1896); "To Build a Bicycle Path," *Pneumatic*," 7, no. 2 (May 1896).

33. "Cycling Cogitation," *Pneumatic* 10, no. 8 (September 1899).

34. Isaac B. Potter, *The Gospel of Good Roads* (New York: The League of American Wheelmen, 1891).

35. Mason, "The League of American Wheelmen," 102.

36. "Observations," *Pneumatic* 1, no. 6 (15 September 1892).

37. Milwaukee City Directory, 1894–1898.

38. "Commentator Commentates," *Pneumatic* 4, no. 4 (January 1894).

39. "We Are Now In the Lead," *Pneumatic* 6, no. 3 (June 1895).

CHAPTER 6: SIDEBAR NOTES

College Bicycle Clubs

1. Junior class of the University of Wisconsin, *Badger* (Madison, WI: 1890–1900); University of Wisconsin–Oshkosh, Polk Library and University Archives, Oshkosh, Wisconsin.

2. Junior class of the Oshkosh Normal School, *Quiver* (Oshkosh, WI: 1897); University of Wisconsin–Oshkosh, Polk Library and University Archives, Oshkosh, Wisconsin.

3. Lawrence University, *Ariel* (Appleton, WI: 1894); Outagamie County Historical Society; History Museum at the Castle, Appleton, Wisconsin.

4. "Untitled," *Pneumatic* 8, no. 4 (July 1897), 8.

CHAPTER 7: Women and Labor during the Boom

1. Susan B. Anthony, "Interview by Nelly Bly," *New York World*, 2 February 1896.

2. "Rage for Wheels: Oshkosh Has It Very Bad," *Daily Northwestern* (Oshkosh), 20 April 1895, 1.

3. "Bicycle Mad," *Appleton Crescent*, 4 May 1895.

4. Christina E. Dando, "Riding the Wheel: Selling American Women Mobility and Geographic Knowledge," *ACME: An International E-Journal for Critical Geographies* 6, no. 2 (2007): 174.

5. Ellen Gruber Garvey, "Reframing the Bicycle: Advertising-Supported Magazines and Scorching Women," *American Quarterly* 47, no. 1 (March 1995): 66–101.

6. Phillip Gordon Mackintosh and Glen Norcliffe, "Flâneurie on Bicycles: Acquiescence to Women in Public in the 1890s," *Canadian Geographer* 50, no. 1 (Spring 2006): 17–37.

7. "Milwaukee's '400' Are Riding," *Pneumatic* 6, no. 1 (April 1895).

8. David Herlihy, *Bicycle: The History* (New Haven: Yale University Press, 2004), 267–273.

9. See Frances E. Willard, *Glimpses of Fifty Years: The Autobiography of an American Woman* (New York: Women's Temperance Publication Association, 1889); *Woman and Temperance* (Hartford, CT: Park Publishing Company, 1883); Ruth Bordin, *Frances Willard: A Biography* (Chapel Hill: University of North Carolina Press, 1986).

10. For more on Willard, see Bordin, *Frances Willard: A Biography*.

11. Frances E. Willard, *A Wheel Within a Wheel: How I Learned to Ride the Bicycle, With Some Reflections by the Way* (Chicago: Women's Temperance Publishing Association, 1895), 11.

12. Ibid., 10–14.

13. Willard, *A Wheel Within a Wheel*, 25, 38. She describes her "philosophy of life," on p. 25 and her feelings about "humanity's mother-half" on p. 38.

14. Willard, *A Wheel Within a Wheel*, 23, 25, 38, 75. For coverage of her death and mention of the book, see "Grand Life Ended," *Fort Wayne Sentinel* (Indiana), 18 February 1898, 1.

15. For a decidedly celebratory look at women and early cycling, see Sue Macy, *Wheels of Change: How Women Rode the Bicycle to Freedom (With a Few Flat Tires Along the Way)* (Washington, DC: National Geographic, 2011). The women listed here are all profiled in this book.

16. Tom Winder, *Around the United States By Bicycle: Entertaining Sketches of the*

Fun, Pleasure and Hardships, the Sights and Scenes Incident to 274 Consecutive Days of Riding (Elmira, NY: Tom Winder, Publisher, 1895), 6.

17. Ibid., 45.

18. Ibid.

19. "Wooden Bicycle Road," *Pneumatic* 6, no. 4 (July 1895).

20. "Wheelmen in Parade," *Pneumatic* 6, no. 7 (October 1895).

21. "Untitled," *Pneumatic* 3, no. 5 (15 August 1893); "A Road Hog Comes to Grief," *Pneumatic* 6, no. 8 (November 1895).

22. See Gregory Bond, "Jim Crow at Play: Race, Manliness, and the Color Line in American Sports, 1876-1916," (PhD Diss., University of Wisconsin–Madison, 2008), 27–28.

23. Ibid., 27–28 ; "Chinamen as Cyclists," *Pneumatic* 7, no. 1 (April 1896).

24. "About Bicycling and a Wife," *Pneumatic* 7, no. 4 (July 1896).

25. "Carload of Bicycles," *Appleton Crescent*, 18 January 1896.

26. "Bicycles Harm Marrying Business," *Pneumatic* 7, no. 4 (July 1896).

27. Maria E. Ward, *Bicycling for Ladies: With Hints as to the Art of Wheeling* (New York: Brentano's, 1896), 12.

28. Ward, *Bicycling for Ladies*, 1–2, 112.

29. Dando, "Riding the Wheel," 191.

30. Halford Erickson, Commissioner, *9th Biennial Report of the Bureau of Labor and Industrial Statistics: State of Wisconsin, 1898–1899* (Madison: Democratic Printing Company, State Printer, 1901), 576.

31. J. Dobbs, Commissioner, *6th Biennial Report of the Commissioner of Labor, Census, and Industrial Statistics of Wisconsin, 1893–1894* (Madison: Democrat Printing Company, State Printer, 1894), 111a.

32. "Trade Pneus," *Pneumatic* 1, no. 2 (May 1892).

33. Original examples of these bicycles are held in the collections of the Milwaukee Public Museum (bamboo-frame) and Racine Heritage Center (wooden-frame).

34. Robert W. Ozanne, *The Labor Movement in Wisconsin* (Madison: State Historical Society of Wisconsin, 1984), 8–13, 26.

35. As an AFL affiliate, the IUBW was later renamed the International Union of Bicycle Workers and Allied Mechanics in 1898 and the International Association of Allied Metal Mechanics in 1900. In 1904 it merged with the International Association of Machinists. Stuart B. Kaufman, Peter J. Albert, and Grace Palladino, eds., *The Samuel Gompers Papers, Volume 4: A National Labor Movement Takes Shape, 1895–1898* (Urbana, IL: Board of Trustees of the University of Illinois, 1991), 559.

36. John D. Buenker, *The History of Wisconsin: Volume 4, The Progressive Era,*

1893–1914 (Madison, WI: Wisconsin Historical Society, 1998), 251. Frederick Winslow Taylor is often credited with developing scientific management. For a good analysis of changes to labor during the era of the bicycle boom, see David Montgomery, *The Fall of the House of Labor: The Workplace, The State, and American Labor Activism, 1865–1925* (Cambridge, England: Cambridge University Press, 1987).

37. *Biennial Report of the State Board of Arbitration and Conciliation of the State of Wisconsin* (Madison: Democrat Printing Company, State Printer, 1901), 11.

38. Erickson, *9th Biennial Report*, 875-895, 936.

39. Ibid.

40. "Table 11—Persons employed, by industries, by months, 1897–1898," in Erickson, *9th Biennial Report*, 428. Cyclical work schedules were common. Labor unions often negotiated similar schedules to avoid working alongside massive boilers and furnaces during the hottest months of the year.

41. Ibid., 296–303.

42. Halford Erickson, Commissioner, *8th Biennial Report of the Bureau of Labor and Industrial Statistics: State of Wisconsin, 1897–1898* (Madison: Democratic Printing Company, 1899), 441.

43. Erickson, *9th Biennial Report*, 299, 624, 647.

44. *Milwaukee: A Half-Century of Progress, 1846–1896* (Milwaukee: Consolidated Illustrating Company, 1896), Milwaukee County Historical Society Pamphlet Collection.

45. Erickson, *9th Biennial Report*, 937.

46. Wisconsin Corporations (Business and Non-Profits) Index, "Bicycle Workers Union No. 1," Domestic Corporations, File No. B 000622, Box No. 0059, Kenosha County, Wisconsin Historical Society Library and Archives.

47. *Biennial Report of the State Board of Arbitration and Conciliation of the State of Wisconsin* (Madison: Democrat Printing Company, State Printer, 1901), 9–11.

48. Ibid., 12–14.

49. "Strike at Beebe Company Is Off," *Racine Journal*, 30 March 1899; *Biennial Report of the State Board of Arbitration and Conciliation of the State of Wisconsin* (Madison: Democrat Printing Company, State Printer, 1901), 18–21.

50. "125 Men Are Out," *Racine Journal*, 27 April 1899.

51. "The First Clash," *Racine Daily Journal*, 8 May 1899; "Trying to Settle," *Racine Daily Journal*, 9 November 1899.

52. "Bicycle Factory Goes Up in Smoke," *Racine Daily Journal*, 8 June 1900.

53. *Biennial Report of the State Board of Arbitration and Conciliation of the State of Wisconsin* (Madison: Democrat Printing Company, State Printer, 1901), 576, 647.

54. *Wisconsin Corporations (Business and Non-Profits) Index,* Domestic Corporations, Wisconsin Historical Society Library and Archives.

55. Ibid.

56. "Bicycles Cause a Strike," *Pneumatic* 7, no. 9 (December 1896).

57. "Rage for Wheels: Oshkosh Has It Very Bad," *Daily Northwestern* (Oshkosh), 20 April 1895, 1.

58. Ibid.

59. "Some Types Chicago Loans Us: Bicycle Girls are Rakish and Reckless," *Milwaukee Sentinel*, 14 August 1898, 5.

60. "Short Skirts," *Weekly Wisconsin Advocate*, 9 July 1898.

61. "Gossip for the Ladies: The Wheelwoman's Errors," *Weekly Wisconsin Advocate*, 30 July 1898, 3.

62. "Meet More People," *Wisconsin Weekly Advocate*, 16 July 1898, 3.

63. "Jacksonville News," *Illinois Record* (Jacksonville), 26 March 1898, 3.

64. "Silenced by the First Shot," *Wisconsin Weekly Advocate*, 4 June 1898, 6.

65. "Sombreros are the Latest: Cowboy's Headgear Now the Favorite with New York Girls," *Wisconsin Weekly Advocate*, 25 June 1898, 8.

CHAPTER 7: SIDEBAR NOTES

Cycling Fashion

1. Herlihy, *Bicycle*, 267–268.

2. "Opinions on the Bloomer," *Pneumatic* 6, no. 3 (June 1895).

3. "Interesting to State Riders," *Pneumatic* 6, no. 2 (May 1895); "The Wheeling Woman," *Pneumatic* 6, no. 3 (June 1895).

4. "The Wheeling Woman," *Pneumatic* 6, no. 3 (June 1895).

5. "Louisa A. Roth—First Bloomer Girl in Milwaukee," *Pneumatic* 6, no. 3 (June 1895).

6. "Brief State Notes," *Pneumatic* 6, no. 3 (June 1895).

7. "Interesting to State Riders," *Pneumatic* 6, no. 2 (May 1895).

8. "Momentary Meditations," *Pneumatic* 5, no. 4 (July 1894).

9. "Untitled," *Pneumatic* 7, no. 1 (April 1896); "Do Not Fear Bloomers Now," *Pneumatic* 7, no. 2 (May 1896); *Pneumatic* 7, no. 5 (August 1895).

10. "The Wheelwoman," *Pneumatic* 10, no. 4 (April 1899).

11. Peter Zheutlin, *Around the World on Two Wheels: Annie Londonderry's Extraordinary Ride* (New York: Citadel Press, 2007).

12. "Bicycle Gossip," *Milwaukee Sentinel*, 30 April 1882; "Whirling Wheels," *Milwaukee Sentinel*, 21 May 1882.

13. Local History Collection, Box: Oshkosh, Sports–Bicycling, "Winnebago Wheelmen, L.A.W. 400: Bicycling 1891–1941," article 51, Oshkosh Public Library.

14. "Cycling Dress for 1899," *Pneumatic* 10, no. 5 (June 1899).

Bicycle Sundries

1. "Four Millions Riders," *Pneumatic* 7, no. 3 (June 1896).

2. "Untitled," *Pneumatic* 8, no. 2 (May 1897).

3. Halford Erickson, Commissioner, *Eighth Biennial Report of the Bureau of Labor and Industrial Statistics: State of Wisconsin, 1897–1898* (Madison: Democrat Printing Company, State Printer, 1899), 234–239, 371, 382, 384–385; an advertisement for the Brandt Weins Company appeared in the *Pneumatic* 7, no. 9 (December 1897). The total number of sundry shop employees excludes workers who made sundries at larger bicycle manufactures.

4. Edward J. Williams, Design for a Bicycle Lamp. US Patent 30,150, filed 10 December 1898, and issued 7 February 1899.

5. Halford Erickson, Commissioner, *Ninth Biennial Report of the Bureau of Labor and Industrial Statistic: State of Wisconsin, 1898–1899* (Madison: Democrat Printing Company, State Printer, 1901), 936.

6. "Strike at Kenosha Settled," *Racine Daily Journal*, 2 May 1899; "Detectives are Fined," *Racine Daily Journal*, 5 December 1907; "Unions are Restrained," *Racine Daily Journal*, 26 November 1907; "Settle Strike: Open Shop," *Racine Journal*, 17 March 1908.

7. "Hall Lamp Company Buys Badger Brass," *Automobile* 36, no. 4 (25 January 1917).

8. "List of Reliable Repair Men in the State," *Pneumatic* 6, no. 1 (April 1895).

9. Julius Andrae & Sons catalog, 1900. Vertical surname files. Milwaukee Public Museum.

CHAPTER 8: Walter Sanger, Major Taylor, and Professional Racing at the End of the Boom

1. "But Once a Year," *Pneumatic* 5, no. 5 (August 1894).

2. Gail Bederman, *Manliness and Civilization: A Cultural History of Gender and Race in the United States, 1880–1917* (Chicago: University of Chicago Press, 1995). Bederman's scope is much broader than professional sports, but her discussion remains relevant for the world of professional cycling.

3. "Walter C. Sanger," *Pneumatic* 1, no. 3 (June 1892): 7.

4. Ibid.

5. One of the rare discussions of Sanger's youth occurs in "Sanger a Coming Cyclist," *Victoria Daily Colonist*, 22 May 1892, 9.

6. Ibid.

7. "Milwaukee's Cyclers," *Weekly Wisconsin Advocate*, 21 March 1891, 9.

8. Pamphlet, "Souvenir, Exposition Bicycle Tournament," (Milwaukee: Arthur B. Lindsley, 1892), Milwaukee County Historical Society Pamphlet Collection; "Exposition Bicycle Track," *Pneumatic* 2, no. 8 (15 November 1892): 7.

9. "C.C.C. Push Get Roasted," *Pneumatic* 2, no. 8 (15 November 1892).

10. "A Thousand Ahead," *Pneumatic* 2, no. 9 (15 December 1892).

11. "The Flying Wheel Will Reign Here Next Week," *Daily Northwestern* (Oshkosh), 2 July 1892.

12. "Flyers on the Wheel: Opening Day of the L.A.W. State Meet," *Weekly Northwestern* (Oshkosh), 9 July 1892.

13. "Get Their Prizes," *Daily Northwestern* (Oshkosh), 9 July 1892.

14. Ibid.; "Cyclist's Last Day," *Daily Northwestern* (Oshkosh), 8 July 1892.

15. "Wooden Shoes Sanger Still Feels Lure of the Bike," *Milwaukee Journal*, 10 January 1932.

16. "Some Hints to Wheelmen," *New York Times*, 13 May 1900.

17. "Doings in Milwaukee," *Pneumatic* 2, no. 11 (15 October 1892).

18. "Trade Pneus," *Pneumatic* 1, no. 6 (15 September 1892).

19. *Pneumatic* 2, no. 9 (15 December 1892): 3.

20. "Racing Men and their Trainers," *Pneumatic* 2, no. 8 (15 November, 1892).

21. Pamphlet, "Souvenir, Exposition Bicycle Tournament."

22. "Wheelmen and Wheeling," *World* (New York), 7 May 1893.

23. "Untitled," *Ironwood Times* (Ironwood, MI), 27 May 1893, 1.

24. "Sporting News," *Daily Gleaner* (Jamaica), 14 July 1893; "Do They Fear Competition?" *World* (New York), 3 June 1894; "Sporting News," *Daily Northwestern* (Oshkosh), 1 June 1893.

25. "Bicyclists Coming Home," *Trenton Times* (Trenton, NJ), 13 June 1893.

26. "Sanger Coming Home," *New York Times*, 20 June 1893.

27. "Sanger Welcomed Home," *Wisconsin State Journal*, 28 July 1893, 1.

28. "Sanger Expelled: Telegram Cycling Club of Milwaukee Ousts Him," *Daily Northwestern* (Oshkosh), 23 August 1893.

29. "Sanger and Culver Part," *Bearings* 8, no. 12 (20 October 1893); "What Milwaukeans are Doing," *Bearings* 8, no. 17 (24 November 1893); "Looking Backwards: A Review of '93 Racing," *Bearings* 8, no. 21 (22 December 1893); "Sanger Losing Flesh," *Bearings* 8, no. 25 (19 January 1894).

30. "Sanger's New Record," *New York Times*, 18 July 1894.

31. "Sanger at Home," *New York Times*, 7 August 1894.

32. "Sanger Now Improving," *New York Times*, 28 March 1895.

33. "Great Year for Cycling: World's Records Will Probably Be Smashed by the Fast Wheelmen," *World* (New York), 21 April 1895, 31.

34. "Sims and Sanger Suspended," *World* (New York), 25 June 1895.

35. "Two Cracks Suspended," *New York Times*, 25 June 1895; "Will Sanger Turn Pro?" *New York Times*, 29 May 1895.

36. "Luscombe Tells Story," *Daily Northwestern* (Oshkosh), 16 July 1895.

37. "Tyler Proves a Flyer," *Boston Sunday Globe*, 28 July 1895, 1.

38. "E. C. Bald the Hero," *Boston Daily Globe*, 12 September 1895. Sanger's victory was featured in a Vim Tire ad that ran alongside the race summary.

39. "Bicycle Racing at Springfield," *Scientific American* 43, no. 17 (26 October 1895): 262.

40. "Slow Watch the Cause," *New York Times*, 9 November 1895.

41. "Walter Sanger's Bride," *Milwaukee Journal*, 4 January 1896.

42. "Bald the Only One," *Appleton Crescent*, 18 July 1896.

43. "L.A.W. Circuit Meets," *New York Times*, 16 April 1896.

44. Waltham Manufacturing advertisement, *American Wheelmen*, 12 March 1896, 64.

45. "Appleton's State Meet," *Pneumatic* 7, no. 4 (July 1896).

46. "Fast Ones Coming," *Appleton Crescent*, 4 July 1896; "Appleton Bicycle Meet Will Be One of the Greatest Events of 1896," *Appleton Crescent,* 4 July 1896.

47. "Appleton Bicycle Meet Will Be One of the Greatest Events of 1896," *Appleton Crescent,* 4 July 1896.

48. "State Meet—Resolutions Adopted Regarding Lawless Riders—Colors of the Club," *Appleton Crescent*, 23 May 1896.

49. Local History Collection, Box: Oshkosh, Sports–Bicycling, "Winnebago Wheelmen, L.A.W. 400: Bicycling 1891–1941," article 58, Oshkosh Public Library.

50. "Eddie in Front," *Appleton Crescent*, 11 July 1896; "Appleton Bicycle Meet Will Be One of the Greatest Events of '96," *Appleton Crescent,* 4 July 1896; "The Meet," *Appleton Crescent*, 18 July 1896. Local History Collection, Box: Oshkosh, Sports–Bicycling, "Winnebago Wheelmen, L.A.W. 400: Bicycling 1891–1941," articles 59 and 60, Oshkosh Public Library.

51. "Eddie in Front," *Appleton Crescent*, 11 July 1896; "Appleton's State Meet," Pneumatic 7, no. 4 (July 1896).

52. Ibid. See also "Bald the Only One," Appleton Crescent, 18 July 1896. The Appleton Crecent and *Pneumatic* both certified Bald's half-time time of 1:00 was a new world record. However, without a major clearing house for record-keeping, it is difficult to determine how long the record stood.

53. "The Meet," *Appleton Crescent*, 18 July 1896. Local History Collection, Box: Oshkosh, Sports–Bicycling, "Winnebago Wheelmen, L.A.W. 400: Bicycling 1891–1941," articles 59 and 60, Oshkosh Public Library.

54. "Walter Sanger Not to Blame: The Tragic Death of a Bicycle Rider at Lima, O[hio]." *Milwaukee Journal*, 31 July 1896, 1.

55. Taylor praised Sanger in his 1928 autobiography. See Marshall Walter Taylor, *The Fastest Bicycle Racer in the World: The Story fo a Colored Boy's Indomitable Courage and Success Against Great Odds* (Worcester, MA: Wormsley Publishing Company, 1928), 6.

56. Gregory Bond, "Jim Crow at Play: Race, Manliness, and the Color Line in American Sports, 1876–1916," (PhD Diss., University of Wisconsin–Madison, 2008), xiii–xvi.

57. G. Grant Williams, "Marshall Walter Taylor (Major Taylor): The World-Famous Bicycle Rider," *Colored American Magazine* (Boston), 1 September 1902, 17.

58. Bond, "Jim Crow at Play," 234–235, 332–336.

59. "Racing at Manhattan Beach," *New York Times*, 15 August 1897.

60. "Among the Wheelmen," Milwaukee Journal, 18 September 1897. Neither athlete appeared in the final meet report in "The State Meet," *Pneumatic* 8, no. 5 (July 1897).

61. "The Cyclist Won," *Graphic* (Pottsville, IA), 8 July 1897; "Bicycling," *Boston Evening Transcript*, 2 July 1897.

62. "Falls Short," *Milwaukee Journal*, 24 September 1897.

63. "How Our Speedy Bicyclists Train," *Stevens Point Daily Journal*, 12 May 1897.

64. "To Pay All Claims," *Milwaukee Journal*, 6 September 1897.

65. "Many Fast Men Will Ride Here," *Green Bay Daily Gazette*, 14 June 1898.

66. Advertisement, "Ladies' 6 Night Bicycle Race," *Green Bay Daily Gazette*, 25 June 1898.

67. "Bicycle Riders Have Left Green Bay," *Green Bay Daily Gazette*, 6 July 1898.

68. "Pastimes Will Call Upon Business Men," *Green Bay Daily Gazette*, 28 June 1898.

69. "Will Take Hold of the Bicycle Meet," *Green Bay Daily Gazette*, 7 July 1898.

70. "Business Men at the Head of the L.A.W. Meet," *Green Bay Daily Gazette*, 11 July 1898.

71. "Pastimes Meet This Evening," *Green Bay Daily Gazette*, 15 July 1898.

72. "First Entries are Made," *Green Bay Daily Gazette*, 1 August 1898; "More Entries Received," *Green Bay Daily Gazette*, 3 August 1898; "Pastime Cycle Club Will Meet Tonight," *Green Bay Daily Gazette*, 1 August 1898.

73. "Bald Will Ride in Green Bay Races," *Green Bay Daily Gazette*, 4 August 1898.

74. "Final Arrangements Made Last Night," *Green Bay Daily Gazette*, 9 August 1898.

75. "More Entries Received," *Green Bay Daily Gazette*, 12 August 1898.

76. "Advertisement: L.A.W. Week," *Green Bay Daily Gazette*, 15 August 1898.

77. Advertisement, "Acetylene Gas Bicycle Lamps: Otto Merkel & Co.," *Green Bay Daily Gazette*, 13 August 1898.

78. Advertisement, "Decorate for the Meet: A. Spuhler Company," *Green Bay Daily Gazette*, 13 August 1898.

79. Advertisement, "Bikes at Less than Cost! Mueller and Man," *Green Bay Daily Gazette*, 16 July 1898.

80. "Fast Racing Men Are Here," *Green Bay Daily Gazette*, 15 August 1898.

81. "Meet Is Surely a Wonder: The Entertainment," and "Notes of the Meet," *Green Bay Daily Gazette*, 16 August 1898.

82. "Black Wheelman Was First to Cross the Tape Line," *Green Bay Daily Gazette*, 16 August 1898.

83. "L.A.W. Meet Continued," *Green Bay Daily Gazette*, 17 August 1898.

84. Ibid.

85. "Nat McDougall Leads in the State Events Today," *Green Bay Daily Gazette*, 17 August 1898; "Races of Today Are Declared Off," *Green Bay Daily Gazette*, 18 August 1898.

86. "Management of the Meet Was a Success," *Green Bay Daily Gazette*, 19 August 1898.

87. "Frank Mulkern," *Pneumatic* 9, no. 10 (December 1898): 231.

88. "Edward Aldridge," *Pneumatic* 9, no. 1 (February 1898): 11.

89. "Cycling Cogitation," *Pneumatic* 10, no. 1 (January 1899): 11.

90. "Tom Eck Praises the Local Track," *Janesville Daily Gazette*, 10 July 1899, 5.

91. "Races at Janesville," *Daily Northwestern* (Oshkosh), 13 July 1899, 8.

92. "Bike Meeting Ends in Total Failure," *Janesville Daily Gazette*, 14 July 1899, 5.

93. "State Cycle Meet Opened Here Today," *Janesville Daily Gazette*, 12 July 1899, 5.

94. "Bike Meeting Ends in Total Failure," *Janesville Daily Gazette*, 14 July 1899, 5.

95. "Janesville Fizzle Has Hurt Sport," *Janesville Daily Gazette*, 15 July 1899, 5; see parallel coverage in "Oshkosh Was Again Fortunate," *Daily Northwestern* (Oshkosh), 18 July 1899, 6.

96. The L.A.W. Magazine and Good Roads 31, no. 93 (August 1900), 6, 15.

97. "Sporting Items," *Weekly Wisconsin Advocate*, 28 June 1900, 6.

98. "Sporting News in General," *Daily Northwestern* (Oshkosh), 2 July 1900, 2.

99. "Track is Defective," *Anaconda Standard* (Anaconda, MT) 12 July 1900; "Sporting," *Racine Daily Journal*, 13 July 1900; "Sporting," *The Racine Daily Journal*, 12 July 1900.

100. "Cyclists Strike at Milwaukee," *Naugatuk Daily News* (Connecticut), 12 July 1900.

101. "Black Wonder of the Wheel," *Weekly Wisconsin Advocate*, 27 September 1900, 7.

102. Although Major Taylor has earned the most attention from scholars and other students of late nineteenth-century sports, he was actually one of several famous black cyclists who built their celebrity during the first boom. Ralph Jackson, son of one of Pittsburgh's most prominent black citizens, Robert Johnson, started racing in 1896. In 1897, according to the Pittsburgh's black magazine, the *Smoky City*, Jackson won the bicycling championship for western Pennsylvania and Ohio. An image from the magazine shows the champion Jackson in a studio atop his wheel, peering straight into the lens. See Oliver G. Waters, "Part II: Glimpses of Social Life," *Smoky City* 4, no. 1 (1 November 1901): 22.

103. For more details on Taylor, including the circumstances of his death, see Todd Balf, *Major: A Black Athlete, A White Era, and the Fight to Be the World's Fastest Human Being* (New York: Crown Publishers, 2008), 250–254; Andrew Ritchie, *Major Taylor: The Extraordinary Career of a Champion Bicycle Racer* (San Francisco: Bicycle Books, 1988), 254.

104. "News of the Cycles: The Steady Decline in the League of American Wheelman Still Unchecked," *New York Times*, 5 June 1898.

105. Ibid.

106. The Sanger handlebar patent was applied on June 6, 1898. George A. Rosenbauer and Joseph P. Schowalter, assignors to The Sanger Handle-Bar and Plating Company, "Bicycle Handle-Bar," U.S. Patent 621,946, 28 March 1899. "With the Trade," *Pneumatic* 10, no. 1 (January 1899): 24–25.

107. "With the Trade," *Pneumatic* 10, no. 3 (March 1899).

108. "Sanger Goes into Bankruptcy," *Janesville Gazette*, 23 April 1901, 6.

109. "Milwaukee Plans for Motor Races," *Janesville Daily Gazette*, 26 June 1902, 1.

110. The Sanger Automobile Company was located at 2578 N. Farwell Ave. See Wright's Directory for Milwaukee for 1929 (Milwaukee: Wright's Directory Company, 1929).

111. "Bicycle Racer Sanger Dead," *Milwaukee Journal*, 6 December 1941. Sanger died on December 5.

CHAPTER 8: SIDEBAR NOTES

Wisconsin's Racetracks

1. "More Excitement at the Rink," *Milwaukee Sentinel*, 28 May 1869; "The Prize Velocipede Tournament," *Milwaukee Sentinel*, 1 June 1869.
2. "Official Handicapper Patitz," *Pneumatic* 3, no. 3 (June 1893).
3. "The Exposition Bicycle Track, Milwaukee," *Pneumatic* 2, no. 8 (November 1892).
4. "Local Pneus," *Pneumatic* 3, no. 1 (April 1893).
5. "The Racing Interests in the State," *Pneumatic* 5, no. 2 (May 1894).
6. Photograph, CF 5071, Charles Van Schaick Collection, Wisconsin Historical Society.
7. "A Grist of State News," *Pneumatic* 3, no. 2 (May 1893).
8. "Madison Road Race," *Pneumatic* 3, no. 3 (June 1893).
9. "State Meet at Ripon," *Pneumatic* 3, no. 4 (July 1893).
10. "Neenah's Big Meet," *Pneumatic* 6, no. 5 (July 1895).
11. "In and Around the State," *Pneumatic* 5, no. 2 (May 1894).
12. "Appleton's State Meet," *Pneumatic* 7, no. 4 (July 1896).
13. "Plan for the Proposed Athletic Fields in Milwaukee," *Pneumatic* 9, no. 6 (August 1898).
14. "A Contest for the 1897 State Meet," *Pneumatic* 7, no. 4 (July 1896).
15. "Racine State Meet," *Pneumatic* 8, no. 3 (June 1897).
16. Ibid.
17. "4-5" indicates four-fifths of a second, and is the unit racing times were most commonly expressed in the 1890s, likely because stop watches could only measure to 1/10 of a second. "The State Meet," *Pneumatic* 8, no. 5 (July 1897).

CONCLUSION

1. Two books are especially helpful in understanding the nature and scope of bicycling in the early twentieth and twenty-first centuries. The first is David V. Herlihy, *Bicycle: The History* (New Haven: Yale University Press, 2004). The other is Jeff Mapes, *Pedaling Revolution: How Cyclists Are Changing American Cities* (Corvallis: Oregon State University Press, 2009). For a recent look at the role of the oil crisis and the role of nature in foregrounding the second boom, see, Mark Fiege, *The Republic of Nature: An Environmental History of the United States* (Seattle: University of Washington Press, 2012), especially 392–395.

2. For more information, see Mapes, *Pedaling Revolution*, 35. See also Robert Penn, *It's All About the Bike: The Pursuit of Happiness on Two Wheels* (New York: Bloomsbury, 2010), 27.

3. "Sale of Secrombe-Bolte's Plant," *The Bearings*, Vol. 8, No. 22 (December 29, 1893); "P. H. Sercombe Now Sought on Fraud Charges," *Milwaukee Journal*, 20 November 1918; "Untitled," *To-Morrow: For People Who Think* 3, No. 11 (November, 1907), 15–16. *To-Morrow* was later called *To-Morrow: A Rational Monthly Magazine*. For more on Sandburg and the visitors to Sercombe, see North Callahan, *Carl Sandburg: His Life and Works* (University Park, PA: Pennsylvania State University Press, 1990), 42.

4. For this brief sketch of the automobile's history, we relied on James J. Flink, "Automobiles," in *The Reader's Companion to American History*, edited by Eric Foner and John A. Garraty (Boston: Houghton Mifflin Company, 1991), 64–68. Also helpful is Penn, *It's All About the Bike*, 94.

5. For more on Major Taylor, see Gregory Bond, "Jim Crow at Play: Race, Manliness, and the Color Line in American Sports, 1876–1916," (Ph.D. Dissertation, University of Wisconsin–Madison, 2008), 328, 347–350. The newspaper article quoted in this paragraph is the *Cleveland Gazette*, 29 July 1901, quoted in Bond, 328.

6. Erika Janik, *A Short History of Wisconsin* (Madison: Wisconsin Historical Society Press, 2010), 127–129.

7. Ibid., 128–129.

8. "Automobiling in Appleton," *Appleton Crescent*, 28 July 1906.

9. "900 Autos within 25 Miles of Here," *Evening Crescent* (Appleton), 30 March 1915.

10. "Bicycle Racer, Sanger, Dead," *Milwaukee Journal*, 6 December 1941.

11. "Andrae Never Disappoints: Automobile Accessories," *Milwaukee Sentinel*, 28 May 1911.

12. Willie G. Davidson, *100 Years of Harley-Davidson* (New York: Bullfinch Press, 2002).

13. Information on the early history of aviation is drawn from Tom D. Crouch, "Aviation," in *The Reader's Companion to American History*, 68–70. See also Penn, *It's All About the Bike*, 95.

14. Janik, *A Short History*, 130–131.

15. Herlihy, *Bicycle*, 323–324, 382–384.

16. "'Pine Dunes Park' to be Big Asset to State," *Sheboygan Press,* 5 December 1928; "Press Photographer Tells Story of Beauties of 'Pine Dunes' Park Given to the State by Mrs. Andrae in Honor of Her Late Husband," *Sheboygan Press,* 21 December 1928.

17. On the reunion of the North Side Cycling Club, see "47 Years of Active Continuing Biking for the North Side Cycling Club, 1891–1936," advertising flyer, H59204 / 29372, Bicycle Materials Box #2, Milwaukee Public Museum.

18. Herlihy, *Bicycle*, 355–360.

19. For details of the accident that injured Dorner, see "Otto Dorner Hurt Severely in Crash," *Milwaukee Journal*, 25 October 1931. For details on his death, see "Shot is Fatal to Otto Dorner," *Milwaukee Journal*, 8 July 1838.

20. See George F. Kennan, *Sketches from a Life* (New York: Pantheon Books, 1989), 36–41. The authors would like to thank University of Wisconsin–Madison Department of History graduate student Athan Biss for alerting them to Kennan's ride.

21. For details on the commemorative road race, see "Souvenir Program: Annual 48 Mile Milwaukee Bicycle Race," held on September 9, 1945, H59192 / 29372 and H59192 / 29372, Bicycle Materials Box #2, Milwaukee Public Museum. Though a complete inventory of its contents does not exist, the story of the Milwaukee Public Museum's fascinating collection of bikes can be found in Michael Horne, "The Greatest Exhibit You've Never Seen," *Milwaukee Magazine,* 15 July 2011. For details on the "old-timer" reunion, see "Gathering of Old Time Bicycle Riders," advertising flier, H59190 / 29372, Bicycle Materials Box #2, Milwaukee Public Museum.

22. For more on Taylor's re-internment, see Todd Balf, *Major: A Black Athlete, A White Era, and the Fight to Be the World's Fastest Human Being* (New York: Crown Publishers, 2008).

23. Details on Wilson and the bike's continuing appeal in the early part of the century are drawn from Mapes, *Pedaling Revolution*, 35.

24. Ibid., 363.

25. For more on the developments of the late 1960s and 1970s as they pertain to cycling, see Mapes, *Pedaling Revolution*, 27–31.

26. While there is no published history of Trek available, the web does provide several starting points, including the website www.vintage-trek.com and an exhibit piece and web information put together by the Wisconsin Historical Society and available at http://www.wisconsinhistory.org/museum/artifacts/archives/001701.asp.

27. Herlihy, *Bicycle*, 368–371.

28. For more information, see Associated Press, "Packers Bike Kids to Work in Unique Tradition," *CBS News*, 30 August 2011.

29. Mapes, *Pedaling Revolution*, 29–31.

30. "A Trek Through Time" was posted on the dealer site almost a decade ago. See http://vintage-trek.com/trek_history.htm.

31. Herlihy, *Bicycle*, 395.

32. Mapes, *Pedaling Revolution*, 49–57.

33. Ibid., 13–18.

34. These numbers are drawn from Maggie Grabow, Micah Hahn, and Melissa Whited, *Valuing Bicycling's Economic and Health Impacts in Wisconsin: Estimating the Value of Bicycling to Tourism and Health in Wisconsin and Reviewing the Potential to Increase that Value in the Face of Changing Demographics, Lifestyles, and Economy* (University of Wisconsin, Madison: The Nelson Institute for Environmental Studies, January 2010), 1.

35. For more on Janesville's plans, see Gina Duwe, "Meetings to Give Residents Look at Proposed Bicycle Trail," *Janesville Gazette*, 9 June 2012.

36. The Bicycle Federation of Wisconsin is online at www.bfw.org. For more information on the state's trails, local industries, annual economic impact, and bicycling events, see the Bike Federation's "Ride Guide: 2012" (Madison: Bicycle Federation of Wisconsin, 2012). Information on the Elroy-Sparta State Trail was drawn from the Rails-to-Trails Conservancy's web page, "Rail-Trail Hall of Fame: Wisconsin's Elroy-Sparta State Trail," http://www.railstotrails.org/news/recurringFeatures/trailMonth/archives/0809.html. For more information on the Janesville bike paths, see "Rock River Parkway Trail," Trail Link by Rails-to-Trails Conservancy, http://www.traillink.com/trail/rock-river-parkway-trail.aspx.

37. Mapes, *Pedaling Revolution*, 62, 86–87.

38. For more on Milwaukee's elevated bike lanes, see Dave Schlabowske, "First Raised Bike Lane in Wisconsin," *The Bicycle Blog of Wisconsin*, Bicycle Federation of Wisconsin, last modified 25 October 2011, http://bfw.org/2011/10/25/first-raised-bike-lane-in-wisconsin/.

39. David Tenenbaum, "Increased Use of Bikes for Commuting Offers Economic, Health Benefits," *University of Wisconsin–Madison News*, last modified 2 November 2011, http://www.news.wisc.edu/19981.

40. Patz quoted in Tenenbaum, "Increased Use of Bikes." David Byrne has also written an entertaining account of his bicycle travels in the United States, which include several of the cities mentioned here. See David Byrne, *Bicycle Diaries* (New York: Penguin Books, 2010), especially his chapter on "American Cities," 7–41.

41. Mapes, *Pedaling Revolution*, 9, 12. For more on Sadik-Kahn, the transportation commissioner for New York City, see Michael Crowley, "Honk, Honk, Aaah," *New York Magazine*, 17 May 2009.

42. Mary Peters told Gwen Ifill of PBS on August 15, 2007 that congressional earmarks often kept taxpayer dollars from being invested in the nation's "in-

frastructure," and noted that she did not believe investments in bike paths counted as infrastructure spending. Peters said, "There are museums that are being built with that money, bike paths, trails, repairing lighthouses. Those are some of the kind of things that money is being spent on, as opposed to our infrastructure." See Mary Peters, "Transportation Secretary Discusses Concerns about National Infrastructure," *PBS Newshour with Jim Lehrer* (Transcript), 15 August 2007, available at http://www.pbs.org/newshour/bb/transportation/july-dec07/infrastructure_08-15.html.

43. See "Governor Signs Bicycle 'Tune-up' Bill," "Bicycle Federation of Wisconsin," last modified 17 November 2011, http://www.bfw.org/2011/11/17/governor-signs-bicycle-tune-up-bill/.

44. Mapes, *Pedaling Revolution*, 19–21. See also Jane Holtz Kay, *Asphalt Nation: How the Automobile Took Over America and How We Can Take it Back* (Berkeley: University of California Press, 1997).

45. Bicycle Federation of Wisconsin, "Ride Guide: 2012." "Events" are listed on pages 10–43 of the guide, easily the publication's largest section.

46. Mapes, *Pedaling Revolution*, 136–139.

47. The state estimated it could claim twenty percent of the entire industry in 2006. More recent data is not available, however. See Bicycle Federation of Wisconsin and the Wisconsin Department of Transportation, *The Economic Impact of Bicycling in Wisconsin*. Prepared for the Governor's Bicycle Coordinating Council, 2006, page 5. The report is available at the Wisconsin Department of Transportation "Doing Business" website, http://www.dot.wisconsin.gov/business/econdev/resources.htm.

48. Both the economic impact and jobs figures estimates come from Grabow, Hahn, and Whited, *Valuing Bicycling's Economic and Health Impacts in Wisconsin*, 5–6. See also the table on page 31.

49. See http://bikewig.nationalmssociety.org/site/TR?fr_id=19765&pg=entry.

50. For information on these rides, see http://www.riverwest24.com; http://www.pedalacrosswisconsin.com; and http://wiki.worldnakedbikeride.org.

50. Gabrow, Hahn, and Whitehead, 13–19.

51. For more on Madison's near miss with the Olympics, see "Wisconsin Would Host Chicago Olympic Cycling Events," *USA Today*, 16 January 2009.

52. Mapes, *Pedaling Revolution*, 8.

INDEX

ABOUT THE AUTHORS

JESSE J. GANT is a PhD candidate in history at the University of Wisconsin–Madison, with research interests in nineteenth-century United States history. A native of Janesville, Wisconsin, he has written for the *History News Network*, the *Indiana Magazine of History*, and the *Wisconsin Magazine of History*. Jesse is a committed cyclist who divides his time between Madison and Saint Louis, Missouri.

Photo by Nick Wilkes Photography

NICHOLAS J. HOFFMAN is chief curator at the History Museum at the Castle in Appleton, Wisconsin, and has written articles for the *Wisconsin Magazine of History*. Born in Hillsboro, his lifelong interest in Midwest history led to a master's in history from the University of Wisconsin–Milwaukee. An avid cyclist, he enjoys exploring the state's landscape on two wheels.

Photo by Nick Wilkes Photography